The Recreation and Leisure Service Delivery System

The Recreation and Leisure Service Delivery System

Christopher R. Edginton
University of Oregon

Charles A. Griffith
Boys and Girls Clubs of Canada

SAUNDERS COLLEGE PUBLISHING

Philadelphia   New York   Chicago
San Francisco   Montreal   Toronto
London   Sydney   Tokyo   Mexico City
Rio de Janeiro   Madrid

Address orders to:
383 Madison Avenue
New York, NY 10017

Address editorial correspondence to:
West Washington Square
Philadelphia, PA 19105

Text Typeface: Optima
Compositor: Caledonia Composition
Acquisitions Editor: John Butler
Project Editor: Sally Kusch
Copyeditor: Merry Post
Managing Editor & Art Director: Richard L. Moore
Design Assistant: Virginia A. Bollard
Text Design: Larry Didona
Cover Design: Larry Didona
Text Artwork: ANCO/Boston
Production Manager: Tim Frelick
Assistant Production Manager: Maureen Iannuzzi

Cover Credit: Photograph of amusement ride at Knott's Berry Farm, Buena Park, CA.
©1982 by Elisa Leonelli.

Library of Congress Cataloging in Publication Data

Edginton, Christopher R.
  The recreation and leisure service delivery system.

  (Saunders series in recreation)
  Includes index.

  1. Recreation leadership — Study and teaching. 2. Recrea-
tion — Management — Study and teaching. 3. Leisure —
Management — Study and teaching. 4. Case method.
  I. Griffith, Charles A. II. Title. III. Series.
GV181.35.E34   1983   790'.06'9   82-60503
ISBN 0-03-052637-7

The Recreation and Leisure Service Delivery System   ISBN 0-03-057637-7

2345   038   987654321

CBS COLLEGE PUBLISHING
Saunders College Publishing
Holt, Rinehart and Winston
The Dryden Press

This book is dedicated to five great kids who have given us unrestrained love, affection and support while we were engaged in this effort and other professional endeavors

Carole Noelle Edginton
David Clifford Edginton
Susan Carol Griffith
Peter Charles Griffith
David Michael Griffith

Preface

During the last few decades, the growth in number and variety of recreation and leisure-related services under the sponsorship of government, private, and commercial auspices has been extremely rapid. It is interesting to note that even in inflationary and depressed economic times, participation in recreation and leisure services continues to increase. As North American society enters the post-industrial era, it appears that the importance of and demand for recreation and leisure services will continue to grow in the future. The ways in which these services are created and distributed is evolving. A prime example of this is the de-emphasis of services provided by governmental agencies paralleled by the growth of services in the commercial sector. This book is directed toward providing the student, practitioner, and educator with contemporary strategies for the delivery of recreation and leisure services.

Starting as a movement primarily concerned with the provision of safe places for children to play in congested urban areas, and from an attempt to provide a formalized park system patterned after European cities, the recreation and leisure movement has now become a multi-billion dollar industry. An analysis of individual major cities in North America would show capital and operating budgets expressed in the millions of dollars per year and organizations whose employees number in the hundreds. The provision of recreation and leisure services by tax-supported agencies as well as by private and commercial agencies is now big business. Clearly, the career person in the recreation and leisure field must now possess a wide array of skills, not necessary during the early years of the movement.

Recognizing that the responsibilities of the professional career person in the recreation and leisure service field have changed drastically in the past decade, this book attempts to provide an introduction to the basic concepts and processes needed to provide efficient and relevant services. The authors believe, first, that the career person providing recreation and leisure services today must understand that the delivery of services is holistic in nature and, second, that the tasks performed by such persons differ only slightly from those performed by individuals in business and industry. Thus, the main purpose of this book is to relate concepts involved in the holistic delivery of services, and to incorporate processes common in business and industry.

This book is divided into ten chapters. The chapters cover a number of basic concepts and processes related to the operation and programming of profit and nonprofit agencies that create and distribute recreation and leisure services and products. Key concepts presented include characteristics of programs and participants, theories of leadership, as well as the processes of planning, organizing, staffing, directing and controlling. In addition, a discussion of financial management is presented with attention devoted to revenue sources for recreation and leisure service organizations. Last, strategies for dealing with organizational dysfunction are discussed.

It should be noted by the reader that various terms related to recreation and leisure service delivery systems have been used in the text. For example, the authors have used the terms "the recreation and leisure service organization," "the human service organization," as well as "profit and nonprofit recreation and leisure service organizations" to describe agencies or businesses that deliver various types of recreation and leisure services. Generally, the concepts and processes presented are relevant to and can be applied to all of these types of recreation and leisure service organizations.

Case Studies

In this book we have used the case study method to assist the student in understanding the material presented in each chapter. The case study method was developed in 1880 by Christopher Langdell at Harvard University. Langdell was interested in developing a method whereby students could engage in independent thinking, could develop an awareness of the universality of some principles of behavior, as well as develop specific skills and knowledge related to problem solving. There are a variety of formats that can be used when employing case studies. The case studies used in this text attempt to involve the student in a number of situations in which he or she can draw upon the principles, theories, and ideas presented in each chapter. The cases are purposefully incomplete and are oversimplifications of the problems and situations they are intended to represent.

The case study method requires active participation on the part of the student. The role of the instructor using the case study method is as a catalyst encouraging group discussion. The instructor should be prepared to help guide the learning process so that individual students are able to discover and understand the broad principles that underlie each of the case studies. The instructor should attempt to engage students in open, informal and expressive interaction. Students should be encouraged to explore alternative solutions to problems, as well as cite their own personal experiences as they relate to the case study situations. Discussion should be comprehensive rather than superficial. Although discussion may involve specific solutions to problems, it should always be focused toward the broad issues and principles that theoretically can be applied universally.

The primary benefit of the case study method is that it allows the student to envision a "real world" situation and to assume the role of decision maker within these settings. This particular case study series offers the student an opportunity to picture what it will be like to assume an entry level position in the park and recreation field. It enables the student to "encounter" some of the problems and questions that are likely to arise when working in such a position.

When using the case studies presented in this book, the student should attempt to assume the role of Chuck Christopher, Assistant Program Supervisor for the Canusa Park and Recreation Department. Canusa is a city of 230,000. The Department's operational budget exceeds 3 million dollars per year and has over 46 full-time employees. Students should use their theoretical knowledge as well as their practical experience and judgement in forming responses to each of the case studies involving Chuck Christopher and his work environment.

When analyzing cases, whether verbally or in written form, the authors would suggest use of a four-step process:

Define the problem or situation. In this initial step, an attempt should be made to identify the problem involved and to inventory information related to it. The problem may not be as obvious as it looks. An obvious problem may be a result of underlying factors that contribute to or cause it.

Identify organizational implications. The second step in the process involves targeting the ramifications of the problem or situation in terms of their impact on the organization. Consideration should be given to the impact of the problem or situation upon human, fiscal, physical and technological resources of the organization. Further, attention should be given to the implications of the problem in terms of its relationship to participants served by the organization and other agencies with ties to the organization.

Analysis of alternative solutions. The third step in the process has students identify and debate alternative courses of action. For any given situation, there may be as many solutions as there are students investigating the problem. Often, this process can highlight the fruitfulness of group problem solving. The sharing of alternative solutions can lead students to the discovery of fresh insights to problems. A good strategy to employ in this third step is to have students formulate alternative solutions individually and then later share these with their class members in order to point out the benefits of collaboration in problem solving.

Choosing a course of action.   The last step in the process involves choosing from among the alternatives. Consideration should be given to both short-term and long-term action. Also an attempt should be made to synthesize the entire process. The instructor should ask students: "What general principles have been learned from analysis of the particular case?" The instructor should also ask: "How might these general principles be applied to other situations and problems?"

In summary, it is the belief of the authors that the case study method can be a valuable learning tool for the student. It provides for the integration of theoretical concepts with practical situations, and enables the student to investigate and analyze principles, ideas and concepts related to the delivery of recreation and leisure services in a stimulating, challenging and meaningful way.

Acknowledgements

This book was intially considered while the authors were employed in the Department of Recreation, University of Waterloo, Waterloo, Ontario, Canada. Much of the material has been based on both the academic and practical experience of the authors. To those individuals who provided an opportunity for previous work experience, as well as a forum to discuss, criticize and formulate our ideas and concepts, we extend our gratitude. Some of the individuals within the academic realm that have contributed to the development of our thoughts are Joseph Bannon, Jim Murphy, Lloyd Heywood, Geoffrey Godbey, John Nesbitt, Allen Sapora, David Ng, Sandy Little, Ken Kim, Ardith Frost, Ted Deppe, and John Lord. Practitioners who have significantly influenced our thoughts and ideas are John Williams, Jack Robinson, Betty Wieseman, John Hannant, Laurie Branch, and Carl Furst.

We wish to extend our appreciation to Eugene K. Beugler and Dawne J. Dougherty and acknowledge the time and energy they spent on preparation of the manuscript. Susan Edginton played an important role in the editing process. She has helped both authors to state their ideas precisely. In addition, she was instrumental in the preparation of the book prospectus by serving as a sounding board. Her insight in the area of motivation was particularly useful in the development of the chapter on human resources. Susan was a continual source of inspiration and her commitment to the completion of this project enabled us to assemble the final product. In addition, the authors would like to thank Sally Kusch, who served as Project Editor, and Merry Post, who served as copy editor, for the book. They were patient and understanding as well as competent and thorough in their handling of the production of the book. Last, we would like to thank John Butler, Acquisitions Editor for Saunders College Publishing. John's interest in the project as well as his faith in the authors' ability to produce this book were appreciated.

Christopher R. Edginton
Charles A. Griffith

Contents

5 Organizing   111

6 Staffing   138

7 Directing Human Resources   165

8 Financial Management   193

The
Recreation and Leisure Service
Delivery System

1

The work ethic may be under fire in the U.S., but another basic drive shows no sign of fading: the right to do as you please—on your own time. Americans, forced in recent years to compromise in many areas of life, remain stubborn about skimping on leisure. Dollars continue to pour out for sports, entertainment and culture, even though incomes for most families have barely kept pace with inflation. . . . Not only is leisure a central part of America's pursuit of happiness, but more and more people use leisure as a way of identifying who they are—a sports enthusiast, an opera buff, a craftsman, a lover of adventure.[1]

The above comments, abstracted from an issue of U.S. News and World Report, reflect the importance of recreation and leisure in today's society. In response to tremendous demand

---

1. *U. S. News and World Report,* August 10, 1981, p. 58

for leisure services and products, numerous organizations have emerged in both the public and private sectors. The variety and scope of leisure products and services is staggering. Increasingly, organizations that provide these services and products are seeking individuals who have the knowledge, competence, and skill to manage them effectively and efficiently.

The tempo of technological, social, and economic change in our society is increasing dramatically. Geographic shifts and demographic changes in population, increased and expanded communication systems, growth and expansion of knowledge, and the unpredictable nature of our economy have set the stage for the emergence of new values. Attitudes, lifestyles, social norms and customs have changed during the past century, and new concepts of individual and collective behavior have emerged, affecting organizations and institutions.

Values associated with work and leisure have undergone significant changes in North American society, especially during the last few decades. Work as a central life focus has been replaced with a leisure ethic that is centered on "the broader goal of providing pleasure and improving the quality of each person's life."[2] Leisure values are influencing the cultural and economic fabric of our society. For example, in the United States expenditures for the consumption of products and services related to leisure now exceed expenditures for defense.[3] Expenditures for goods and services related to leisure are now estimated to exceed 244 billion dollars a year.[4] When adjusted for inflation, this reflects a 47 percent increase between the years 1956 and 1981.

With increasing demand for recreation and leisure products and services, a host of new business opportunities has been created in the private sector and, until very recently, governmental services in this area were expanding. The operation of today's recreation and leisure service delivery system requires a high degree of skill, knowledge, and ability in order to achieve organizational goals while adapting to cultural and economic changes in society. Although total expenditures for goods and services related to leisure have risen substantially, professionals working in recreation and leisure service organizations are increasingly being asked to do more with less. To provide more services of a higher quality, with fewer resources, is the challenge that currently faces those individuals operating recreation and leisure service organizations.

---

2. Marvin D. Dunnett, *Work and Nonwork in the Year 2001* (Monterey, California: Books/Cole Publishing Company, 1973), p. 91.

3. *U. S. News and World Report*, August 10, l981, p. 61.

4. *U. S. News and World Report*, August 10, 1981, p. 62.

BASIC CONCEPTS

There are numerous terms and concepts that can be associated with the delivery of recreation and leisure services. The identification of terms is useful, providing a starting point from which an understanding of the concepts, practices, and functions involved in the delivery of recreation and leisure services can be developed. Some of the terms and concepts that will be discussed are the recreation and leisure service organization, the goals of recreation and leisure service organizations, recreation and leisure products and services, recreation and leisure service delivery systems, recreation and leisure service management, effectiveness and efficiency, and fusion and goal displacement.

The recreation and leisure service organization.   A review of the literature defining organizations reveals many and varied terms. Some of the key terms cited are "a structured process," "a social unit," "the formal framework for the role environment," "the rational coordination of people," "a system of cooperative human activities," "a complex of relationships," and "a network of systems." Most definitions also include a reference to the fact that organizations exist in order to achieve or accomplish a set of specific goals or objectives. Therefore, we can think of a *recreation and leisure service organization* as *a set of structured roles that have been deliberately constructed for the purpose of acquiring and transforming human, physical, fiscal, and technological resources in order to achieve a goal or set of goals.* There are two types of recreation and leisure service organizations: service-oriented and profit-oriented.

The goals of recreation and leisure service organizations.   *Goals are the ends toward which organizational actions are directed.* The goals of the service-oriented agency focus on human well-being, life satisfaction, and happiness. The emphasis of the profit-oriented agency is on promotion of the same values, but in a way that ensures a profit. Agencies organized for profit are service-oriented in that they attempt to create products or services that have value to society. Their *primary* goal, however, is economic gain.

Recreation and leisure products and services.   In the broadest sense, the *products and services* that are created and distributed by recreation and leisure service organizations are *vehicles that are used to produce a leisure experience.* Generally speaking, people are offered experiences, not products or services. This is an important distinction to make. As professionals, we tend to focus almost exclusively on the products or services we create and distribute, rather than the experiences that we are attempting to provide for our constituents.

The recreation and leisure service delivery system. In general, a delivery system may be thought of as a process whereby resources are transformed to produce products or services. *The recreation and leisure service delivery system* can be defined as *a process whereby human, fiscal, physical, and technological resources are transformed to produce the leisure experience.* A delivery system can usually be displayed in a graphic way and its components identified, defined, and measured. We will present a discussion of all of the components of a recreation and leisure service delivery system model later within this chapter.

Recreation and leisure service management. Although there are numerous definitions of the term management, there are common factors in nearly all attempts to define the term. One common factor is the manager's concern with the attainment of organizational objectives. Another factor common to all definitions is the realization that managers accomplish or reach objectives primarily as a result of their relationships with people.

Thus, for the purposes of this text we will operationally define *management* as *the process of working with and through individuals and groups within organizational structures to establish and subsequently accomplish organizational goals.* This definition does not differentiate between the various types of organizations in which managers may be employed, nor does it differentiate on the basis of the sizes or the objectives of the organizations. Such a definition implies the following: (1) management is the process of working with people in the establishment and subsequent attainment of objectives; (2) management expertise, at least to the degree that the manager has an understanding of the organization's objectives, is transferable from one organization to another; (3) the processes of management that facilitate the establishment and attainment of objectives remain the same, regardless of the organization in which these functions occur. Operationally, we may define *recreation and leisure service management* as *the process of working with and through individuals within a formalized organizational structure to achieve goals related to the provision of recreation and leisure services.*

Effectiveness and efficiency. The terms effectiveness and efficiency have become increasingly important in the operation of recreation and leisure service organizations. Inflation, taxpayer concern, economic austerity, and dwindling resources have forced a heightened consciousness concerning the way in which organizational resources are expended. *Effectiveness is the extent to which an organization achieves its stated goals.* Profit-oriented organizations often state their goals in terms of economic profit or loss. Service organizations historically have relied on user participation rates to determine effectiveness. However, neither of these methods offers an accurate reflection of the extent to which a person achieves a leisure state of mind and experiences a sense of satisfaction, happiness, and well-being. *Efficiency* can be defined as *the prudent use of organizational resources—human, fiscal, physical, and technological—to achieve organizational goals.* An agency can be very effective, that is, achieve its goals and still be inefficient, if it uses an inordinate amount of resources to achieve these goals.

Fusion and goal displacement.   The effective operation of recreation and leisure service organizations is tied to an understanding of fusion and goal displacement. Since management essentially involves working with and through individuals and groups, it is important to understand the personal needs, behavior, and concerns of people. Further, since we can think of an organization as a set of structured roles, the integration of these two variables—the personality and disposition of the individual and the organizational structure—becomes the major responsibility of the manager. *When the need disposition of an individual is consistent with the role that has been created for that person, fusion occurs. Goal displacement occurs when the personal needs of individuals come in conflict with the roles that have been created for them, adversely affecting their contribution to the goals of the organization.*

RECREATION AND LEISURE SERVICE ORGANIZATIONS IN POST-INDUSTRIAL SOCIETY

Management has been practiced since people first organized in groups. However, the study of management and the development of a body of knowledge related to management did not occur until the industrial revolution. The industrial revolution started in England and covered a 300-year period, from 1650 to 1955. During this period of time, a number of basic principles evolved that were applied in the management of businesses, industries, and government agencies. These basic principles included division of work, specialization of labor, unity of command, centralization, and chain of command. These principles, when applied, enabled the efficient mass production of goods and services.

In 1955 many developed countries entered a new era. This era was identified as the post-industrial society by Daniel Bell, and more recently, as the technological revolution by Alvin Toffler in his book *The Third Wave.* Two major factors have moved developed countries from the industrial revolution into post-industrial society. First, as of 1955, more people in North America are working in service-oriented positions than in labor-intensive or product-oriented jobs. This has resulted in a dramatic change in the work force, forcing a redefinition of concepts of work, leisure, and job satisfaction. The second factor precipitating the post-industrial society has been the development of the computer and other technological advances. In addition, profound social and cultural changes have helped to bring about the transition from the industrial revolution to the post-industrial society. Increasingly, individuals in society have become more highly educated. The percent of high school graduates increased from 14 percent in 1910 to over 60 percent in 1976. The availability of political, social, and cultural events through the mass media has created a more sophisticated, aware public.

These and other factors have dramatically changed the strategies used in the management of organizations. No longer is it possible to apply a basic set of principles to all organizational situations. Consider the characteristics of employees of post-industrial organizations.

- These employees are highly educated individuals who use work as a means of self-development, self-satisfaction, and self-fulfillment. The possibility exists of an overqualified and undersatisfied work force if proper care is not taken to design work opportunities commensurate with the skills of employees.
- Workers possess a high level of sophistication as a result of increased access to political, social, and cultural events. It is not unusual for employees to bring their social, political, and ethical concerns to the work environment.
- Employees are seeking opportunities for fulfillment through intrinsic, rather than extrinsic rewards. This means that reward systems (the motivation process) will need to be redefined if they are to be effective.
- Increasingly, employees are seeking autonomy within organizations as an extension of freedom of expression or lifestyle. Traditional mechanisms of control, performance appraisal, and the organization of work tasks may have to be reconsidered.
- Work is no longer necessarily viewed by employees as a means to an end, but as an end in itself. As a result, employees want satisfying work experiences that provide opportunities for personal growth and development. There has been a fusion of work and leisure values.

What do such changes in the work force mean to today's recreation and leisure service manager? What abilities will the contemporary manager need in order to succeed? First, he or she should possess human relations skills. The manager should be able to influence people through his or her personality, rather than solely by virtue of the position he or she holds. The manager should also understand the process of delegation of authority. This is especially important since employees are demanding more responsibility, and organizations in general are hiring more specialists. Further, the manager will need to be able to coordinate tasks between work units and resolve conflicts that occur. Conflict resolution will be particularly important. The work environment will be more open and permissive and, as a result, the coordination function will be necessary to ensure that work units are merged together effectively. Managers should also possess skills that help them develop the human resources of the organization. They may need to act as teachers, instructors, and facilitators in order to encourage the growth of individuals. Managers will engage more in long-term planning and, as a result, should be schooled in creative thinking. Last, managers should know how to employ technology, especially the computer, in decision-making.

UNDERSTANDING RECREATION AND LEISURE

It is important that the recreation and leisure service manager understands the bases upon which services and products are created and distributed. In other words, the manager should have a clear concept of "recreation" and "leisure." This portion of the book will define leisure and recreation, discuss the antecedents to the leisure experience and link the definition of terms with practical management considerations.

To fully understand the leisure experience and, in turn, provide services and products that will produce it, the manager must be able to define and measure this elusive phenomenon. A manager who does not understand the cause-and-effect relationship between the provision of a service or product and the resulting outcomes may waste resources or be unable to produce the desired outcomes or behavior. The manager who knows that provision of a summer playground program will result in the demonstration by the consumer of certain behaviors, skills, and knowledge can invest resources to produce the service and have a high degree of certainty that the resources will achieve the desired ends. If this cause-and-effect relationship is not known, then the recreation and leisure service manager may not be able to predict, with any degree of confidence, that the resources invested will be used as intended, in an efficient and effective manner.

Defining Leisure

Leisure has been defined from a number of perspectives. There are four theories that have emerged in the recreation and leisure service literature in the past several decades. They suggest that leisure can be defined as a block of time, a state of mind, an activity, or as a holistic way of life. Following is a brief discussion of each of these approaches to the definition of leisure:

Leisure as time.   Defining leisure as time suggests that life can be divided into segments according to use. Leisure, in this sense, is *an unobligated block of time* in which a person is free to choose activities, passive or active. Thus leisure is regarded as discretionary time, as distinguished from time spent working or sustaining existence.

Leisure as a state of mind.   This approach to defining leisure suggests that leisure is a *style of behavior or an attitude.* An individual's state of mind or condition of existence is the focus of this orientation. This definition is especially useful since the leisure experience is often individually defined.

Leisure as an activity. This approach to defining leisure suggests that leisure can be identified by viewing the *nonwork activities* that one participates in that are associated with leisure services and products. This approach assumes that the leisure experience is limited to *a select number of activities*, such as reading, swimming, walking for pleasure, traveling, and so forth.

The holistic model of leisure. The holistic model of leisure suggests that *all of one's life experiences* have the potential for leisure. Especially important in this definition is the supposition that work and leisure values can be fused, and satisfying life experiences may be derived from either.

Antecedents to the Leisure Experience

In the past several years, a number of social psychologists have begun to identify and isolate the critical components of the leisure phenomenon. They have asked such questions as How do we measure leisure?, Can leisure be measured?, and How can we determine if one is at leisure? Basing their investigations on the theory that leisure is a state of mind that results in behavior or the development or demonstration of an attitude, they found several criteria that can be identified in order to measure the leisure experience. These criteria focus on the individual's disposition prior to the leisure experience. They can be thought of as the antecedents to leisure. The term "antecedent" can be defined as the condtions (in this case, state of mind) that must precede the event or experience. Four variables have been identified as being central to the leisure experience. They are: perceived freedom, intrinsic motivation, perceived competence, and optimal arousal. A brief discussion of each of these variables follows.

Perceived Freedom. When individuals do not feel forced or constrained to participate in activities and do not feel inhibited or limited by the environment, they are said to be perceiving a degree of freedom. Perceived freedom is measured in terms of the concept of *locus of control*. Individuals experiencing an internal locus of control feel that they have control over their behavior and are responsbile for their actions. Individuals who attribute outcomes or events in their lives to external factors such as chance, fate, or luck are said to have an external locus of control. The greater the internal locus of control, the higher the degree of perceived freedom, hence the greater the probability that the leisure experience will occur.

Intrinsic Motivation. The way in which individuals are motivated will also affect the leisure experience. Two types of motivation—extrinsic and intrinsic—have been postulated to explain human behavior. Extrinsic motivation exists when individuals respond to external reward and punishment mechanisms. That is, they are motivated by incentives such as financial rewards, grades, trophies, etc. Intrinsic motivation exists when individuals are motivated from within by inner drives and needs. Intrinsic rewards occur as a result of the experience itself rather than a tangible memento of that experience. Theoretically, intrinsically motivated individuals will gain a greater sense of satisfaction, enjoyment, and gratification from leisure experiences, since extrinsically initiated participation reduces perceived freedom.

Perceived Competence.   Perceived competence refers to individuals' perceptions of their skill levels or abilities. Whether or not individuals have high or low skill levels according to external standards is irrelevant. What is important is the individuals' actual perceptions of themselves, their skills, and their competence in participating in given activities. In order for individuals to experience leisure, they must perceive a degree of competence. The provision of recreation and leisure activities at different skill levels is an example of how agencies have responded to this particular variable, for example, the provision by an agency of two basketball leagues—slow break and fast break. If activities demand a skill level beyond a person's perceived competence or ability, the participant may become anxious. An activity that is too simple may result in boredom.

Optimal Arousal.   Optimal arousal theory is based on the premise that individuals will seek stimulation in order to satisfy their needs for activity. Optimal arousal theory is used to explain human play behavior and offers an hypothesis accounting for behavior after basic survival needs have been met. This theory defines three basic components that determine the attractiveness of an activity: novelty, dissonance and complexity. The concept of *novelty* explains man's desire for unfamiliar stimuli or situations. This suggests that individuals will seek out new adventures. *Dissonance* refers to the element of surprise that can occur within an activity. Individuals are attracted to activities where the outcome is uncertain. *Complexity* refers to the amount of challenge inherent in a given activity. An activity must be either psychologically or physically challenging to the individual, or participation will decrease or stop.

What do these variables (antecedents of leisure) mean in terms of the work of the recreation and leisure service manager? If the presence of these variables results in the leisure experience, then they may serve as guidelines for the development of leisure services and products. Consider the development of a product that has been popular within the last few years— *Rubik's Cube.* This puzzle offers the consumer many of the variables that we have suggested are necessary for a leisure experience. Certainly the cube presents elements of novelty, dissonance, and complexity. It can be easily manipulated, and therefore the perceived ability of the individual to master the game seems (at least initially) within reason. Outside of tournament competition, motivation to solve the problem is intrinsic in nature. Locus of control also remains with the individual. As can be seen, this game has many of the elements necessary to produce a successful leisure experience.

It is obvious that it is important for the recreation and leisure service manager to understand the variables that influence the leisure experience. By understanding these variables, social and physical environments can be created that will ensure, with a relatively high degree of predictability, that given leisure experiences are attained by those consumers that the organization serves. Without knowledge of the variables that influence the leisure experience, the probability of success is reduced or becomes a chance occurrence. Although research in this area is new, these variables should be considered in the development of services and products. Professional recreation and leisure service managers should encourage continued research in this area to ensure an expanded body of knowledge to aid them in making effective and efficient use of agency resources.

Figure 1.1 demonstrates the relationship between *pure research* that is directed toward the understanding of the leisure phenomenon, *applied research* that is directed toward the improvement of service and product delivery, and *organizations* that deliver these services. Scientists who conduct pure research in order to develop theoretical models that can be supported by empirical investigation are concerned with explaining the phenomenon of leisure but not with the way in which this knowledge

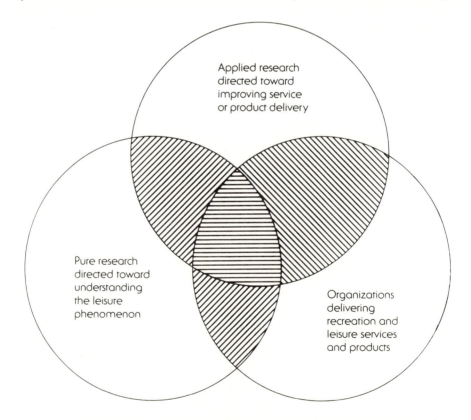

Applied research directed toward improving service or product delivery

Pure research directed toward understanding the leisure phenomenon

Organizations delivering recreation and leisure services and products

Figure 1.1 The interactive relationship between pure research directed toward understanding the leisure phenomenon, organizations delivering recreation and leisure services and products, and applied research directed toward improving service and product delivery.

affects the delivery of leisure services. Scientists who conduct applied research are concerned with acquisition of knowledge that can be practically applied, resulting in an improvement of product and service delivery. Applied research, unlike pure research, is directly concerned with determining the ways in which theories concerning the leisure phenomenon can affect the delivery of recreation and leisure services and products.

The recreation and leisure service manager will probably have a greater affinity for applied research; however, it is important to acknowledge the value of pure research. The recreation and leisure service manager must take the initiative in reviewing and understanding theoretical constructs to determine their potential for application within a leisure delivery system. In the recreation and leisure service field, professionals rarely apply pure research or applied research findings. Further, colleges, the major institutions responsible for conducting pure and applied research, often are negligent in establishing such research programs. One of the important responsibilities of the social scientist is to interpret his or her findings in such a way that they can be understood and used by the practitioner.

The expansion of knowledge in today's society is staggering. Within seven years, half of the current knowledge in the management area will be obsolete. This is also true of the knowledge related to the management of recreation and leisure service organizations and the phenomenon of leisure. Staying abreast of developments and new research is a major responsibility of the recreation and leisure service manager, and perhaps one of the most glaring deficiencies within the profession.

Defining Recreation

Recreation is a term widely used to describe the leisure experience, with particular emphasis placed on it as a form of activity. Recreation comes from the Latin word *recreatio*, which means "to refresh." Most definitions of recreation suggest that recreation is an activity voluntarily engaged in that is satisfying to the individual. Many definitions of recreation suggest that recreation activities are socially acceptable or wholesome.

Use of the term "recreation" may have evolved from two sources. First, it may have been used to describe the desired goal of the leisure experience (rejuvenation) in an era that was tied to the organization of work. During the industrial revolution, the behavior of the worker was regulated by the needs of the organization. Workers no longer adjusted their own work efforts to their own desires, needs, and abilities; instead, they were attached to machines, time clocks, and managers. Individuals worked in a mechanical rhythm: that is, their work, play, and sleep were regulated by the work environment. Time was divided into three components: time spent working (subsistence); time spent in sustaining bodily functions such as eating, sleeping, and sex (existence); and discretionary time (leisure). Discretionary time, like work time, was regulated by the organization and viewed as a commodity that could be manipulated by the organization. Employers viewed recreation activities as a way of restoring or refreshing employees (re-creation) so that they would become more productive.

A second explanation for the use of the term recreation is that it may have evolved from the need to promote socially acceptable uses of leisure. The term leisure has no value orientation; leisure can be used for either good or evil. The term recreation, however, carries a value direction suggesting that activities must be socially and culturally acceptable and contribute to the betterment of the individual and society. The use of the term recreation may have suggested that organizations offering recreation services were engaged in a worthwhile endeavor. Historically, the development of organizations offering recreation services was tied to disadvantaged populations. Recreation activities were often used to socialize individuals to common societal values, such as citizenship, fair play, and cooperation. Furthermore, recreation activities have been used as social instruments to solve certain social problems. Juvenile delinquency in the tenement slums of New York in the 1890s was addressed by providing wholesome outlets for play. The support of the Aristotelian notion of leisure may also be a factor influencing the use of the term recreation. Leisure in the classical sense was used for the development of mind, body, and spirit and was seen, therefore, as a commodity that should be used wisely by the individual.

Regardless of the definition, recreation is a term that has come to be identified with our field. Contemporary theorists would suggest that the use of the phrase "recreation and leisure" is redundant because the term leisure encompasses recreation. This is especially true if the Aristotelian notion of leisure is rejected for a broader, holistic definition that suggests that everything has the potential for producing satisfying leisure experiences.

Organizations, especially government agencies, do not have the luxury of being all things to all people. Organizations must define their scope of services and often must respond to ethical, environmental, and social limits imposed by society. The recreation and leisure service manager is often the individual who charts the course of action for an agency or business. It is his or her job to respond to the legal and philosophical mandate within which the agency or business operates.

TYPES OF RECREATION AND LEISURE SERVICE ORGANIZATIONS

Although there are many types of organizations delivering recreation and leisure services, two major categories of organizations emerge with distinctive values and orientations. The first category includes those organizations for which the basic value orientation is service to people. Organizations with this goal focus on human care needs and are known as human service organizations. Many government agencies providing recreation and leisure services fall into this category. The second category includes those organizations for which the primary objective is profit. Such businesses are also interested in providing a service and meeting the needs of the consumer; however, the success of the organization is usually measured quantitatively, in terms of financial gain or loss.

Recreation and Leisure as a Human Service Profession

Many individuals working in recreation and leisure service organizations are a part of the human service profession. Human service professionals are concerned with the facilitation of human happiness, life satisfaction, and the mental, physical, and social well-being of individuals. It is often said that human service workers are altruistic in the provision of services, deriving their satisfaction from the gains made by individuals receiving services.

In a general sense, organizations in the fields of health, education, and social welfare are considered to be human service organizations. These three general types of organizations include agencies and institutions such as "hospitals, medical centers, mental health centers, social service agencies, public health agencies, public schools, universities, and nursing homes. They also include police departments, correctional institutions, employment services, and probation departments."[5] Human service organizations are pervasive in our society and provide many of the services which North Americans have come to accept as a part of their culture. Certainly recreation and leisure services should be considered to be human services. As a profession, recreation and leisure service workers are involved in providing physical and social environments that affect the behavior and well-being of individuals.

There are a number of different types of recreation and leisure service organizations with similar historical roots. As institutions, they were created either to protect our natural resources or to provide activities, often to disadvantaged populations. Five types of recreation and leisure service agencies are detailed below.

County and local government.   County and local governments are one of the major vehicles for provision of recreation and leisure services in North America. There are nearly 400 counties throughout the United States with park and recreation departments. In addition, special districts at the local level of government whose sole mission is providing park and recreation services are prevalent in California, Illinois, and Oregon. The primary purpose of these types of agencies is to provide recreation programs and services and to acquire, develop, and maintain recreation

---

5. James M. Kouzes, and Paul R. Mico, "Domain Theory: An Introduction to Organizational Behavior in Human Service Organizations," *Journal of Applied Behavioral Science*, (1979): pp. 449–475.

areas and facilities. School districts have increasingly played an important role in the provision of recreation and leisure services, especially those with community education or continuing education programs.

State and federal government.   There are numerous federal agencies engaged in the provision of recreation and leisure services. The primary purpose of many of these agencies is the acquisition, protection, and maintenance of our nation's scenic and historic areas. Some of these agencies are the National Park Service and the U.S. Forest Service. There are many federal agencies for which recreation is a by-product of their primary function, such as the Bureau of Land Management, the U.S. Army Corps of Engineers, the Bureau of Reclamation, the Tennessee Valley Authority, and the Fish and Wildlife Service. Various branches of the armed forces have organized recreation services for their members. State governments are also involved in the provision of recreation and leisure through the management of resources and programs, as well as the creation of enabling legislation to assist the expansion of services at the local level of government.

Voluntary agencies.   This type of organization is nongovernmental and nonprofit. The two types of organizations generally considered to be voluntary agencies are youth-serving agencies and religious social agencies. Youth-serving agencies include such organizations as the Boy Scouts of America, Boys and Girls Clubs, Girl Scouts of America, Camp Fire Inc., and 4-H Clubs. Religiously oriented social agencies may be associated with a particular religious denomination or may be interdenominational in nature. Such agencies as the Y.M.C.A., Y.W.C.A., Y.W.H.A., Y.M.H.A. and C.Y.O. are examples of this type of agency. Voluntary agencies provide educational, recreational, spiritual, and vocational development for their memberships.

Private agencies.   Private membership organizations that are nonprofit are within the category of voluntary agencies. Their primary purpose is to provide opportunities for socializing within the membership of the group. Often these types of agencies have extensive facilities, services, and programs for their membership. Usually members pay an initial membership fee and an annual maintenance fee. Golf clubs and fraternal organizations such as the Elks and Moose are perhaps the most obvious examples of this type of agency.

Advocacy associations.   Advocacy associations usually exist to promote the interests of the disadvantaged or disabled. Although their primary purpose is initiation of community action on behalf of the disadvantaged or disabled, recreation and leisure services may be provided as a by-product of the association's efforts. The Easter Seal Society and the National Association for Retarded Citizens are examples of this type of association.

Recreation and leisure service organizations have often defined their purpose in terms of the products that they create or deliver. This approach to understanding the basic mission of the profession has limited the scope of the movement to the provision of recreation activities and recreation and park areas and facilities. Philosophers in our field, such as Gray and Grebin[6] and Murphy and Howard,[7] have suggested that the focus of the movement should be broader and should center on the creation of humanistic services that promote individual and societal well-being. This reorientation of the recreation and leisure service movement from the products or services that it delivers to an emphasis on human well-being is resulting in a restructuring of organizations, methods of service delivery, and basic assumptions of the profession. In addition, and perhaps more important, linkages between recreation and leisure service organizations and other human service professions are being established.

Within the past decade, the mission of many recreation and leisure service organizations has broadened. Many organizations feel that the traditional provision of recreation and leisure activities and facilities is too narrow. Instead, they view themselves as being concerned in a broader, more holistic sense with the development and well-being of an age group or a unit such as the family. Many volunteer agencies are concerned with nutritional care, family counseling, employment, individual job satisfaction, and self-improvement, as well as recreation and leisure services. The Boys Club does not see itself as being primarily a recreation and leisure service agency, but rather as an organization concerned with the development of youth, crime prevention, and other more broadly conceived services. The Y.M.C.A. movement has expanded its services to include women and families rather than just services for men. Municipal park and recreation departments are being restructured and given a broader mandate. Life enhancement, cultural development, social development, and environmental preservation and protection are becoming dominant themes for which local governments are reorganizing their resources. It is no longer accurate to view agencies that provide recreation and leisure services as only being concerned with the provision of activities or facilities.

Another change that has resulted from the broadening of the mission of recreation and leisure service organizations is in the way in which services are delivered. Traditionally, most recreation and leisure service workers have engaged in a role that resulted in the direct delivery of services. This direct provider role has found the recreation and leisure service professional involved in needs assessment, organizing, promoting, and implementing activities. The job of the direct service provider basically has been

---

6. David Gray and Sy Greben, "Future Perspectives: An Action Program for the Recreation and Park Movement," *California Parks and Recreation,* June/July, 1974. *Future Perspectives II: Earning a Place in National Priorities,* (Institute for Leisure Behavior, Department of Recreation, San Diego State University, 1981).

7. James F. Murphy and Dennis Howard, *Delivery of Community Leisure Services: An Holistic Approach,* Philadelphia: Lea and Febiger, 1977.

one of determining what people want to do; locating appropriate leadership, facilities, supplies and equipment; publicizing the activity to attract participants; and ensuring that the program is carried out in a way satisfactory to both the participants and the agency providing the programs or services.

More recently, another role has emerged for the recreation and leisure service worker—that of the facilitator or enabler. As an enabler, the professional does not use his or her expertise to provide services for individuals, but instead is concerned with promoting initiative by helping individuals discover their own talents and abilities. In other words, professional expertise is redirected from providing activities and facilities to counseling individuals in such a way that they will have the opportunity to use their skills to provide for themselves. This reorientation is changing the role of the recreation and leisure service professional as well as the type and nature of services provided.

Also dramatically affected by the reorientation of the profession are the collaborative relationships or *linkages* that have been, or are being, established with other human service organizations. A linkage implies a sharing of human, physical, and fiscal resources. It involves the development of a cooperative partnership of people, agencies, and institutions. The development of linkages among human service organizations requires planning, organizing, and development of programs on a cooperative basis with participating agencies. In the recreation and leisure service field we have often been involved in the development of agreements for joint use of facilities. The notion of establishing linkages between human service agencies is similar to the concept of shared facilities, however the linkages concept is broader and deals with people in a more holistic, less fragmented manner. All organizational resources have the potential to be linked with other agencies. With the development of programs of communication and interaction, the probability that human service organizations will work on a collaborative and cooperative basis has increased.

Why are linkages among human services important? There are a number of practical reasons. In economically austere times, there is a need to use community resources more effectively. It is important to share human, physical, and fiscal resources, thereby reducing competition between agencies for the same funds. Linkages also result in less duplication of services and more accessibility of services. In addition, the creation of linkages helps to avoid the fragmentation of services.

The legal basis of public recreation and leisure service organizations.   In order for public recreation and leisure service organizations to exist, they must be granted the authority to operate. This authority can be thought of as the sovereignty or right that a government maintains to exercise certain powers and responsibilities. The constitutions of the United States and Canada retain certain rights for the federal government and cede other rights to state and provincial jurisdictions. State and provincial governments, in turn, establish laws that provide the authority for the operation of services at the state and provincial levels and at the local level of government.

Statutory laws established by a legislative body are especially important in the establishment of recreation and leisure services at the local levels of government. At the local level, the most important type of statutory law is that of the enabling act. An enabling act authorizes a local government to establish a recreation and leisure service organization. This type of act specifies methods of taxing, land acquisition, administration of services, and so forth. This permissive type of legislation sets the broad parameters for the operation of a recreation and leisure service system within a city government. Another type of statutory law affecting the provision of services at the local level of government is the *special district*. Special districts are independent, autonomous units serving local jurisdictions. These types of agencies have their own taxing power and governing boards and focus exclusively on specialized services, such as parks and recreation. At the state and federal levels, statutory laws are also used to create agencies that deliver recreation and leisure services. For example, the United States Congress can enact legislation that results in the creation of a federal agency. State legislatures can also enact legislation to establish agencies to provide recreation and leisure services (e.g., departments of conservation, parks and recreation, natural resources, tourism, and so on).

Recreation and Leisure as a Business or Industry

Equally as dramatic as the changes that have occurred within public or semi-public human service organizations is the growth of businesses and industry in the recreation and leisure service and product areas. Over 21 million dollars is spent for television, radios, records, and musical instruments. Over 29 million is spent for toys, sports equipment, and boats. Admissions to amusement parks, theater and opera result in expenditures of over 6 million dollars.[8] These figures indicate the tremendous market in this area.

There are numerous businesses that can be considered part of the recreation and leisure service industry. The diversity and scope of businesses providing recreation and leisure services are great, ranging from the manufacture and distribution of games and toys, to the organization of tours and trips, to the management of ski resorts and theme parks. Some of the general categories of such businesses are travel services, hospitality and food services, leisure products, and entertainment services. A description of these follows:

Travel and tourism services.   Travel has become a large industry in this country. Transporting an individual or group to a particular place of interest

---

8. *U. S. News and World Report,* August 10, 1981, p. 63.

is often termed tourism. Individuals engaged in this type of business are instrumental in transporting individuals to one or more attractions. This might involve working for an airline, a tour bus service, or a car rental agency. Individuals engaged in the travel and tourism business are also involved in the promotion, operation, or administration of tourist agencies or attractions and act as counselors, tour guides, or interpretors.

Hospitality and food services.   Hospitality services are those services that are available to individuals for their comfort while they are away from home. There are a variety of agencies that provide hospitality services, such as resorts, convention centers, hotels, motels, campgrounds, and guest houses. An individual engaged in this type of business might serve as a convention manager, reservations clerk, salesperson, host or hostess, or front office manager. Although these types of services can be associated with activities other than leisure ones, lodgings with appropriate support facilities, such as tennis courts, swimming pools, stables, golf courses, hiking trails, and so on are often the location for recreation and leisure activities. The consumption of food and beverages as a leisure experience is also becoming an important industry. The growth of the fast food industry serves as evidence of this phenomenon, as does the increase in restaurants that create a festive, leisure-oriented environment to complement the provision of their food services.

Leisure products.   Businesses in this area of the industry are primarily concerned with the manufacture, promotion, and distribution of toys, games, sporting equipment, books, vehicles, and souvenirs. North Americans' consumption of such leisure goods is rapidly increasing. Corporations like Mattel Toys, Wilson's Sporting Goods, Nike Shoes, and Winnebago Recreational Vehicles, are examples of successful companies based on the leisure market. A certain area of growth in the years to come will be electronic devices, such as televisions, stereos, and computers. It is likely that nearly every family will be able to have a comprehensive home entertainment center. Such games as Dungeons and Dragons, Top Secret, and Gamma World are increasingly popular with their youthful participants.

Entertainment services.   The entertainment category is comprised of those businesses that create entertainment, amusement, and development opportunities for leisure consumers. There are a variety of these types of businesses, including race tracks, night clubs, rodeos, movie theaters, bowling alleys, carnivals, music centers, dance studios, fitness centers, hobby shops, and tennis or racquetball clubs. Professional sports is an entertainment area that has influenced the leisure patterns and perspectives of North Americans. Attendance at sporting events continues to grow. The amusement or theme park is another entertainment service that is very visable and has set standards for the entire industry in terms of quality of service.

What is the role of recreation and leisure service businesses in society? Basically, such businesses are involved in the creation and distribution of a recreation and leisure product or service for a profit. Businesses have obviously fulfilled this role. Today, one out of every eight dollars spent by Americans is related to the leisure experience. Certainly the quality of life for all North Americans has been enhanced by the availability of products and services that are provided by recreation and leisure businesses. Our economic system of free enterprise has been a major force in producing both material bounty and an increased availability of leisure. Discussing the contributions that businesses have made to society, Mondy et al. have written the following:

Businesses have been able to make significant contributions to the rising living standards primarily because of the manner in which the free enterprise economic system operates. The profit motive provides incentive to business to produce products and services as efficiently as possible. Business firms try to improve the quality of their products and services, reduce cost and prices, and thereby attract more customers to buy from the firm. By earning profits, the successful firm pays taxes to government and makes donations to provide financial support for charitable causes. Because of the efficient operation of business firms, an ever increasing number of people have the means and the leisure time to enjoy the good life.[9]

Recreation and leisure businesses may be in a more favorable position than public agencies to provide quality leisure experiences. They have access to financial resources for capital investments; and the voluntary nature of involvement in the leisure experience makes the application of marketing concepts very appropriate. Because the leisure experience is individually determined, there is a need to create many avenues through which it can occur. Businesses are generally more open, flexible, and capable of diverse services than public agencies and often can more easily respond to individual leisure preferences that differ according to interests, economic status, and other variables.

Because recreation and leisure service businesses operate within society and draw from society, there are many who would say that they have a number of responsibilities to society as a whole. Ethical, environmental, and human social responsibilities should be addressed by recreation and leisure service businesses. Ethical responsibilities require behavior on the part of the organization that is open, honest, and free of deceit and fraud. In other words, all recreation and leisure businesses have a responsibility to represent themselves accurately, by providing forthright information concerning their products or services. Environmental responsibilities are central to many of the values of the recreation and leisure service movement. The preservation, protection, and responsible use of our environment must be a primary concern of the recreation and leisure service business. "The public's environment is the businesses' environment; the people who make up corporations have to breathe the same air, drink the same water, and gaze at the same scenery as the people they work

---

9. R. P. Wayne Mondy, Robert E. Holmes, and Edwin B. Flippo, *Management: Concepts and Practices* (Boston: Allyn and Bacon, 1980), p. 591.

among."[10] The misuse or abuse of the physical environment will ultimately lead to problems within the business environment. Businesses also have a responsibility to people within their organizations and the people they serve. Every business has an obligation to help its employees develop as well as an obligation to participate in and contribute to programs that are directed toward the betterment of the community.

The growth of recreation and leisure service businesses will provide diverse career opportunities for those interested in the recreation and leisure field and will create many new, creative, and diverse opportunities for consumers. The impact of Disneyland as a high quality, profit-oriented venture, for example, has been great. As a leader in this type of industry, Walt Disney Productions has set high standards and has produced an extremely effective model for other recreation and leisure service businesses to emulate. Furthermore, the services delivered by the Disney organization have affected consumer behavior and expectations. Its creative energy has catalyzed other types of services, led to the creation of other theme parks, and opened up new and challenging career paths. These effects have all occurred in a relatively short period of time, as Disneyland recently celebrated its twenty-fifth anniversary.

Organizing the recreation and leisure service business.   There are a number of ways in which recreation and leisure services can be organized as a business enterprise: as a sole proprietorship, partnership, corporation, or cooperative. These approaches to organizing the business activity are based on practices initiated in England. Historically most businesses were run by one individual or a family. As business ventures grew, there was a need to involve other people in order to provide more capital and reduce the risks associated with loss.

The most common form of business ownership is that of sole proprietorship. The *sole proprietorship* can be thought of as one-person ownership. One individual owns and manages the business, is entitled to claim all of the profits, and is responsible for all of the losses. The advantages of the sole proprietorship are that it provides a high personal incentive for the individual, it provides freedom to act, it is less expensive to establish, it is private, and it can be dissolved simply. However, the sole proprietorship has a number of serious disadvantages, including unlimited personal liability, limited capital and talent, and lack of continuity.

A *partnership* is established when two or more individuals combine their resources to establish a business. A partnership has a number of advantages, including increased capital and talent. It also provides an opportunity for valuable employees to be taken in as partners, thereby ensuring stability. The establishment of a partnership is relatively simple and has few legal restrictions. The disadvantage of a partnership is the possibility of disagreement between owners.

A business that has a legal existence of its own is termed a *corporation*.

---

10. R. P. Wayne Mondy, Robert E. Holmes, and Edwin B. Flippo, *Management: Concepts and Practices* (Boston: Allyn and Bacon, 1980), p. 594.

Corporations have the highest sales volume of the three different types of organized businesses. The advantages of a corporation are that it provides limited liability, increased capital, and the opportunity to employ professional management. Further, a corporation can transfer ownership from one party to another simply by selling shares of stock. The major disadvantages of a corporation are that it is expensive to establish and it must pay a corporate income tax.

The last way of organizing a business is as a *cooperative.* A cooperative allows a number of individuals to supply themselves with services or commodities at low cost. Cooperatives are advantageous in that they are usually democratically controlled and can reduce the cost of products in such areas as retail goods, foodstuffs, and insurance. A major disadvantage of cooperatives is that they are not viewed as being profit-oriented corporations, and consequently capital for such ventures is often limited.

Attributes of Recreation and Leisure Service Organizations

Table 1.1 contrasts the attributes of the two types of recreation and leisure service organizations: recreation and leisure as a human service organization and recreation and leisure as a business. The primary motive of

TABLE 1.1   Contrasting Attributes of HSOs and Business Industry*

Dimensions	Human Service Organizations	Business/Industrial Organizations
Primary motive	Service	Profit
Primary beneficiaries	Clients	Owners
Primary resource base	Public taxes	Private capital
Goals	Relatively ambiguous and problematic	Relatively clear and explicit
Psychosocial orientation of work force	Professional	Instrumental
Transformation processes	Staff-client interactions	Employee-product interactions
Connectedness of events and units	Loosely coupled	Tightly coupled
Means-ends relation	Relatively indeterminant	Relatively determinant
Outputs	Relatively unclear and intangible	Relatively visible and tangible
Measures of performance	Qualitative	Quantitative
Primary environmental influences	The political and professional communities	The industry and suppliers

* (From James M. Kouzes and Paul R. Mico, "Domain Theory: An Introduction to Organizational Behavior in Human Organizations." The Journal of Applied Behavioral Sciences, 1979, p. 454.)

one is service, of the other, profit. The primary beneficiaries are, in one case, the clients who receive the services and, in the other case, the individuals who own the business. Human service organizations draw their primary support from public taxes, whereas businesses derive their capital from private sources. An important distinction between the two types of agencies can be found in the types of goals pursued by each. Human service organizations tend to establish highly ambiguous, unattainable goals. The result is services that are difficult to measure, unclear, and intangible. This often is a problem when decisions must be made concerning the distribution of funds. Recreation and leisure businesses focus on more clearly defined, attainable goals. They tend to have tangible products or services, and their measurement of effectiveness is often related to their measure of profit. Thus businesses focus more on quantitative aspects in measuring performance, and human service organizations focus more on qualitative aspects of performance.

It is important to recognize that there are profound differences between the two types of organizations. Their goals, resources, means of production, outputs and measures of effectiveness differ. Each type of agency requires the application of different management strategies and techniques. The successful manager understands different management techniques and strategies and knows when to apply them. It is important to remember that management techniques are not universal. In one situation, one technique may be more appropriate than another; in another situation, the reverse may be the case. It is not uncommon to hear pleas from public recreation and leisure service managers for effective business principles to solve their problems. However, the business environment is different from the environment in which human service organizations operate and business techniques that are successful in running a corporation may not work effectively within public agencies.

RECREATION AND LEISURE SERVICE ORGANIZATIONS: A SERVICE AND PRODUCT DELIVERY MODEL

A model can be thought of as a concrete representation of a concept or idea. The purpose of model development is to represent the component parts of, in this case, a process—the delivery of recreation and leisure services. The model is an abstraction and is presented to help you to understand and to analyze those factors that influence the delivery of recreation and leisure services. Although the model, as represented on paper, is unidimensional and linear, it is important to note that the management process itself is multidimensional, requiring the manager to integrate and synthesize a number of functions simultaneously.

Figure 1.2 presents various components of a model for recreation and leisure service organizations. The model has six major components: (1) the

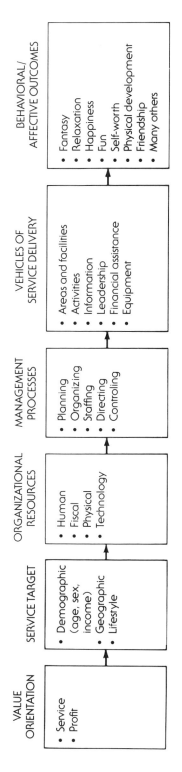

Figure 1.2 The recreation and leisure service delivery system.

value orientation of the organization, (2) the service targets, (3) the resources, (4) the management processes, (5) the vehicles of service delivery, and (6) the behavioral and affective outcomes. The following paragraphs will discuss each of the model's units.

Value orientation.   As previously discussed, the value orientations of recreation and leisure service organizations can be divided into two categories—service and profit. In addition to these two general categories organizations can also have values that are concerned with protection of the environment, reduction of juvenile delinquency, preservation of open space, maintenance and stability of the family, fellowship, citizenship, promotion of physical fitness, promotion of mental health, intellectual development, and employment.

How important is an organization's value orientation? The values held by an agency will determine the types of individuals served by the agency, as well as the methods or vehicles of service delivery. An organization's values provide the conceptual and philosophical foundation from which its actions are initiated and justified. It is important for recreation and leisure service organizations to clearly articulate their value orientations. Failure to do this may create problems both within and without the organization. Within the organization, internal disharmony can result. Outside of the organization, there may be confusion if the organization is not consistent in its actions.

Service targets.   Service targets can be thought of as the people served by the recreation and leisure service organization. Whereas some organizations may serve specific age groups, others may perceive their constituency to include all members of a community. Careful analysis of the service targets to be addressed by a recreation and leisure service organization is important. The idea that an agency can effectively serve all members of a community is a philosophical ideal that is extremely difficult to achieve. Further, in these economically austere times it is much more efficient to concentrate on specific groups in order to make the best use of organizational resources.

The process whereby service targets are identified is known as market segmentation. Market segmentation involves an analysis of the potential recipients of services by demographic, geographic, and lifestyle variables. The idea of market segmentation was first practiced on a large scale by the General Motors Corporation when they discovered that markets could be segmented by income. Rather than producing one car model with one price, General Motors produced a full line of cars from Chevrolet to Cadillac priced at different levels to accommodate different consumer incomes. Car companies have further segmented the market by designing cars that appeal to different lifestyles. Thus, a car could have racing stripes or be styled as a family sedan, depending on the lifestyle of the consumer. Demographic variables—age, sex, and income— are very useful in predicting leisure behavior. Lifestyle variables, such as a person's risk-taking propensity, and qualities such as introversion/extroversion, aggression/submissiveness, and liberalism/conservativism are also predictors of leisure behavior.

Organizational resources.   Recreation and leisure service organizations have four primary resources—human, fiscal, physical, and technological. *Human resources* are the most important resources in any organization. The personalities, dispositions, interests, and ambitions of individuals within organizations will greatly influence the extent to which the organization succeeds or fails. It is through its human resources that the organization achieves its goals. In turn, it is through the management process that human resources are recruited, trained, and motivated. *Fiscal resources* refer to the financial capital available to the organization. Recreation and leisure service organizations have two primary fiscal sources—subsidies from government and user fees paid by individuals who consume services or products. Financial management is extremely important both in agencies subsidized by taxes and those businesses that measure their success or failure by their financial profit or loss. *Physical resources* refer to the facilities, areas, equipment, and supplies that the organization acquires or possesses. Organizations need a place to conduct business as well as space to provide services and to store items needed for various activities. *Technology* includes all of the knowledge, skills, and methods used to produce various services. The technology of some agencies is highly refined and developed. For example, the organization of leagues and tournaments that have precise rules and definable structures is said to have achieved a highly refined state of technology.

The types of resources needed by a recreation and leisure service organization will vary according to its value orientation, its service target and, ultimately, the methods that it employs to deliver services. A park system may require herbicides and pesticides to be used in the maintenance of park areas, whereas a recreation department may be more concerned with the acquisition of sports equipment. No two agencies will have the same resource needs. Even if their services are directed toward the same age group, their geographical location will affect the types of resources needed.

Management processes.   Once a recreation and leisure service organization has acquired necessary resources, it must transform these resources into services or products. This transformation is the management process. In order to accomplish this transformation, the recreation and leisure service manager performs a number of functions: planning, organizing, staffing, motivating, budgeting, and controlling. A separate chapter is devoted to a detailed discussion of each of these management functions, so we will only briefly define them here.

Planning involves the identification of goals and objectives and the methods that are used to achieve them. *Organizing* finds the manager establishing roles, developing structures and merging work units in a coherent fashion. The process of recruiting, screening, interviewing, testing, and developing individuals can be thought of as the process of *staffing*. Staffing also involves appraising the performance of individuals and determining the extent to which they are performing effectively and efficiently in their assigned duties. The management process of *motivation* can be thought of as a dynamic process involving the basic interaction between the manager and his staff. *Controlling* is a management function that involves the establishment of standards and the measurement of performance as contrasted with such standards. *Financial management* focuses on the management of an organization's fiscal resources. This management function is multidimensional, incorporating components of each of the other management functions. For example, the budget is a mechanism of control as well as a planning tool that reflects the programs of the organization.

The emphasis that a manager places on each of these functions will vary, depending upon the type of organization involved and the specific position of the manager within the organization. In larger organizations top level managers spend more time on long-range planning than do top level managers in smaller organizations. It is interesting to note that successful managers spend a higher percentage of their time with managers at the same level. Poor managers must focus their attention on subordinates who have been inappropriately recruited or trained.

Vehicles of service delivery. Vehicles of service delivery can be thought of as the programs or products that the recreation and leisure service organization produces. Of course, the basic value orientation of an agency will greatly influence the types of programs or products produced. A company that manufactures toys will have a product line different than a sporting goods manufacturer.

Some of the products or programs created and distributed by recreation and leisure service organizations are: areas and facilities, activities, information, leadership, equipment, and financial assistance. *Areas and facilities* refer to the acquisition and development of land and physical structures for recreational use. Some of these facilities are parks, swimming pools, ice rinks, tennis courts, racquetball courts, amusement rides, ski hills, toboggan runs, arboretums, aquariums, zoos, recreation centers, airports, bird sanctuaries, marinas, drag strips, youth centers, conservatories, gymnasiums, libraries, athletic fields, botanical gardens, campgrounds, playgrounds, riding and hiking trails, and fitness centers. Recreation and leisure *activities* can be thought of as structured experiences, including sports, games and athletics, visual arts, crafts, performing arts (dance, drama, and music), hobbies, outdoor recreation, social recreation, volunteer services, literary self-improvement programs, and travel and tourism. These activities can be organized in numerous ways: competitively, on a drop-in basis, as an instructional effort, as a club, a special event, a workshop or conference, or as an outreach program.

The provision of *information* by recreation and leisure organizations is directed toward helping individuals identify available leisure pursuits. At its most sophisticated level, information is offered through a leisure counseling program. A recreation and leisure service organization may provide *leadership* to a group wishing to organize around a special interest or concern. Agency leadership is directed toward the development of individual and group skills. The agency leader serves as a catalyst, encourager, process expert, and instructor. Yet another type of service is direct *financial assistance* to individuals and groups. An example of direct financial assistance is the service operated by Ontario's Ministry of Culture and Recreation, which gives direct financial assistance to individuals and groups wishing to pursue leisure interests. For example, if an adult basketball team in a southern part of the province wanted to participate in a tournament in the northern part of the province, the ministry might subsidize a portion of the travel costs. *Equipment* manufacture is a major business area in the recreation and leisure field. We use the term equipment in the broadest sense to include toys, games, apparel, sports apparatus, recreation vehicles, electronic gear, books, magazines, plants, tools, and so on.

Behavioral and affective outcome.   Behavioral or affective outcome can be thought of as the end result of the recreation and leisure experience. *Behavioral* outcomes are those outcomes that can be demonstrated in such a way that they are observable by the recreation and leisure service manager. *Affective* outcomes are the feelings, emotions, and satisfaction derived by the individual that are not necessarily observable or measurable. Both public and profit-oriented recreation and leisure service organizations have goals that focus on producing satisfying experiences for consumers. In public agencies, the goal of service is primary, and the well-being and happiness of customers is the focus of organizational efforts. In the profit-oriented organization, on the other hand, profit is the focal point, but there is a symbiotic relationship between the desire for profit and the desire to satisfy consumers. The two variables, profit and consumer satisfaction, are inseparable. Consumers who are not pleased with a service or product will not participate in the service or consume the product in the future, resulting in lower sales and declining profit.

There are numerous behavioral and affective outcomes that can result from the leisure experience. These include behaviors that manifest a sense of accomplishment and achievement, increased body awareness, changes in self-esteem, development of confidence, creative expression, development of friendships, enjoyment, entertainment, excitement, expanded awareness of self, exhilaration, increased feeling of self-worth, fun, happiness, improvement of mental health, and increased use of one's imagination. Other outcomes include opportunities for risk-taking, mental achievement, reflection, rejuvenation, relaxation, relief of tension, escape and fantasy, and alleviation of boredom and anxiety.

SUMMARY

Technological, social, and economic change in our society has produced a new set of values based on leisure. This new value orientation is focused on enhancing life satisfaction. The corresponding growth of agencies and institutions providing recreation and leisure services has produced a need for competent, knowledgeable, and skilled managers.

The recreation and leisure service organization can be thought of as a social unit that has been deliberately constructed to achieve a set of predetermined goals. The goals of recreation and leisure service organizations can be identified as either service- or profit-oriented. Service organizations focus on human well-being, life satisfaction, and happiness. Profit-oriented organizations have an economic motive, as well as one directed toward successfully meeting leisure needs. These organizations produce many different types of products and services through which the leisure experience is achieved. In an ecological sense, the recreation and leisure service delivery system can be thought of as a process whereby human, fiscal, physical, and technological resources are transformed to produce the leisure experience. A key element in the transformation of resources is the manager, who works with people to achieve organizational goals. In the transformation process there is a need to use resources effectively and wisely.

Central to the effective and efficient management of recreation and leisure organizations is an understanding of the leisure experience. Leisure can be defined as time, a state of mind, or as an activity. Further, it can be defined in a holistic way, suggesting that many, if not all, of our life experiences have the potential for leisure. In order to help the reader understand the leisure phenomenon, several antecedents to the leisure experience have been defined. These include perceived freedom, intrinsic motivation, perceived competence, and optimal arousal. Understanding these variables can help the recreation and leisure service organization produce environments that result in the leisure experience.

There are many types of recreation and leisure service organizations. Those focusing on service as a central goal include agencies and organizations at the local, county, state, and federal levels of government; voluntary agencies; private, nonprofit membership organizations; and advocacy associations. Those organizations with profit as a primary purpose include travel and tourism services, hospitality and food services, manufacturers of leisure products, and entertainment services.

The recreation and leisure service delivery system has six major components. These include the value orientation of the organization, the service targets, resources, management processes, vehicles of service delivery, and behavioral and affective outcomes. This delivery system is the process whereby resources are transformed and services are produced.

STUDY QUESTIONS

1. Define recreation and leisure service organizations, leisure products and services, and the recreation and leisure service delivery system.
2. How do the concepts of efficiency, effectiveness, fusion, and goal displacement relate to one another?
3. What are some of the characteristics of individuals working in post-industrial society?
4. Why must the recreation and leisure service manager be able to define and measure leisure and recreation?
5. How can knowledge of the antecedents to the leisure experience affect the development of vehicles for service delivery?
6. What are the differences between service-oriented human service agencies and profit-oriented recreation and leisure service businesses? Identify different types of recreation and leisure service agencies and locate specific agencies in your own community.
7. List four ways in which recreation and leisure services can be organized as businesses.
8. Discuss the attributes of the two types of recreation and leisure service agencies.
9. Identify and discuss the major components of a recreation and leisure service delivery system.
10. What social, cultural, and economic variables do you think will influence the operation of recreation and leisure service organizations in the year 2001?

CASE STUDY 1

Three Steps Toward Professionalism and those Ticky-Tacky Boxes

It was June and Chuck Christopher was uncomfortably warm in his rented hood and gown. "Well, this is it!" he thought as his line moved slowly toward the three steps leading to the stage of the university auditorium. As Chuck heard the registrar call his name, he mounted the steps to the stage and walked to the podium. The dean shook Chuck's hand, smiled, and wished him luck as he handed Chuck a rolled diploma. "Finally!" thought Chuck, "after four years of study, four field work experiences, and a four-month internship in Canusa, I have graduated!"

Happy as he was to be graduating and starting a new position as assistant program director for the Canusa Parks and Recreation Department, Chuck was rather sad to realize that his undergraduate days were over. "Monday morning when I report to work at the Municipal Building, I will be starting a new chapter in my life," he thought as the dean commenced his final remarks to the graduating class. Similar thoughts were occupying Ron Levy, newly appointed recreation therapist for the Canusa Mental Health Center, and fellow graduate Barb Quarry who only that morning had accepted the position of youth work director at the Canusa Family Y.M.C.A.

At the same time that Chuck and his classmates were receiving their diplomas,

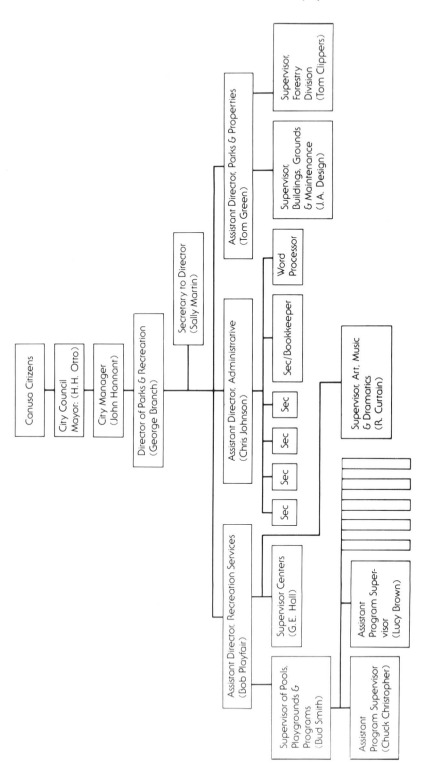

Partial organizational chart: Recreation and Parks Department, City of Canusa.

George Branch, due to retire in three months as commissioner of Recreation and Parks for Canusa, was making last minute changes to the notes he had prepared in preparation for his weekly senior staff meeting at four o'clock. Each Friday for the past three months George; the director of Recreation Services, Bob Playfair; the director of Parks, Tom Green; and the director of Administration Services, Chris Johnson, met in George's office to discuss the happenings of the last week and to plan the next week's activities.

George glanced at his notes once again and reread the items for discussion: a complaint from Mr. Gardner about vandalism after the teenage dance last Friday, a request from Bud Smith for a new filtration plant at the pool complex, the ordering of new playground equipment for Central Park, the request from the city manager for preliminary estimates for the next year's budget, the request from the local service club council for use of the skating arena for a carnival night, the request from the Canusa Athletic Council for the use of the lighted athletic field during July, and, finally, the request from the mayor and council for an up-to-date organization chart of the department.

"It was so much simpler in the old days," thought George. When he became director, the department consisted of himself, his secretary, and part-time program leaders. "How this operation has changed. In those days we operated primarily summer programs, worked closely with the Y.M.C.A. and the schools, had our budget set each year by the city council, without too much fuss, and had no need for fancy organization charts, specialized personnel, union negotiations, neighborhood councils and pension plans. Life has changed in these past 20 years," he mused as he turned to the revised organization chart, the preparation of which had caused him reluctantly to miss his weekly poker game, and had involved two lenghty sessions with his secretary, Sally Martin. "What do these boxes and lines really mean?" he asked himself. Noting the latest box to be added, designated as "assistant supervisor of programs," and bearing the name "Chuck Christopher" he wondered if this newest member of his growing staff would help solve, or simply add to, the many problems he was having in his twentieth year with the department—a period during which the municipality had grown from a small town of 15,000 to a still-growing municipality of 230,000 persons. "Our operational budget is now over three million per year," he thought, "at last count we had 46 full-time personnel in the department, and that figure doesn't even include the union personnel in the parks section. In many ways, I am glad to be leaving this job before it gets even more involved. In two more months my only worry in regard to recreation and parks will be whether my drives are straight and I read the greens right on my putts."

As he waited for the three senior staff members to arrive, he reviewed the organization chart and tried to picture each of the persons listed in the boxes. "Some of these people I don't even know personally," he said aloud as he distributed the charts in front of the three empty seats around his desk. "Boxes, boxes, ticky-tacky boxes," he thought, "what do they really mean?"

QUESTIONS

1. What do those "boxes and lines" really mean?
2. How can Chuck Christopher's university preparation help him in his new job?
3. How specifically can this course you are enrolled in prepare you for a professional career in the recreation and leisure field? What do you expect to learn? What do you want?
4. What can the instructor do in this course to help you understand the concepts more effectively?

Participants and Programs

2

Carl Kloninger, a professor of mathematics at a local university, has a keen interest in dancing. New in town, he would like to meet other people. He is from the southwestern area of the United States.

Karen Smith, a young telephone worker, enjoys solitude in her nonwork hours, as well as being outdoors. Living in a large urban area, she has been frustrated in her attempts to meet her leisure needs.

David Clifford, a 12-year-old boy, is gregarious and enjoys solving complex intellectual problems. He also enjoys interacting with other children his age. His mother would like to involve him in a community recreation program.

The above scenarios point out the wide variety of leisure needs. It is the function of the recreation and leisure service manager to determine what participant needs are and then to structure program offerings and services that will meet these needs. In the case of Carl, the mathematics professor, square dancing may be an appropriate program to meet his particular needs. For Karen, the telephone worker, a backpacking trip into the wilderness might help her to find the solitude she desires in the outdoors. David Clifford, the 12-year-old boy, might be best served by a club activity focusing on Dungeons and Dragons or a class in computer operations. In short, the programs that are created and distributed by the recreation and leisure service organization enable individuals to achieve leisure experiences and meet leisure needs.

DETERMINING PARTICIPANT NEEDS

How can the recreation and leisure service manager predict whether a participant is likely to benefit from services provided by his or her organization? Why are some services consumed by large numbers of individuals and others not? How can the manager attract participants to programs and services? Answers to these questions are complex and are at the heart of the success or failure of a recreation and leisure service organization. There are numerous factors that can influence the behavior of individuals. An understanding of some of the processes that explain human behavior can be useful in predicting the leisure patterns of participants.

Understanding Human Needs

Human beings are active; they are continually striving to meet certain needs, wants, and interests. These needs, wants, and interests give direction to human behavior. In other words, most human behavior is goal-directed. It is directed toward alleviating physical hunger, physical discomfort, anxiety, boredom, lack of social contact, lack of self-esteem, lack of security, and so on. Some of these needs, wants, and interests are biological; others are psychological and social. In other words, some of these are innate needs; others are culturally defined and can be learned. To develop programs and services effectively, it is important for the recreation and leisure service manager to differentiate between needs, wants, and interests of participants. The manager can influence wants and interests, but cannot influence innate needs. A brief description of needs, wants, and interests follows.

- Need. A need is an innate, inherent characteristic of the individual (nature of the person). Needs must be satisfied to attain happiness or contentment.

- Want. A want is culturally learned and results in defined patterns of behavior (nurture for the person).

- Interest. Interests are innate and learned ideas, motivations, attitudes and goals. Interests are things that attract and hold the attention (the intensity and duration of the attention dependent on the source of interest and motivation) of the participant.[1]

Motivation to satisfy these needs, wants, and interests is characterized by the following: (a) energy arousal, (b) direction of effort toward a particular goal, (c) . . . attention (focused) on relevant stimuli, (d) organization of response . . . into an integrated pattern or sequence, and (e) persistence of this activity until the initiating conditions are changed.[2] Where in this process can the recreation and leisure service manager intervene effectively? *Cues* can be given by the recreation and leisure service manager that affect nearly all of the components of the motivation process. Cues can be thought of as an arrangement of the physical and social environments by the leisure service manager in order to stimulate the participant to give a certain response. For example, initial energy arousal (e.g. sparking an individual's interest and desire to participate) can be facilitated by promotional activities. A visual cue, such as a logo that has become associated with a desirable outcome, can trigger a positive response, such as registration for an activity. The role of the manager is to arrange such cues, especially those that relate to culturally learned ideas, patterns of behavior, and goals to motivate the participant to meet his or her needs.

Once energy arousal has been achieved, e.g. a participant is involved in an activity, the recreation and leisure service manager can intervene with cues that help the participant direct his or her effort toward a particular goal or meeting a particular need in a concentrated and organized fashion. For example, a need for social contact might be met by offering a social recreation activity. Once a participant's need, want, or interest has been met successfully, reinforcement has occurred, and the participant will be more likely to seek out similar experiences in the future. Again, managers should look for cues that can be used to reinitiate action and participation on the part of participants.

Qualifying Dimensions: Developing Service Targets

Chapter 1 discussed qualifying dimensions that can be used to predict recreation and leisure needs, wants, and interests more accurately. These qualifying dimensions include an analysis of the potential recipients of services by demographic, geographic, and lifestyle variables. Demographic variables refer to such factors as the age, sex, and income of potential participants. Lifestyle variables can be thought of as personal preferences for a manner of living that may or may not be related to demographic and

1. Peter Witt and Rhonda Groom, "Damages and Problems Associated with Current Approaches to Developing Leisure Interest Finders," *Therapeutic Recreation Journal*, 13:1 (1979), p. 23.

2. Philip G. Zimbardo and Floyd L. Ruch, *Psychology and Life*, 9th ed. (Glenview, Ill.: Scott, Foresman, 1976), p. 198.

geographic variables. Lifestyle variables might include one's propensity for risk, desire to be fun-loving, degree of introversion or extroversion, degree of active or passive behavior, and so on. Geographic variables refer specifically to the location of individuals. Different regions spawn different cultural patterns, norms, and values.

The process of sorting out needs, wants, and interests in terms of the qualifying dimensions of demography, geographic location, and lifestyle is done through the process of *market segmentation*. Market segmentation involves dividing the market into homogeneous groups. These homogeneous groups then become potential service targets that can be served by the recreation and leisure service organization. Each distinct homogeneous group will have unique needs, wants, and interests. Program services should be designed and priced in a way that is consistent with these distinctions. It is a faulty assumption to believe that a recreation and leisure service organization should cater to everyone, simply because everyone has leisure needs. Some segments of the market will be more responsive to the services that the organization provides than others. Individuals vary in their commitment to leisure pursuits and, logically, limited organizational resources and promotion should be directed toward those individuals most likely to become involved in the programs and services offered by the organization.

An Alternative Approach to Determining Needs

Another approach to determining needs has been developed by Bradshaw[3] and applied to the recreation and leisure service field by Mercer,[4] and later by McAvoy[5] and Godbey[6]. They have suggested that defining recreation and leisure service needs has been extremely difficult and that there has been a need for a taxonomy that would help identify approaches for determining needs, especially in the public sector. Whereas Bradshaw suggested that needs could be classified into four categories: *normative, felt, expressed, and comparative*. Godbey expanded the concept and added a fifth classification: *created needs*. Following is a brief description of each of these terms.

Normative needs. Normative needs can be thought of as general established standards with which comparisons to actual behavior can be made. They are established by experts using professional judgement to

3. Jonathan Bradshaw, "The Concept of Social Need," *New Society*, 30, no. 3 (March 1972), pp. 640–643.
4. David Mercer, "The Concept of Recreational Need," *Journal of Leisure Research*, 5:1 (Winter 1973), p. 37.
5. Leo H. McAvoy, "Needs of the Elderly: An Overview of Research," *Parks and Recreation*, 12:3 (March 1977), pp. 31–4, 55.
6. Geoffrey Godbey, "Recreation and Park Planning: The Exercise of Values." (Paper presented at a graduate seminar, University of Waterloo, Waterloo, Ontario, January 1976), p. 2.

determine what constitutes the most appropriate or most effective number of facilities, acres of parkland, and so on. Normative standards are often criticized as being irrelevant to local, specific needs.

Felt needs.   When an individual expresses a desire to participate in an activity, program, or service in which he or she has not previously participated, the desire is known as a felt need. Felt needs are useful predictors of leisure behavior, although not always accurate. Individuals may indicate a preference for an activity, but may not actually participate in it if it is made available.

Expressed needs.   The activities, programs, or services that an individual actually participates in can be thought of as expressed needs. In developing programs and services, it is useful for the manager to determine what activities individuals have participated in the past in order to accurately predict the likelihood of future participation. Of course, by offering only services or programs that have been offered successfully in the past, the manager narrows the experiences available to participants.

Comparative needs.   Comparative needs are determined by comparing the program offerings of one agency with those of a similar agency, or by comparing the leisure preferences of one individual with those of a similar individual. The premise is that similar individuals and communities will tend to enjoy similar activities. Comparative needs are often used in the park and recreation field as a basis for the establishment of programs and services. The comparison of like communities and individuals may not take into consideration the differences that may be present and, thus, may offer inaccurate information for program planning.

Created needs.   Created needs are determined by engineering social and physical environments and providing appropriate cues to influence the wants and interests of individuals. In other words, created needs are needs that have been determined by professionals, or through the market segmentation process, and presented to participants. The value orientation of the manager can affect the validity of this approach.

These strategies for determining needs can supplement the market segmentation process. Recreation and leisure service organizations use a variety of techniques or tools to collect information concerning needs, including surveys, questionnaires, polls, personal interviews, observation, plebiscites, petitions, briefs, and advisory groups.

A PRODUCT OR PROCESS?

Recreation and leisure organizations can provide services by using either *direct service delivery* or *enabling or indirect service delivery.* Direct service delivey is product-oriented; that is, it involves the planning, organization, promotion, and implementation of activities, facilities, and information resource systems. In this approach to providing services, the recreation and leisure service manager identifies consumer needs, manages resources within complex bureaucratic structures, and creates and distributes services. The work of the manager is often evaluated in terms of the number of participants served, the number of facilities, programs and activities offered, and the amount of parkland provided. These criteria provide quantitative measurements from which effectiveness and efficiency can be determined.

The relationship between the participant and the recreation and leisure service manager using the direct service role is one of provider and consumer. The recreation and leisure service agency and the professionals operating the organization are veiwed as the experts who have the knowledge to acquire resources and transform them into specific facilities or activities. The direct service approach to delivering services is also known as the *social-planning process*. Social planning is a rational approach that is systematically directed toward identifying and solving social concerns and problems. It is a procedure whereby the recreation and leisure service manager engages consumers or participants in decision making. The extent to which the participant is involved in any of these mechanisms varies according to the needs of the organization.

Enabling or indirect service delivery suggests a different relationship between the professional and the consumer. It involves the development of a cooperative relationship wherein the professional works with participants in order to help them acquire the knowledge, skills, or attitudes necessary to control, provide, or influence variables that affect individual or community leisure experiences. The work of the professional using this approach to service delivery is not oriented toward the creation and distribution of facilities and activities, but rather is focused on helping individuals to attain appropriate knowledge and skills. Individuals are encouraged to help themselves control their own leisure, and to operate independently of the formal recreation and leisure service delivery system.

The enabling or indirect service approach is also known as the *community-development* or *locality-development* process. Community development can be thought of as a way in which broad participation of community members can be encouraged in the planning, organization, and implementation of recreation and leisure services. It is based on the assumption that professionals are not the only members of society who have appropriate knowledge, skills, and ability to plan and implement recreation and leisure activities. In fact, it presumes that these skills are widely distributed throughout society and can be taught to individuals by the professional recreation and leisure service manager. The recreation and leisure service manager plays many roles when employing the community development strategy: enabler, catalyst, facilitator, educator, group monitor, problem solver, and so on.

The organization of a community sports program can serve as an example of how these two strategies (direct and indirect service delivery) can be employed. Using the social-planning process or direct-service approach, what would the work of the recreation and leisure service manager involve? Basically, in this situation the manager would first determine whether or not there was a need for the program. This would be a fact-finding process. Assuming that there was a need for the activity, the manager would acquire the resources to build appropriate facilities. The manager would then plan the program. For an athletic activity, this might involve establishing the rules and parameters of the activity; determining the number of teams and the type of tournament; locating and hiring officials, scorekeepers, timers, and coaches; and promoting the activity. After planning the program, the manager would oversee implementation of the activity. All of the management processes would be within the parameters or jurisdiction of the organization and most likely would be financially subsidized by the organization, as well as supported by participant fees and charges. The participant in this process consumes the service and has extremely limited involvement in the planning and implementation of the activity. Basically, the agency acts as the provider, taking care of all details regarding program organization, promotion, and implementation; the consumer is the recipient of this process.

Using the community-development or indirect-service approach, the work of the professional would be vastly different. The basic set of assumptions that the manager uses to create and distribute services changes, as does the relationship with the participant. Rather than planning for people, the role of the manager is to plan *with* people so that participants can assume the control of and responsibility for the organization, promotion, and implementation of the program. Using this approach, the manager would not plan activities for individuals, but instead would help interested persons develop their own skills, knowledge, and ability to run a community sports program.

Specifically, the manager might work with community members to incorporate as an independent, nonprofit organization, perhaps affiliated with a community recreation and leisure service organization. The manager might also help the group understand the fundamentals of fund raising and help in the actual implementation of a fund-raising event. The manager might provide groups with access to the latest product information and rule modifications made by local, state, and national organizations. The manager might also help groups understand the process of acquiring, for temporary use, facilities operated by other government agencies, such as school districts. Further, the manager might help sports groups establish workshops and training programs for coaches and officials.

In other words, using the community-development approach, the manager would assist the group by helping it identify and assimilate all relevant information necessary to plan, organize, promote, and implement the community sports program. However, the recreation and leisure service manager would not actually plan and implement the program. This would be the consumer's responsibility, and thus the control of the program would rest with the consumer, rather than the recreation and leisure service agency or professional. The participant would play an active role rather than a passive one in the participation and implementation of the sports program. The community-development approach encourages independence on the part of consumers, rather than promoting a dependent provider/consumer relationship.

Both of these strategies for service delivery—community development (indirect service) and social planning (direct service)—are employed in recreation and leisure service organizations. The social-planning process is more widely used, as indicated by studies of the perceptions of municipal park and recreation directors of the goals of parks and recreation departments conducted in Canada and the United States.[7] In fact, goal statements relating to indirect service activities, such as providing consultation services, direct financial support, equipment for nonprogram activity use, leisure counseling, and so on were rated in the bottom 25 percent by the respondents in these studies for both actual level of importance and future level of importance. In other words, the respondents in these studies viewed themselves primarily as direct service providers, not only in terms of their present work, but also in terms of their future work activities.

Many contemporary philosophers in the recreation and leisure service field suggest that the community-development strategy will be more frequently employed in the future. Murphy,[8] Gray and Greben,[9] and Foley and Benest[10] have suggested that strategies that promote self-help and participant independence should be employed by recreation and leisure service delivery systems. Further, the idea of self-help programs independent from government agencies is currently being encouraged by conservative political groups and has been advocated in the past by liberal groups. It seems as if there is considerable support for this strategy.

When using the community-development strategy, the recreation and leisure service manager attempts to establish a network of groups and organizations that independently provide recreation and leisure services. Once the manager assists in the development of one independently functioning group or organization, he or she would move on to others, thereby assisting in the creation and distribution of new and diverse recreation and leisure services.

It could be argued, however, that North Americans, who are very efficiency- and task-oriented, would not be interested in a community-development approach to recreation and leisure services. Many consumers tend to want services that are prepackaged in such a way that they are able

---

7. Christopher R. Edginton, "Organizational Goals—What Directors Think They Should Be, and Are," *Recreation Canada*, no. 36/5/1978, p. 33; *A National Study of Goals*, (Center for Leisure Studies, University of Oregon, 1980).

8. James J. Murphy, *Concepts of Leisure* (Englewood Cliffs, N.J.: Prentice-Hall, 1981), p. 25.

9. David Gray and Seymour Greben, "Future Perspectives," *Parks and Recreation*, (July 1976): p. 49; David Gray and Seymour Greben, *Future Perspectives II: Earning a Place in National Priorities* (Institute for Leisure Behavior, Department of Recreation, San Diego State University, August, 1981).

10. Jack Foley and Frank Benest, "Proposition 13 Aftermath—A Crisis in Recreation and Parks Leadership?" *Parks and Recreation*, 15 (January, 1980): pp. 87, 98.

to enter and exit the leisure experience with a minimum of effort. Interestingly, this attitude may account for the tremendous increase in business for companies that provide recreation and leisure services and products such as theme parks, fast food restaurants, and fitness centers. Social planning is an efficient way of packaging and delivering services, and this may account for the dominance of this strategy in government agencies that provide recreation and leisure services.

Another factor that might hinder the use of the social-planning process is the desire of recreation and leisure service agencies to control program offerings. Theoretically, one could argue that the involvement of the recreation and leisure service agency in the planning and organization of programs entails a continuing responsibility on the part of the agency for the actions of the satellite organization, even though it may be operating independently. This could be a difficult situation for the recreation and leisure service organization, in that it would have no control over a satellite organization that was operating in opposition to the philosophy of the parent organization, although the parent organization might well be held accountable. Using the community sports program as an example, the satellite organization could develop a philosophy emphasizing competition that might be in opposition to the philosophy of the parent organization of promoting fun and skill development. In this case, the parent organization might still be associated with the satellite organization in the mind of the public, but would have no control over the actions of the sports group.

ORGANIZING RECREATION AND LEISURE SERVICES

The process of developing a recreation and leisure service can be undertaken on a step-by-step basis. Basically, it involves the determination of program objectives; the specific area in which a program is to be developed; the format; the length, duration, and time factors of the service; the facilities, areas, and equipment to be used in providing the service; the cost of the service; the leadership or personnel to be employed; the methods of promotion to be used; the factors necessary to ensure participant safety; and program evaluation. Both nonprofit and profit-oriented organizations use the same methodology. It is important to note that a different emphasis will be placed on various parts of the process, depending on the goals of the organization. Some organizations will place a great deal of emphasis on the development of activities, whereas others will focus more strongly on the creation of facilities. However, in either case, consideration of all parts of this methodology would be appropriate.

Establishing Objectives

The first step in the process of program development is the establishment of program objectives. Program objectives must be stated in measurable, quantifiable terms in order to serve as a basis from which accurate evaluation can take place. This step in the program-planning process is often ignored or underemphasized by recreation and leisure service organizations. It is an important step in the planning process, and program objectives should be linked to broader organizational goals and statements of purpose. The process of establishing organizational goals and objectives is outlined in Chapter 3.

Objectives for program development should be written in behavioral or performance terms. That is, they should be written in terms that define the behavior, values, attitudes, and knowledge that should be demonstrated at the conclusion of an individual's involvement in a given leisure activity. One may argue that the establishment of program objectives is difficult because the leisure experience is often individually defined. However, from a theoretical as well as practical basis, the recreation and leisure service manager must have criteria in order to determine whether or not the agency's effort has achieved its goals. In an age of accountability, it is simply not acceptable to provide services without determining what they are intended to accomplish and what they do, in fact, accomplish.

Program Areas

Program areas refer to the general content of the service to be delivered. There are numerous ways of classifying program areas: passive versus active, formal versus informal, or by more descriptive terms, such as educational, cultural, and physical. In this text, we have chosen to adopt a classification system developed by Edginton et al.[11] These authors suggest that program areas can be divided into visual arts; crafts; new arts; performing arts (including music, drama, and dance); hobbies; sports, games, and athletics; outdoor recreation; social recreation; volunteer services; literary and self-improvement; and travel. The following is a brief definition of each of these program areas:

Visual arts.   Visual arts are art forms that are decorative and aesthetically pleasing. They can be either graphic representations, such as an oil, watercolor, or acrylic painting; a pen-and-ink drawing or sketch; or a block printing; or objects with dimension, such as sculptures.

Crafts.   Crafts are very similar to visual arts in that they are also decorative in nature. However, a craft also serves some utilitarian purpose, and it is this factor that distinguishes it from purely visual art. Making a lampshade, a belt, a vase, a candle, an item of clothing, can all be classified as crafts since each of these items has a functional purpose aside from the decoration that they provide.

---

11. Christopher R. Edginton, David M. Compton, and Carole J. Hanson, *Recreation and Leisure: A Guide for the Professional* (Philadelphia: Saunders College, 1980), pp. 97–9.

New arts.   In the nineteenth and twentieth centuries, technological developments have provided new avenues for leisure expression. Consider the invention of photography and the artistic and leisure-related spinoffs related to this technological invention of the 1800s. Certainly, the computer, television, and radio have provided and will continue to provide additional avenues for artistic expression, as well as opportunities for leisure enjoyment.

Performing arts.   The performing arts include music, drama, and dance. The important factor distinguishing this category from others is that the artist is the mode of expression. Such things as singing, playing, and performing are modes of expression within this area.

Hobbies.   A hobby is a leisure activity that is pursued over an extended period of time with intense interest. There are a variety of different kinds of creative and educational hobbies ranging from collecting stamps, to traveling, to running. Most other program areas can be hobbies.

Sports, games, and athletics.   Sports, games, and athletics involve fine and gross psychomotor coordination and muscle control. A game usually involves some combination of luck, physical endurance, and skill. Sports and athletics involve similar elements, but are more formal and, especially in the latter case, are competitive in nature.

Outdoor recreation.   Outdoor recreation services are those that are tied to interpretation, awareness, and use of natural resources. Thus, outdoor recreation can occur both indoors and outdoors, as long as the focal point of the service is concerned with the environment. Generally, outdoor recreation services are divided into two categories: activity-oriented and resource-oriented.

Social recreation.   Recreation and leisure services that focus on bringing people together and the resulting interaction between individuals can be defined as social recreation. Thus, other program areas can be included in this category if their primary objective is social interaction. Festivals, picnics, reunions, retreats, parties, and dances are all examples of social recreation services.

Volunteer services.   The number of North Americans contributing their leisure to a variety of agencies and institutions on a voluntary basis is increasing every year. A volunteer is an individual who contributes his or her time, energy, and skills without financial remuneration. Examples of volunteer services in the leisure area include working with youth-serving agencies, serving as cultural and historical guides, and working with senior citizens.

Literary and self-improvement programs.   Perhaps the greatest growth area of leisure products and services has been in literary and self-improvement programs. Reading for pleasure is a popular leisure activity as evidenced by the growth of paperback book sales. Self-improvement programs have also grown by leaps and bounds. These programs are directed toward intellectual development, as well as personal and spiritual development.

Travel and tourism.   Travel and tourism are involved with the support services provided for people who travel from one area to another for recreation. This includes services offered at primary tourist attractions, such as historical sights, cultural areas, natural wonders, and novelty attractions, as well as support services such as hotels, travel agencies, restaurants, and transportation.

Program Format

The program format refers to the way in which a specific program area is organized. It is the structure within which the program is contained. Program formats are varied and can facilitate different opportunities for leisure expression. Some formats are highly structured, requiring specifically defined responses from participants, whereas other formats provide opportunities for broader responses from participants. Following are some of the program formats that can be employed by recreation and leisure service organizations: instructional class; competition; club; drop-in; special event; outreach; and workshop and conference. A brief description of each of these program formats follows:

Instructional class.   Many recreation and leisure service organizations attempt to teach participants leisure skills, knowledge, and attitudes. This is usually accomplished through a highly structured learning situation wherein participants study a given topic over a fixed period of time. Instructional classes are usually didactic in nature, in the form of expository lectures.

Competitive.   Many recreation and leisure services are organized on a competitive basis. There are a number of ways that services can be organized competitively, including contests, meets, or tournaments. We usually think of competitive organization as occurring in sporting events, where leagues are formed or duel competitions established. Competitive activities can be thought of as a way to compare the performance of one individual or team with the performance of another individual or team, or to assess one's own performance as compared to past performance or standards.

Club.   Club organization is widespread in North American society. Clubs are organized around special interests such as square dancing, bridge, sports, and amateur radio with leadership primarily provided by group members. Clubs offer a way for members to exchange information and resources and create opportunities for participants to socialize with others with whom they have common interests. There are many different types of clubs, including travel, service, fraternal, sport, spiritual, hobby, and self-improvement.

Drop-in.   The drop-in format is used to provide services in which the participant retains a high degree of control. Participants select those activities that they would like to pursue within a facility, area, or other structure that has been made available by the recreation and leisure service organization. A park, in a broad sense, provides opportunities for individuals to drop in and use the facility at their discretion (within reasonable limitations) to pursue activities of their choice, such as picnicking, jogging, relaxing, viewing natural beauty, walking, and so on.

Special event.   A special event is a format for organizing recreation and leisure services in which the participant engages over a relatively short period of time—a day, a week, or a few hours. It lacks the regularity of involvement that other program formats may demand. Further, a special event usually involves special planning that departs from the routine planning associated with other organizational functions. It is a powerful program format and usually elicits strong participant interest and response, if carefully and appropriately organized. Special events may include such activities as an Easter egg hunt, an art show, or a carnival.

Outreach.   The outreach program format implies that the agency provides a service to the participant directly within his or her own environment. This could be the participant's home, neighborhood, street, or place of work. Outreach programs in the recreation and leisure service field have been manifested primarily through the use of mobile recreation units, including bookmobiles, sportsmobiles, mobile swimming pools, zoomobiles, portable stages, and sciencemobiles.

Workshop/conference.   The workshop/conference method of organization can be thought of as a process wherein information is disseminated, problems solved, and attitudes formulated in an intense program of interaction. This format also includes the convention, institute, seminar, and clinic methods of organization and is often preferred by individuals who seek intense short-term leisure experiences. It is very popular in the self-improvement program area.

Length and Time Factors

Length refers to the number of days, weeks or months necessary to implement a program. Time factors refer to the number of hours per session that are necessary to implement a given service. Obviously, the needs of the participant must be taken into consideration when determining these factors, since they may spell the success or failure of a given activity. Increasingly, program services are being scheduled to accommodate new patterns of work, as well as changes in leisure lifestyle patterns.

Facilities, Areas and Equipment

In order to conduct a given service, there is often a need to construct or locate an appropriate area or facility. Specifically, an activity must be housed in a structure that is conducive to its successful implementation. A candlemaking class, for example, should be housed in a facility with appropriate lighting, seating, work space and heating in order to provide the best possible environment for learning. Likewise, there is a need to have the appropriate equipment available to conduct the activity. In the case of the candlemaking, running water, burners or hotplates, and other supplies such as wax, coloring, and wicks would be needed. In times of financial austerity, the recreation and leisure service manager may need to be creative and seek out those resources that can be employed in the most cost-effective manner. This will be discussed later in this chapter.

Cost

The financial outlay, in terms of both operating and capital expenditures is obviously an important consideration of the recreation and leisure service manager in the program-planning process. In profit-oriented organizations, the manager wants to ensure that expenditures do not exceed revenues, and in nonprofit organizations the manager wants to ensure that expenditures are consistent with the mandate of the governing body of the organization. Cost is also a determinant of participant involvement. Often the price of a particular product or service is associated with its value. Consequently, offering a free program may not necessarily attract the numbers or type of participants desired. Careful consideration should be given to fees in the establishment of pricing strategies. It is important to convey the value of a program to the public.

Leadership

The single most important factor in the organization of programs and services is the leadership provided. It is interesting to note that in the operation of theme parks such as Disneyland, careful consideration is given to the appearance, presence, and cordiality of employees. These organizations recognize the importance of ensuring that appropriate leadership is available to complement the provision of facilities and activities within the park. Not only is leadership the most important factor in program success, it is also the most costly. Therefore, the recreation and leisure service manager must pay close attention to the recruitment, screening, selection, placement, and training of employees. Chapter 6 discusses staffing in detail.

Methods of Promotion

Program promotion can be basically thought of as a process of communication. The recreation and leisure service manager must communicate a message to the prospective participant. For example, an agency might focus its promotional activities on the benefits or value that an individual could derive as a result of participation or involvement in a program or service. The communication can be either a verbal or written expression or some type of visual stimulus. There are five basic ways to promote a program: through advertising, publicity, sales promotion, personal selling, and public relations.

Advertising.   Advertising can be thought of as a paid message that informs or persuades an individual to participate in a service. There are two types of advertising: direct action and indirect action. The first encourages the participant to consume the service immediately; the second attempts to instill long-term interests in the organization's services or products. Advertising is usually done through television, radio, magazines, newspapers, and billboards.

Publicity.   When the media report the various events or activities of a recreation and leisure service organization, they are reporting the news of the agency to interested individuals. Therefore, publicity can be thought of as news about the agency that is of interest to its consumers. News is not manufactured; however, recreation and leisure service organizations can help those organizations reporting the news, such as newspapers and television and radio stations by providing them with accurate, useful information through news releases, photographs, press conferences, and other media opportunities.

Sales promotion.   Sales promotion attempts to generate consumer interest in an activity through such strategies as sampling, coupons, contests, and demonstrations. Sampling and demonstrations are similar, in that they both allow the participant to preview the activity prior to purchase. Coupons are used to generate interest by providing reduced rates for consumption of a service. Last, contests stimulate interest by directing attention toward a product by promising the consumer an attractive payoff.

Personal selling.   Personal selling involves face-to-face contact with consumers to persuade them to participate immediately in an organizational activity. Personal selling is a dynamic way to interact with the consumer and has become essential in the operation of most profit-oriented organizations. Because personal selling has a poor image, a concerted effort should be undertaken to train personnel effectively in this area. Personal selling usually involves two steps: order taking, and support or servicing of clients. Order taking involves identification of new consumers for the organization and, of course, taking initial orders. Servicing or supporting established consumers involves ensuring that products are operating effectively, as well as taking reorders.

Public relations.   The image that an organization projects to its consumers is of extreme importance. This image is cultivated through the process known as public relations. Public relations should affect every aspect of an organization's operation—not only the way in which employees interact with the public, but also the way in which facilities are maintained, products created, and so on. Most organizations develop a strategy to cover the area of public relations. A public relations strategy may include such activities as the releasing of staff to work on projects in the public interest or the standardizing of stationery and logos that can produce a favorable image.

Participant Safety

The safety of the participant is of extreme concern for two primary reasons. First, each participant has the right to engage in programs with the assumption that safe conditions exist. This means that consideration has been given to the design of equipment, the condition of facilities, the competence of the leader, and the skill level of participants. Consideration of participant safety is especially important in high-risk activities such as sky diving, scuba diving, spelunking, hang gliding and skiing. Discussing participant safety, Ford suggests that each program plan should include the following:

1. Participants: limited by number, ages, abilities, qualifications, physical condition, experience.
2. Activity: location, distance, dates, time, alternate routes.
3. Transportation to and from the activity.
4. Permission of authorities (if needed).
5. Equipment: mandatory/optional.
6. Identifiable hazards.
7. Policies to manage risk potential in light of 1 through 6 above.[12]

The second reason that participant safety is important is that a recreation and leisure service organization exposes itself to potential financial loss by not considering risks or hazards. For example, a recreation and leisure service organization may be liable for its failure to protect the participant from injury or harm that occurs as a result of poor program organization, use of poor or hazardous equipment, or lack of responsible leadership. Management programs designed to address the issues of consumer safety and protection of the organization from financial loss are

---

12. Phyllis M. Ford, *Principles and Practices of Outdoor/Environmental Education* (New York: John Wiley, 1981), pp. 134–5.

known as *risk-management programs.* These types of programs are concerned with the identification of hazards that can result in financial loss to an organization. The key in determining how to manage these risks is the identification of the likely severity and frequency of each risk that may be encountered by the organization. Once this is determined, the organization may choose an effective management program. Situations that could be defined as high risk and high severity might be avoided completely by an organization.

Program Evaluation

The last step in the process of program development is that of program evaluation. Evaluation can be thought of as a process wherein the organization attempts to assess the extent to which it has achieved its stated goals and objectives. Evaluation should be an ongoing activity that takes place not only during the organization and implementation of an activity, but also at its conclusion. Evaluation that is directed toward assessing the step-by-step process of program development, as it occurs, is known as *formative evaluation.* Evaluation that takes place at the conclusion of a program effort or that attempts to assess the concluding impact of a program on individuals or groups is known as *summative evaluation.*

In the recreation and leisure service field, most of the evaluation that has occurred has focused on the quantitative aspects of service delivery. There is a tendency for a recreation and leisure service agency to count the number of acres of land that it has developed and maintained, the number of individuals that participate in programs offered by the agency, and so on. In profit-oriented organizations, evaluations activities are expressed in quantitative terms as the profit margin. *Qualitative* evaluation of the impact of programs on individual leisure behavior, values, and attitudes is lacking.

THE LIFE CYCLE OF PRODUCTS AND SERVICES

Change is prevalent in North American society. This is reflected in leisure as well as other behavior. The leisure tastes, interests, and needs of North Americans change rapidly. How can the recreation and leisure service manager prepare effectively for the changes that are necessary in the products and services offered by a delivery system? One of the most useful techniques available to recreation and leisure service managers is the *product life cycle* concept. This simple concept suggests that products and services, like people, go through stages of growth and development. As the life changes of a person may be categorized and predicted, so may the life span or cycle of products or services. By understanding each of the stages that a product or service passes through, more effective plans can be developed for its management and marketing.

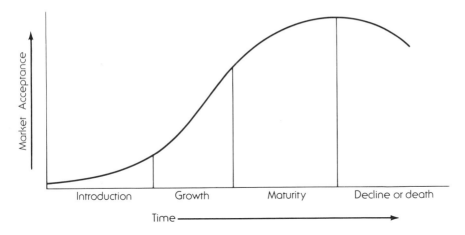

Figure 2.1 Stages in the product life cycle. (Adapted from Philip Kotler, *Marketing for Non-Profit Organizations*, Englewood Cliffs, N.J.: Prentice-Hall, 1975, p. 168.)

Figure 2.1 presents the stages in the product life cycle. These four successive stages are known as introduction, growth, maturity, and decline. Following is a discussion of each of these.

Introduction.   The introductory stage in the product life cycle attempts to gain acceptance of the product or service by the consumers for whom it is intended. Basically, the consumer or participant must be informed of the availability of the new product or service, as well as its features or value. Usually, this is a period of heavy product promotion and involves the extensive investment of funds for the development of the product.

Growth.   Once the product has been successfully introduced to the market, the next step in the process is rapid growth. The growth stage of the product life cycle can be thought of as the period in which the product or service becomes adopted broadly by the target market. It is also a period during which competition emerges from other organizations and agencies.

Maturity.   Following the growth stage, the product or service enters the stage of maturity. This is a period of time characterized by consumer familiarity with the product or service. Further, since competing products and services may differ only slightly from one another, promotional activities are geared toward emotional appeals as a way of attracting consumers. Competition is very keen between organizations at this stage of the product life cycle.

Decline.   The last stage in the product or service life cycle is known as decline. This is a period of time when consumer interest in the product dies. It is at this point that new replacement products are cycled into the system.

Often, competition to sell dying products results in a lowering of the prices of products and services.

Product life cycles may be short or long. However, product life cycles seem to be short for leisure products and services. Consider the short life cycles for leisure products and services such as pop music, skate board parks, trampoline centers, tennis apparel, activities and facilities, roller skating apparel and facilities, video games, and children's toys and games.

The recreation and leisure service area appears to be *style-* and *fad-oriented*. The term style can be thought of as a distinctive method of expression that has been accepted broadly during a relatively long period of time. Fads, on the other hand, are adopted by a narrow segment of the population for a very short period of time.

There are trends that can be detected within the population as a whole that reflect the style of the times. We often think of this as the culture embraced by the majority of individuals within our society and define it as popular culture. For example, in past decades, the popular culture in North America, as it related to leisure, centered on group activities. Individuals were likely to engage in group-related activities such as sewing bees, quilting parties, parlor games, and church-related activities. More recently, the popular culture in North America emphasizes individual expression of leisure interests. Individuals today are more likely to pursue leisure interests such as jogging, meditation, bike riding, reading, use of individualized home entertainment units, watching TV and listening to the radio.

Fads, in the areas of leisure, provide a means by which individuals can express new and different forms of behavior with public sanction. This diversity of expression has resulted in a greater variety and number of avenues for the leisure experience. There are more leisure fads, occurring more rapidly today. Fads have very short life cycles. Consider the hula hoop craze of the late 1950s. This leisure product went through a life cycle of very short duration and now is in a state of decline.

How can the recreation and leisure service manager use the product life cycle? By understanding that products and services go through a life cycle, the recreation and leisure service manager can exercise management action in order to complement each stage of the process. As the product life cycle progresses, an agency will want to devote an appropriate portion of its resources to it. This will ensure that the organization's resources are used in an efficient and effective manner. It is important to note that different products and services will have different life cycles. The target market being served will also influence the life cycle.

Social movements also have life cycles. The play movement may have followed such a life cycle. During the late 1800s and early 1900s, playground programs were introduced in such cities as Boston, Chicago, and New York. The period between 1910 and 1960 saw tremendous growth of recreation services. Municipal park systems may be following a similar life cycle. Again, there was a period of introduction of municipal park services in the 1850s, followed by a period of rapid growth. Both the play and recreation and park movements may be at a level of maturity and, in fact, may be declining somewhat, especially when per capita expenditures for services are compared.

Recreation and leisure services provided by the private sector seem to be at the introduction or growth stages of the product life cycle. Theme parks, for example, were introduced just over 25 years ago. During the 25 year period since then, there has been a tremendous increase in the number and variety of theme parks in the United States. Nearly every major metropolitan area today has a theme park. The prospects that this market will continue to expand, at least in terms of new theme parks, is unlikely, and therefore the maturity portion of the life cycle is in effect at this time. However, it is interesting to note that within theme parks themselves there is a consideration of the effects of the life cycle in terms of the park attractions. New rides are frequently being introduced and older rides are cycled out as they become less attractive to the consumer. In this way, the theme park remains a popular leisure entity.

JOINT USE OF ORGANIZATIONAL RESOURCES

What does joint use of organizational resources suggest? The joint use of organizational resources implies a sharing of resources. As indicated in Chapter 1, organizations work with four types of resources: human, fiscal, physical, and technological. Sharing these resources simply means that an organization commits some of its resources to another organization in order to provide a program, build a facility, or organize a community activity that might not be possible or cost effective without this relationship.

Without question, the joint use of organizational resources is becoming increasingly important in these changing times. Reductions in government spending as well as changes in the basic patterns of service delivery (involving a more broadly defined organizational mission) require that recreation and leisure service organizations cooperate with other agencies and institutions. Not only is it important for public agencies to cooperate with one another, but also for public agencies to cooperate with private organizations. Historically, cooperation between municipal park and recreation departments and, for example, public school systems has been seen as desirable, if not mandatory. Many states have enacted enabling legislation that provides opportunities for governmental agencies to cooperate with one another. The collaborative relationship between local park and recreation departments and school systems has been well established. However, newer patterns of cooperation are emerging. As the mission of recreation and leisure service organizations has expanded, newer collaborative relationships have been developed with other governmental units, including social welfare, health, police, environmental service agencies, and so on. Further, cooperation between the public and private sectors is being promoted. Private investments, beyond the traditional concession type operations, are being pursued. Numerous ventures that combine private capital with public lands, facilities, and other resources are being carried out.

The parks and recreation department in Plano, Texas has developed a number of strategies to encourage cooperation with other public agencies and the business community. This city has experienced tremendous growth during the past two decades. In 1960 Plano's population was 3,695. In 1980 its population was estimated to be in excess of 75,000. The challenge of providing municipal park and recreation services at low cost to the taxpayers of Plano was enormous. The park and recreation department initially sought to work closely with the Plano Independent School District to establish programs operated in schools. This initial program venture met with success and encouraged the development of a collaborative relationship that ultimately led to the joint purchase and development of land and buildings and joint operation of these areas and facilities. Today, eight school/park sites exist throughout the community, as well as numerous joint recreational facilities, including two swimming pools that are located adjacent to schools. The park and recreation department has also actively pursued collaborative relationships with business. Today, an outstanding golf course has been developed and is operated on public lands with private capital. In addition, the city has utilized undeveloped private lands for a youth soccer program. Private business also operates and maintains a municipal tennis center. The city developed the facility and shares in the profit with the professional manager who runs the center. Each of these ventures has expanded services to the citizens of Plano, while at the same time minimizing the cost to taxpayers. Without these collaborative ventures with other public and private organizations, Plano's park and recreation department would have not been able to develop these areas and facilities without a substantial increase in their costs. This is especially significant in light of the tremendous increase in Plano's population over the past two decades.

The sharing of organizational resources requires the development of a cooperative partnership between parties or agencies, based on the assumption that each benefits from the sharing process. In other words, there must be an exchange between parties or organizations that is beneficial to each. Cooperative partnerships between government agencies benefit taxpayers by lowering the cost of services, providing opportunities to extend the impact of available fiscal resources, and theoretically providing more and better services. Cooperative arrangements with businesses can provide a public organization with capital that would not otherwise be available to develop facilities. They can provide a business with a means to generate a profit through the provision of land that would not otherwise be available.

There are a number of reasons that recreation and leisure service organizations are being encouraged to share resources. Some of the more important ones include the following: to avoid duplication and fragmentation of services, to use resources and facilities most effectively, to reduce competition among agencies for funds, and to develop new programs and strategies through synergistic planning.

Duplication of services.   To avoid duplication of services, government agencies are being encouraged to plan their programs, services, and facilities collaboratively with other organizations. In tight financial times, it is inexcusable for a program provided by a government agency to expend resources to compete for the same clients as a program of another government agency within the same geographic area.

Avoiding fragmentation of services.   A lack of coordination between agencies providing services tends to fragment services, resulting in waste, frustration, and a feeling on the part of the participant of being pulled between competing agencies. Joint use of resources can alleviate this by encouraging the planning, organizing, and development of programs that group services together logically, based on the holistic needs of the participant.

Efficient and effective use of resources.   The need to expend organizational resources efficiently and effectively is obvious. A management strategy directed toward joint use of resources implies the need for agencies to communicate with one another. Communication may lead to more efficient and effective planning and, hence, more cost-effective use of resources.

Improving accessibility of facilities and services.   Most agencies operate on limited budgets and may not be able to provide all of the services that they would like to. By pooling resources, two or more agencies can work together to extend the use of facilities by expanding the hours of operation, the variety of program services, or the number of locations at which services are offered. This leads to increased accessibility of facilities and services to participants.

Reducing competition among agencies for funds.   Joint use of resources can reduce the competition for funds among agencies providing similar or duplicate services. In addition, cooperation between agencies seeking funds can be advantageous, increasing the likelihood that they will receive them. If, for example, two agencies approach the taxpayer with referendums to purchase bonds at the same time, the taxpayer, in all likelihood will support only one of the referendums. Therefore, if the two agencies (for example, a school district and a park and recreation department) pool their planning and approach the taxpayer with a jointly developed referendum, it is more likely to pass.

Synergistic planning.   The joint use of organizational resources leads to synergistic planning. Synergy implies that blending different resources will lead to innovations and new methods for solving problems. Combining the thinking of two agencies can lead to new programs and strategies, as well as an understanding of current methods of management that have been successfully employed and utilized in other organizations.

Building Collaborative Relationships

The key to joint use of organizational resources is the establishment of cooperative relationships. Several factors must be taken into consideration in the development of these types of relationships. Initially, there must be a commitment to the need for linkages between organizations. If the recreation and leisure service organization is not committed to the idea that joint use of resources is not only necessary but desirable, collaborative relationships will be difficult to establish. Total commitment implies a willingness to give time, energy, and resources to the development and maintenance of collaborative partnerships. This requires that the philosophy of joint use be embedded in the organization's planning process and that staff be coached in its importance.

When working with other organizations, there is a need to develop a high level of honesty, trust, and respect. This usually occurs when individuals are mutually committed to the objectives of a given program, both formally and informally, and may involve the development of formal and informal agreements that are mutually subscribed to and understood by the parties involved. Staff time may be used to clarify agreements, underscoring the various expectations that each of the parties involved have of one another and their roles and responsibilities. Further, it is important to recognize that some conflict may be inevitable between agencies operating on a collaborative basis. Strategies to handle conflict effectively must be developed by the recreation and leisure service manager and employed when necessary.

There are a number of specific steps that can be taken by recreation and leisure service managers in order to develop cooperative relationships with other organizations. Some of the management strategies are very simple and can be carried out with little effort or expenditure of organizational resources. Others are more complex and require considerable planning and organization. Following are some ideas that managers can use to build cooperative relationships:

1. Determine the status of existing agreements and relationships with other organizations.
2. Contact other agencies and individuals to determine interest.
3. Assess your own organization's readiness to engage in cooperative relationships with other agencies.
4. Inventory existing community and organizational resources, including human physical, fiscal, and technological ones.
5. Review local and state laws that promote and mandate the joint use of organizational resources.
6. Develop role expectations (job descriptions) that require individuals to pursue and promote joint use of organizational resources.
7. Organize a network of agencies concerned with the joint use of resources. Establish meetings, workshops, and clinics.

8. Promote joint use of organizational resources to the public by establishing a public awareness program.
9. Examine model programs that emphasize joint use of organizational resources.
10. Calculate the potential financial savings that could result from joint use of resources.

Developing cooperative partnerships requires a proactive posture on the part of the recreation and leisure service manager. This is because the recreation and leisure service organization often has the most to gain from such partnerships. A proactive posture suggests that recreation and leisure service managers take the initiative in pursuing collaborative relationships. It is important to recognize, however, that barriers may be encountered. Some of the barriers might include territoriality, competition, poor communication, tradition, politics, and lack of trust. These barriers can be overcome by establishing management strategies that allow for the identification of barriers, as well as strategies to surmount them.

SUMMARY

This chapter has focused on two important concerns in the delivery of leisure services: determining participant needs and organizing programs. Human behavior is goal-directed; that is, it is directed toward the fulfillment of needs, wants, or interests. These can be innate or learned. The role of the recreation and leisure service manager is to identify various needs, wants, and interests of participants and then provide cues that trigger responses or behavior designed to fulfill these needs, wants, and interests.

A number of qualifying dimensions can be used by the recreation and leisure service manager to better understand the interests, needs, and wants of individuals. These qualifying dimensions include the age, sex, and income of participants (demographic variables), the location of participants (geographic variables), and the personal preferences of participants (lifestyle variables). The process of sorting out needs, wants, and interests, using the various qualifying dimensions, is known as market segmentation. The goal of this process is to identify homogeneous groups of individuals, in order to meet their needs.

There are two vehicles that can be used by recreation and leisure service organizations to deliver services. Direct service delivery, or social planning, is a process whereby the manager applies his or her expertise to plan systematically and to solve societal problems and concerns. Indirect service delivery, or community development, emphasizes the creation of broad opportunities for citizen participation and finds the manager acting as an enabler, catalyst, facilitator, educator, group monitor, and problem solver.

The actual process of program planning involves ten steps: (1) establishing objectives; (2) determining program area; (3) determining program format; (4) establishing the length, duration, and time of the program; (5) securing necessary facilities, areas and equipment; (6) establishing the price or cost of the service; (7) securing and training leadership; (8) promoting the activity; (9) ensuring participant safety; and (10) evaluating the program. A useful technique in determining the life of a given program can be accomplished by applying the product life cycle concept. This concept suggests that products and services, like people, go through stages of growth and development. One of the most important concerns in the development of programs is the effective joint use of organizational resources. Joint use of resources implies a sharing of resources and the establishment of a cooperative partnership.

STUDY QUESTIONS

1. Define human needs, wants, and interests, and discuss how the recreation and leisure service manager can affect them.
2. Describe the motivation process as it relates to participant needs.
3. Discuss market segmentation and identify the primary qualifying dimensions that can be used by the recreation and leisure service manager in this process.
4. What does the question "Recreation and leisure services—a product or process?" mean?
5. What is the difference between social planning and community development?
6. Identify and define eleven program areas.
7. Identify and define seven program formats.
8. Identify and define five methods for promoting a program.
9. Identify and discuss the product life cycle. What leisure activities do you think will have short or long product life cycles?
10. Discuss why joint use of organizational resources is important. What are some things that the manager can do to promote joint use of organizational resources?

CASE STUDY 2

The First Day: Morning

It was Monday morning and Chuck Christopher's first day as the assistant supervisor of programs at the Canusa Recreation and Parks Department. Chuck had been looking forward to this day for a number of reasons. It was great to be finally working full-time, with a chance to put into practice many of the ideas that had been discussed in class over the past four years. Chuck was also looking forward to working with George Branch. George Branch had been a frequent guest lecturer in some of Chuck's classes, popular with the students because of his entertaining presentations. "After working 20 years with the department, five of those years as commissioner, he knows just about everyone on the city council and in Canusa. He should really be able to give me good direction," thought Chuck as he neared City Hall. When the former commissioner had moved to a large metropolitan park system, the popular and experienced George, who at that time was the director of the Recreation Services Division, had been the first choice of the selection committee for the vacated position. George's good-natured manner, his years of experience as director of the largest division in the department, and his knowledge of the community and the members of the committee had made the choice an easy one.

Chuck pulled his somewhat battered car into the city parking lot, parked in the space allocated for staff and entered the new building. Familiar with the building, Chuck soon found his small but neat office. Just as he was getting settled behind his desk, his phone rang. Sally Martin, the director's secretary, was on the line and informed Chuck that Mr. Branch was on his way over to pick him up and take him to the personnel department to complete the forms required of all new personnel. As Chuck hung up his phone George appeared with an outstretched hand and said, "Welcome aboard Chuck, and let me be the first to congratulate you on your new position."

As they walked the short distance to the personnel department, George introduced Chuck to several secretaries, the maintenance man for their floor, and then to Mr. Hiriam, the director of personnel. After Chuck had picked up the necessary forms he was escorted back to George's office and over coffee was introduced to his new responsibilities.

"Chuck," said Mr. Branch, "you may call me George, and before you get involved with anything else in the department, I did want to ask you to pay particular attention to a pet project of mine, the Jackson's Park development, which is situated in the east area. It is my feeling that we should put all our efforts into seeing that the east area gets the new combination pool and library that has been suggested for the city. As a resident of that particular area I know the need exists and I would like you to spend at least one day per week for the next few months developing a brief that could be submitted to council. I know that Bob Playfair and Tom Green are not as enthusiastic as I am about this particular project, but I want you to concentrate your efforts on development of this brief. When you meet with community groups you can also help to get the community involved. I want you to report directly to me on this matter and will expect a progress report at the end of this month. I've mentioned my interest in the project to Bob Playfair, but since Tom Green feels that he should share his program objectives with the other two assistant directors, I have not told him as yet that you are going to develop this report. I'll let him know in a couple of weeks however, so it would be appreciated if you could work on this quietly for at least two months. Okay? Thanks, and if there is anything you need during your first few weeks with us, please feel free to come over to my office and have a chat. Now, let's go back to work. Perhaps you might see Bob Playfair or Bud Smith and let them know you have arrived. They will have all the necessary forms to complete."

As Chuck walked back to his office he could not help thinking, what a good guy George was. He did have some second thoughts about the assignment given him, however.

QUESTIONS

The First Day: Morning

1.a) What are the possible disadvantages inherent in a situation where a selection committee makes an internal appointment, as was the case with George Branch?
  b) What are the possible advantages?
  c) How do you decide if the possible advantages outweigh the possible disadvantages?
2.a) How was Chuck's initial welcome to the organization handled?
  b) What was wrong with the welcome?
  c) How could it have been improved?
3.   Was George right in asking Chuck to put all efforts into seeing that the east area got the new pool and library?
4.   If you were Bob Playfair, what would be your reaction to Chuck's first few hours on the job?
5.   Do "good guys" make good managers?

CASE STUDY 3

The First Day: Afternoon

Chuck, Lucy Brown, and Bud Smith were meeting over coffee to discuss programs offered by the department in the east area.

"I have a strange case to talk about today," said Lucy. "It appears that there is a group in our area who enjoy swimming, but they have added one new twist. Apparently, during the summer months, this group swims at the nudist camp on the north of town. While they have not as yet approached me concerning the use of our pool, the grapevine has it that they will. Do we have any departmental policies on the use of our pool by such outside groups?" she asked Bud.

"Not that I know of," said Bud, "but I'll check with Bob Playfair and let you know. Well, Chuck, welcome to the Department. Lucy and I meet each Monday at 1:30 to plan for the week ahead and let each other know what is happening. Since this is your first day on the job we thought we could best spend the time talking about what has been going on in this area and what some of the plans for the future are. You will be responsible for all the programs, with the exception of aquatic activities, in the east area of the city, and so I guess the first thing you should do is to study the files and brochures so that you know what is going on. I've arranged a staff meeting of all part-time staff and volunteers for Wednesday evening after the close of programs. This will be a good opportunity for you to meet the people who will be reporting to you. I would suggest that you spend your first week getting acquainted and visiting those programs that have already started. I also want you to go through all our files and the part-time staff activity reports so that you will know what has happened in the past few months. There are some very interesting reports submitted by the neighborhood associations and one in particular I believe you should read. The report in question concerns the need for the development of the Jackson's Park area, and it is my belief that this project should receive top priority. The original request came from the neighborhood council, and I would like you to follow it up in any way you see fit. As you know, developmental funds are becoming harder and harder to obtain, and thus I think we should move quickly on this project. I am not sure that either Bob Playfair or George Branch are really keen on this type of expenditure, but let's first find out the facts concerning the project, and if it looks justifiable then we can take appropriate action. So, Chuck, your first assignment will be to prepare a preliminary feasibility report on the need for the redevelopment of Jackson's Park. If your initial report is positive, then I'll see that you get the necessary support to conduct a full report. Please have your report include the pros and cons of proceeding, the estimated costs of conducting a feasibility study, a ball-park figure on anticipated expenses, and a preliminary assessment of the need by yourself, immediate neighbors of the park, and by any of the local groups. We will need this report within six weeks, so please have your report ready for me on or before six weeks from today. Any questions? No? Okay then, proceed, and if either Lucy or I can help please call on us.

"If there is nothing more, I would suggest that we adjourn until we meet on Wednesday evening with the part-time personnel. Don't forget that there is a Recreation Division meeting scheduled for Friday at nine o'clock. Bob Playfair tells me that there is an interesting agenda being prepared. It's the first meeting this fall, and with the large turnover in staff that we have had during the last three months, it will provide an opportunity of meeting the new staff. I also heard that George is going to be there to talk about the new organization chart and the new task force that he has recommended. He will also be giving us some idea of the funds available for next year. Meeting adjourned."

QUESTIONS

The First Day: Afternoon

1. Should groups be allowed to rent public facilities for the type of program that Lucy described? How are policies arrived at in a case such as this?
2. What is a grapevine? Where does it exist?
3. Did Bob Playfair give Chuck enough guidance on the Jackson's Park situation?
4. Should Bud Smith know more about the agenda than he does? Why?
5. Is a large turnover in staff any indicator of the health of an organization?

CASE STUDY 4

The Inner-City Problem

It was Wednesday night of the second week since Chuck had started working for the Canusa Parks and Recreation Department. Tonight he was attending a meeting called by a community group in the downtown area. The purpose of the meeting was to discuss the apparent lack of recreation facilities and programs for inner-city children between the ages of 8 and 18. Chuck had been asked by his supervisor to attend the meeting and to bring in recommendations to the next staff meeting. Persons in attendance included, the Rev. David Hart, chairman, and representatives from the school board, the downtown merchants' association, two service clubs, the single parents association, the police, the local Y.M.C.A. and a government-sponsored inner-city project for teenagers. During the meeting the following allegations were made.

1. Children from the low-income inner-city area did not have as many programs or facilities available to them as did the children living in other areas of the city.
2. Children spent most of their leisure time at the local electronic amusement center.
3. The use of drugs and alcohol was widespread in the downtown area.
4. Most children came from single-parent homes.
5. Crime, including theft, breaking and entering, and muggings were on the increase in this area of the town.

While some persons at the meeting felt that it was the responsibility of the city to provide facilities and programs, many felt that much more would be accomplished by forming a private voluntary organization such as a Boys and Girls Club and soliciting help from government, private industry, and interested citizens.

At the conclusion of the meeting, a steering committee was established and given the responsibility of bringing a plan for action within 30 days to another public meeting that would be widely publicized. Chuck, along with a representative from the police department, a single parent, a member of the downtown merchants' association and the Rev. David Hart, was appointed to the committee.

QUESTIONS

1. Can you think of any other individuals or groups who should have been in attendance at the meeting?
2. If the allegations given were true, is the responsibility for overcoming the problems primarily that of the city government or of a volunteer community group?
3. If you were Chuck what recommendations would you make to the next Parks and Recreation staff meeting?
4. What additional kinds of information will Chuck and the newly formed steering committee need before bringing in a plan for action?
5. What kinds of action seem warranted by this situation?

Leadership

3

How many times have we heard statements asserting that many, if not all, of the problems of a particular organization could be traced to something termed "poor management"? We quite often hear remarks such as, "If the Y.M.C.A. had been better managed, the board of directors would not be in the current poor financial position," or "The constant turnover of employees at the Parks and Recreation Department is due to poor management, nothing more."

If we were to investigate these statements more thoroughly, we might find that what is really at the heart of such complaints is the lack of appropriate leadership. Because of this lack of leadership, the organizations involved are unsuccessful in reaching goals and objectives. With further consideration we might discover that not only is appropriate leadership missing, but action that should have been facilitated by the presence of that leadership has not been taken.

THE RECREATION AND LEISURE SERVICE LEADER

In order to be effective, recreation and leisure service leaders should have the responsibility, the authority, and the combination of skills necessary to facilitate actions that enable an organization to accomplish leisure-related goals. There will be some leaders who, for one reason or another, have the authority to initiate goal-directed action, but who are unsuccessful because they lack necessary skills. It is the hope of the authors that this text will at least point the way toward the acquisition of such skills since everybody in the recreation and leisure service career field becomes a leader at one time or another. There are two basic functions that are common to all leaders: first, they work through and with people, and, second, this work is directed toward the accomplishment of organizational objectives.

Recreation and leisure service agencies have leaders at many levels. The director of recreation and parks is a leader; the executive director of the Y.M.C.A. is a leader; the supervisor of recreation programs at the community center is a leader, as is the camp director at the Y.M.C.A. resident camp and the head recreation therapist at the county hospital. To be identified as a leader, two criteria must be met: first, the leader's organization must pursue goals and objectives, and, second, the organization must hold the leader accountable for the job performances of others as they attempt to reach organizational goals. Leaders have the right to act with authority for the actions of others. The President of the United States and the Prime Minister of Canada are both leaders, as are deans, college presidents, and heads of government agencies. Just about all of the individuals whose names appear on the brochures of municipal recreation and leisure service organizations can be identified as leaders. The leader, then, is simply the person who ensures that the organization meets its objectives and its long-range goals.

Of course, this is primarily a working definition and might be considered somewhat simplistic when applied to modern organizations, whether profit- or service-oriented. What about the comptroller for the metropolitan Y.M.C.A.? This individual's primary responsibility is long-range financial planning for the organization, which does not require the direct supervision of subordinates. The comptroller is, however, considered to be a member of the senior management team and thus, by implication, must be considered a leader. Perhaps another important criterion for the identification of leaders should be that the individual contributes to the organization, rather than just having command over others. All organizations will have persons who fit the traditional concept of a leader, which is to have influence over others. Some organizations, however, will also have persons who contribute to the attainment of organizational goals through planning, organizing, and controlling, without having direct command over subordinates.

Types of Leadership

As indicated, leadership is pervasive within all levels of recreation and leisure service organizations. There are three distinct types of leadership that can be identified in most recreation and leisure service organizations— direct service, supervisory, and management.

Direct service.   Direct-service leadership involves face-to-face contact with the organization's constituents. The leader in this situation could be a ticket taker, playground leader, sports official, instructor, coach, tour guide, or one of the other numerous positions found within profit and nonprofit recreation and leisure service organizations that directly deliver services to consumers. Direct-service delivery also may involve the preparation and maintenance of areas and facilities. Thus, a park laborer may be thought of as a direct service employee.

Supervisory.   Supervisory leadership is also known as mid-level management. The supervisor often manages a program component within an organization, entailing the supervision of other individuals, areas, or facilities. Providing direction to others, planning, organizing, staffing, and controlling within the supervisor's area of jurisdiction are all supervisory functions. The success or failure of a supervisor as a leader is often related to his or her ability to manage other individuals.

Management.   Management is also a form of leadership. The successful manager must be able to understand the process of leadership in order to guide an organization toward the accomplishment of its goals. Leadership is evident in the way in which a manager interacts with his or her subordinates, establishes productivity standards, and represents the interests of the organization to other organizations and the general public. The identification and development of managerial leadership skills has been a focal point of management theorists during the past several decades. The search for effective leadership strategies that can be employed in the managerial role has been exhaustive.

These three primary levels of leadership do not include all of the potential levels of leadership within recreation and leisure service organizations. Numerous authors have suggested that community leadership is also an essential type of leadership. It is prevalent in public agencies. However, we have focused on direct, supervisory, and management leadership, as they are perhaps the most accepted categories when discussing both profit and nonprofit organizations.

Leadership Skills

Leadership skills are those personal attributes that enable individuals to influence others toward certain predetermined ends. They are those skills or attributes possessed by individuals who successfully accomplish objectives through the efficient use of organizational resources.

It is worth noting that, though management positions within organizational structures have inherent authority, defined by the particular roles that managers play, this is not necessarily the case for leadership positions. By definition, an individual is considered to possess leadership abilities when he or she is able to influence a group to accomplish objectives. However, when a manager assumes a particular position within an organization, he or she automatically inherits the authority that is vested in that position and, because of this authority, is able to influence subordinates toward certain actions. The waterfront director at a youth camp is given the authority to take such action as he or she deems necessary to ensure that the program will provide for the safety of participants and achieve recreational values, such as enjoyment, accomplishment, and progressive learning. In other words, within the organizational structure of the camp there is a position designated as waterfront director, and inherent within that position lies certain authority. If, in addition to possessing the authority inherent in the position, a waterfront director possesses outstanding leadership abilities, then it is quite possible that this particular individual will have the ability to influence the waterfront staff, waterfront counselors, other camp counselors and staff, and campers toward the achievement of overall camp and program objectives. In short, this person would be a much more effective leader that an individual who was entirely dependent on the authority inherent in his or her position. In a broader sense, an individual who possesses good leadership skills has the ability to influence others to perform activities necessary to achieve group and individual objectives.

Most writers in the management sciences would agree that there are at least three kinds of skills that are needed by all leaders. These include skills that Hersey and Blanchard define as technical, human, and conceptual.[1] As an individual progresses upward from face-to-face supervisory to management positions, the amount and type of skill needed will change. As one advances from lower to higher levels within the organization, one needs to have more conceptual and less technical skill to be an effective leader. At lower authority levels, leaders need enough technical skill to train and supervise their subordinates. However, as they progress up the management ladder and away from the operational or administrative level, they no longer need to know how to perform specific tasks and instead become more involved in conceptual concerns.

---

1. Paul Hersey and Kenneth H. Blanchard, *Management of Organizational Behavior: Utilizing Human Resources* (Englewood Cliffs, N.J.: Prentice-Hall, 1969), p. 6.

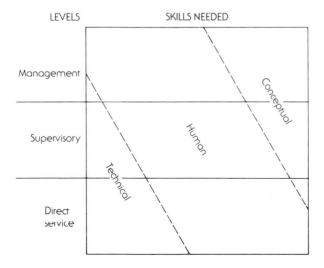

LEVELS   SKILLS NEEDED

Management

Supervisory

Direct
service

Conceptual

Human

Technical

Figure 3.1   Skills needed in a recreation and leisure service organization. (Adapted from Paul Hersey and Keith H. Blanchard, Management of Organizational Behavior: Utilizing Human Resources,
Englewood Cliffs, N.J.: Prentice-Hall, 3rd edition, 1977, p. 7.)

Hersey and Blanchard define these three types of skills as follows:

Technical skill. Ability to use knowledge, methods, techniques and
equipment necessary for the performance of specific tasks as acquired
from experience, education and training.

Human relations skill. Ability and judgement in working with and
through people, including an understanding of motivation and an application of effective leadership.

Conceptual skill. Ability to understand the complexities of the overall
organization and where one's own operation fits into the organization.
This knowledge permits one to act according to the objectives of the
organization as a whole, rather than on the basis of the goals and needs
of one's own immediate group.[2]

The degree of skill that the leader should possess in each of these
areas varies with his or her position within the organizational structure. In
terms of recreation and leisure service management, this would suggest that
a different mix of managerial skills would be needed by a director of
recreation and leisure services than would be needed by the foreman of a
park maintenance crew. The skills needed by the recreation and leisure
service manager at various levels within a municipal agency are illustrated in
Figure 3.1.

---

2. Paul Hersey and Kenneth H. Blanchard, *Management of Organizational Behavior:
    Utilizing Human Resources* (Englewood Cliffs, N.J.: Prentice-Hall, 1969), p. 7.

An analysis of Figure 3.1 suggests that as an individual progresses to higher levels within the organization, the need for conceptual skills increases. Also, as an individual progresses to more senior positions, the need for technical skills decreases. Thus, though the director of recreation and leisure services for a large municipal system does not need the technical skills necessary to operate an effective aquatic program, the director must have a thorough understanding of the overall goals of the city for which he or she works. The director must also know how individual departmental objectives fit into the overall objectives of the city. At lower levels of the organizational structure, the supervisor of aquatics must have the technical knowledge necessary to perform at the operational level. In addition, individuals at this level should be aware of the objectives of their particular unit and how these objectives relate to the overall departmental objectives.

It should also be noted that, though the amount of conceptual and technical skill needed by the leader varies in the relation to his or her level of management within the organizational structure, the amount of human skill needed to function as a leader remains approximately the same at all levels. The essence of management, after all, is simply working with and through people and thus, to be effective, all managers must possess the ability to lead and motivate people.

Management and Technical Work

As the previous discussion indicates, the skills needed by recreation and leisure service leaders vary according to the level of their position. The higher an individual progresses within a recreation and leisure service organization, the more technical work he or she should be delegating. Time and effort at the highest levels should be devoted almost entirely to managerial work. Louis Allen states that the chief executive in an organization should devote at least 90 percent of his or her time to what could be classified as managerial work, and, thus, no more than 10 percent of his or her time should be devoted to technical work.[3] He maintains that the percentage of time spent in managerial work should decrease from the chief-executive level to the lowest managerial level. The first line supervisors, such as parks supervisors, should spend approximately 50 percent of their time performing managerial work and 50 percent of their time performing technical work. However, as Allen points out, there is a distinct difference between what should occur in terms of the allocation of work time and what actually does occur. This difference is known as the *management gap*, which is illustrated in Figure 3.2.

Figure 3.2 suggests that leaders at all levels within organizations are not performing the type of work that their positions in the organizational structure dictate. Although the amount of technical work that a manager performs will vary according to factors such as the size of department; the

---

3.   Louis A. Allen, *Professional Management* (New York: McGraw-Hill, 1973), p. 57.

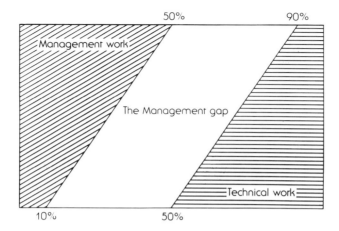

Figure 3.2 The management gap. (From Louis A. Allen, Professional Management: New Concepts and Proven Practices, **New** York: McGraw-Hill, 1973, p. 58.)

number, qualifications, and experience of subordinates; seasonal demands; and departmental objectives; it is probably safe to assume that in most recreation and leisure service organizations, as in other organizations, a management gap appears because managers are spending too much time doing technical work. The effective leader will detect this and will instigate action to ensure that the management gap is reduced to a reasonable level. It should be recognized that Figure 3.2 represents an ideal toward which organizations should strive. Managerial delegation of the more technical types of work is one method of reducing the management gap; however, the complete solution to this problem depends on the degree to which the organization follows sound management practices in all aspects of its operations.

MANAGERIAL LEADERSHIP

What is Managerial Leadership?

How does the waterfront director at camp induce the other staff members to cooperate in and contribute to the goals of the aquatic program? How does the director of recreation and leisure services persuade his or her subordinates to work together for the good of the total department, rather than for the good of their individual units? By personality? By the authority inherent in the role of director? By friendship? By all of these? All of these variables can play a part in an individual's leadership style. In any particular situation, one or more of these variables may be useful and may contribute to the development of one's leadership style.

Although leadership is an important aspect of management, an individual can be a good leader yet still be a very poor manager. Leadership involves the persuasion of others. It is the ability to get others to follow. This does not, however, always mean that the leader knows the right direction. Even though a leader is able to get others to follow, he or she may not have the managerial skills of conceptualization and planning to establish clear-cut objectives and determine the best methods of achieving them. On the other hand, an individual can be a poor leader, but still be a reasonable manager, depending primarily upon the caliber of the individuals who are accountable to him or her. If, for instance, a director of recreation and leisure services has three immediate subordinates who are highly motivated and skilled in their own particular areas, then the director could be a poor leader, but because of his or her ability to plan, to organize, and to maintain an effective control system, he might still be an effective manager. In practice, however, leadership skills are usually prerequisite to good management. Excellent managers usually have good leadership qualities, and it is difficult to picture a manager being successful for very long without them.

Theories of Leadership

Leadership by inheritance.   *Leadership by inheritance* is probably the oldest source of leadership authority. In all studies of leadership researchers ask the question, "Why do people follow any given leader and accept that person as possessing authority?" When tradition dictates the choice of leaders, the answer is easy. "Simply because it has always been that way." Tribal chiefs can pass along their authority to their eldest sons; a king or queen is marked for a leadership role from birth. In modern times, however, very few leadership positions are secured through inheritance.

The trait or great man approach.   Many early writers have attempted to isolate specific traits that characterize persons who were considered to be successful leaders. From this approach emerged what has been termed the *trait theory*—a theory that postulated that leadership ability was dependent upon the presence of inherent characteristics, such as physical energy, human-relations skills, physical strength, education, speech, intelligence, overall health, social maturity, and internal motivation. Thus, persons who inherited these characteristics only needed an opportunity to demonstrate their leadership ability. In other words, great leaders were born and not made.

Unfortunately, research that attempted to isolate these characteristics failed to find significant relationships between these traits and successful leadership. Gradually, researchers came to the conclusion that, though these personality traits did help individuals assume leadership roles, they did not account for all the attributes needed by a leader in any given situation.

Situational leadership theory.   One important factor that was missing from these early attempts to explain leadership was the role played by the environment in which the leader functioned. Gradually, researchers began to realize that the environment played a major role in the determination of who would be best suited to assume a leadership role in a given situation. From this realization has come what is now termed the *situational leadership theory.* The situational theory of leadership simply states that leadership is dependent in large measure on the environment. It is contingent not only upon personal characteristics, but also upon the whole environment within which the leader operates.

This concept can be related to management: different styles of management will be more or less effective, depending upon the situation and upon such variables as size and make-up of the group, size and type of organizational framework within which the group operates, the primary and secondary objectives of the group, plus a host of other factors. Thus, effective management, like effective leadership, can be said to be at least partially the result of the particular situation in which the manager attempts to function.

Leadership Characteristics

Even though trait theories of leadership are now considered to be somewhat less than accurate, it does appear possible to isolate some characteristics that help an individual to assume the leadership role. Keith Davis lists these characteristics as including intelligence, social maturity and breadth, inner motivation and achievement drives, and positive human-relations attitudes.[4]

Since leaders must have considerable analytical skills and be able to visualize the total environment in which a problem exists and the complicated relationships that are present in this environment, it is logical to assume that intelligence is a characteristic of good leadership. Leaders tend to have a somewhat higher level of intelligence than the average of the group in which they operate. Leaders must also have communication skills in order to convey their ideas and to receive communications back from the persons they are leading. The leader must also have the ability to motivate members of the group toward group goals. Leaders tend to be socially mature and to have self-respect and a broad interest in the activities of society. The successful leader also tends to be a self-motivated individual whose rewards tend to be intrinsic rather than extrinsic. Finally, the successful leader has to possess human-relations skills. The leader must be people-oriented and have the ability to work for and with people.

It is not surprising that a great deal of research has been conducted in

---

4. Keith Davis, *Human Behavior at Work* (New York: McGraw-Hill, 1972), pp. 103–104.

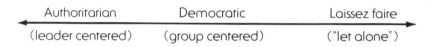

Figure 3.3 Single-dimension leadership theories. (From Daniel A. Wren and Dan Voich, Jr., *Principles of Management: Process and Behavior*, New York: Ronald Press, 1976, 2nd edition, p. 536.)

relation to leadership. Leadership is common to all organizations and, in all cases, the level of leadership that exists will in large measure determine the success of the organization. In reviewing early and contemporary approaches to the study of leadership, Wren and Voich[5] have set forth a number of classifications on the basis of what they term single- and two-dimensional theories. The following paragraphs will review some of these classic studies that have attempted to explain the nature of leadership within organizational structures.

Single-dimensional theories.   By the 1930s the great man theory was on the decline, and, instead of focusing attention on leaders, emphasis was shifted to the group and to the social climate in which the group operated. The effects of different styles of leadership were studied as researchers attempted to understand the relationship of the leadership process to the group and the leader's effect on the group process.

These *single-dimensional* approaches viewed leadership as being along a continuum of possibilities, as shown in Figure 3.3. Generally speaking, research in this area tended to view the democratic leader as portraying the best leadership style.

The Lippitt and White studies.   In the late 1930s two researchers, Ronald Lippitt and Ralph K. White, conducted one of the first leadership studies at the University of Iowa.[6] In this early study, under the general direction of Kurt Lewin, the researchers observed hobby clubs for ten-year-old boys. Each of the hobby clubs was subjected to one of three leadership styles: authoritarian, democratic, and laissez-faire. The club that was assigned an authoritarian style was given a leader who was very directive in his approach and allowed the club members no participation in planning. Although the authoritarian leader was friendly, he tended to remain impersonal and very authoritative in his dealings with the boys. The second group of boys had a democratic leader who encouraged discussion and group action on any important decisions of the club. The democratic leader attempted to be objective in his dealings with club members and stressed

---

5.   Daniel Wren and Dan Voich, Jr., *Principles of Management: Process and Behavior* (New York: Ronald Press, 1976), pp. 538–45.

6.   Kurt Lewin, Ronald Lippitt, and Ralph K.White, "Patterns of Aggressive Behavior in Experimentally Created Social Climate," *Journal of Social Psychology*, (May, 1939): pp. 271–76.

the importance of group decision and esprit de corps. The third group was given a leader who gave complete freedom to the group in all projects. This laissez-faire type of leadership provided very little, if any, actual leadership.

This early experiment, held under experimental conditions with controls to ensure that the type of leadership involved accounted for differences in group satisfaction and aggression, was one of the classic experiments in group behavior. Lippitt and White reported that the boys had an overwhelming preference for the democratic leader. The boys resented the authoritarian style of the autocratic leader and chose the laissez-faire leader as being less acceptable than the democratic leader, but more acceptable than the autocratic leader.

Though these studies leave something to be desired in terms of modern experimental design, they do contain valuable information from a historical viewpoint. The studies marked the first time that scientific methods, though somewhat crude by today's standards, were applied to the study of leadership. If nothing else, in addition to their historical significance, the studies showed that different types of leaders can produce different types of results in similar groups.

Because of the rudimentary research methodology used in the Lippitt and White studies, it is not possible to generalize upon the findings. However, the studies will be remembered as marking the first serious attempt to study leadership styles; they formed an informational base upon which other more sophisticated studies could build.

Two-dimensional approaches.   In the mid 1940s research on leadership was beginning to challenge the trait, or great man, and *uni-dimensional* views of leadership. Studies at Ohio State University and at the University of Michigan were comparable in certain respects: (1) both held a new view that was in opposition to the trait or single-continuum approach, and (2) both identified two dimensions of leader behavior.[7]

Ohio State leadership studies.   In 1945, a series of investigations into the nature of leadership commenced at the Ohio State University. From the results of this research came the development of the situational approach to leadership. These studies, conducted by an interdisciplinary team from the fields of psychology, sociology, and economics, attempted to study leadership in a wide variety of situations. Using a research instrument that they termed the Leader Behavior Description Questionnaire (LBDQ), the interdisciplinary team sought data from armed forces personnel, civilian administrators in the Navy Department, foremen employed in industry, executives, college administrators, teachers, principals and school superintendents, and a variety of leaders from a number of student and civilian groups.[8]

7.   Wren and Voich, *Principles of Management: Process and Behavior* (New York: Ronald Press, 1976), pp. 538–45.

8.   Fred Luthans, *Organizational Behavior* (New York: McGraw-Hill, 1977), p. 436.

The Ohio State Studies determined that regardless of the situation studied, two dimensions of leadership continually occurred. One factor that was perceived as being an important dimension of leadership behavior was *consideration* for group members. This consideration was translated into actions that resulted in friendly, trusting, respectful, and warm relationships between the leader and the group. Another dimension of leadership that occurred was what the researchers termed *initiating structure*. Stated simply, this phrase meant that the leader took the initiative and defined the relationships between the leader and the group and, in addition, organized the group so that each member knew the role that he or she was to play, the channels of communication available within the group, and the ways that members would help reach the objectives of the group.

The leadership studies at Ohio State, like the earlier studies with Lippitt and White at the University of Iowa, were important historically. The studies at Ohio State were the first studies to point out and to emphasize the importance of considering each group member's individual needs and the importance of defining roles.

University of Michigan studies.   Using a grant from the Office of Naval Research, the University of Michigan Survey Research Center initiated a leadership study in 1947 at the home office of the Prudential Insurance Company in Newark, New Jersey. The purpose of this study was to determine the principles that contribute to group productivity and to the satisfaction of group members from their participation. The researchers in this study, having noted the questionable methodology used in previous studies, took particular care in the research design.

The study included both supervisors and workers and attempted to measure perceptions and attitudes in relation to performance. The Michigan study was designed so that a high degree of control was placed on nonpsychological variables that might influence attitudes and productivity. Variables such as type and conditions of work and work methods were controlled. Individuals in the study were divided into high-low productivity pairs, with each pair representing a high-producing section and a low-producing section. Other variables such as type of work, conditions, and the method of work used were the same for each pair. A total of 419 clerical workers and 24 section supervisors were included in the study. The results showed that supervisors of high-producing sections were significantly more likely to conform to the following pattern:

1. To receive general, rather than close, supervision from their supervisors.
2. To like the amount of authority and responsibility they have in their jobs.
3. To spend more time in supervising.
4. To give general rather than close supervision to their employees.
5. To be employee-oriented, rather than production-oriented.[9]

---

9. Fred Luthans, *Organizational Behavior* (New York: McGraw-Hill, 1977), pp. 437–38.

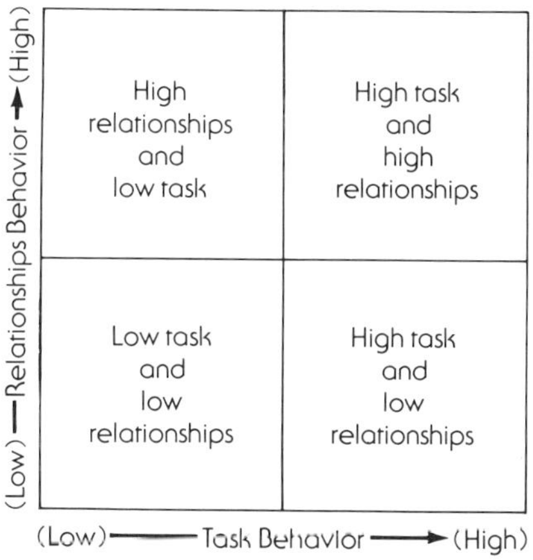
High relationships and low task
High task and high relationships
Low task and low relationships
High task and low relationships
(Low) — Relationships Behavior → (High)
(Low) —— Task Behavior → (High)

Figure 3.4 Leadership styles. (From Paul Hersey and Keith H. Blanchard, Management of Organizational Behavior: Utilizing Human Resources, Englewood Cliffs, N.J.: Prentice-Hall, 3rd edition, 1977, p. 301.)

When the results of interviews with the low-producing supervisors were analyzed, it was found that such supervisors had essentially the opposite characteristics and techniques of the high-producing supervisors.

The Michigan leadership studies indicated that the presence of employee-centered rather than production-oriented supervisors resulted in higher production. Another important finding was that there was no direct relationship between employee satisfaction and productivity. From these studies and from the hundreds of similar studies soon conducted in a variety of organizations, came the realization that the possession of human-relations skills by supervisors is extremely important. The Michigan studies were landmarks in the growth of the human-relations approach to managerial leadership.

Over a period of years, the research at the University of Michigan led to a two-dimensional approach to leadership. Two different leadership orientations were identified: (1) an employee orientation in which the supervisor stressed interpersonal relationships on the job, and (2) a production orientation in which the supervisor stressed production and was concerned primarily with the technical rather than the human aspects of the job.[10]

Results from both the Michigan and Ohio studies negated the trait, or single-continuum, approach, and researchers at both universities identified two dimensions of leader behavior.

In Figure 3.4 (Hersey and Blanchard), one dimension is a production-oriented initiating structure (task-centered axis), and the other dimension is an employee-oriented consideration structure (interpersonal, relations-oriented axis). The two dimensions are not mutually exclusive; a leader could combine a high initiating structure with high consideration. This advanced the understanding of leadership by viewing every leadership situation as an interaction between the leader and the group. This, in turn, resulted in a realization that, rather than there being one leadership style

10. Wren and Voich, *Principles of Management: Process and Behavior* (New York: Ronald Press, 1976), p. 537.

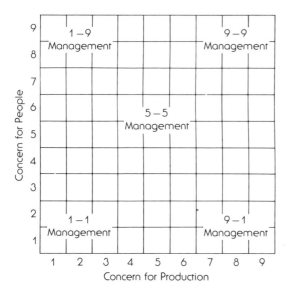

Figure 3.5 The management grid. (Adapted from Robert R. Blake and Jane Srygley Mouton, *The Managerial Grid*, Houston: Guld Publishing, 1964, p. 10.)

that achieved the best results, there were in fact a number of dimensions that could facilitate success in every leadership situation.

The Management Grid

The work completed at Ohio State and the University of Michigan was a logical prerequisite to the work of Robert Blake and Jane Mouton.[12] The concepts postulated by these two researchers represented an attempt to avoid the extremes inherent in the Ohio and Michigan studies. The Blake and Mouton management grid is depicted in Figure 3.5. The work of Blake and Mouton was a logical extension of the two-dimensional models and was an attempt to avoid the "either-or" styles of leadership, such as production-centered or employee-centered. In the management grid, concern for production is illustrated on the horizontal axis, with a rating scale from 0–9. Five different styles of leadership are represented in the four quadrants and in the center of the grid.

The five leadership styles are impoverished, country club, task, middle-of-the-road, and team. Following is a description of each:

- *Impoverished.* Exertion of minimum effort to get required work done is appropriate to sustain organization membership.
- *Country club.* Thoughtful attention to needs of people for satisfying relationships leads to a comfortable, friendly organization atmosphere and work tempo.
- *Task.* Efficiency in operations result from arranging conditions of work

---

11. Hersey and Blanchard, *Management of Organizational Behavior: Utilizing Human Resources* (Englewood Cliffs, New Jersey: Prentice-Hall, 1969), p. 75.

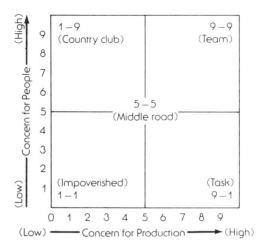

Figure 3.6 Management grid leadership styles. (Adapted from Paul Hersey and Keith H. Blanchard, *Management of Organizational Behavior: Utilizing Human Resources,* **Englewood Cliffs**, N.J.: Prentice-Hall, 3rd edition, 1977, p. 96.)

in such a way that human elements interfere to a minimum degree.

- *Middle-of-the-road.* Adequate organization performance is possible through balancing the necessity to get out work while maintaining morale of people at a satisfactory level.
- *Team.* Work accomplishment is from committed people; interdependence through a "common stake" in organization purpose leads to relationships of trust and respect.[12]

The development of the management grid popularized the leadership components identified in the Ohio state studies. A diagram depicting the merger is shown in Figure 3.6.

In the nine–one, task-oriented management style, high emphasis was placed on task and job requirements, with the leader assuming a high degree of authority. In this type of leadership, the leader assumed prime responsibility for planning, directing, and controlling. In the one–nine country-club style of leadership, the emphasis was on meeting the needs of the employee with little concern for either people or production. In the middle-of-the-road style of leadership, the manager was concerned with the functions of planning, directing, and controlling, but this five–five leadership style did not directly command or direct subordinates as much as lead, motivate, and exchange communication with employees in an effort to accomplish organizational objectives. A goal of this style of leadership was maintaining high morale, in addition to accomplishing organizational objectives.

The nine–nine team approach assumed that the job of the manager was to create a work environment where people understood the objectives of the organization, had a personal stake in the outcome, and became

---

12. Robert R. Blake, et al., "Break Through in Organization Development," *Harvard Business Review,* (Nov.–Dec. 1964): p. 136.

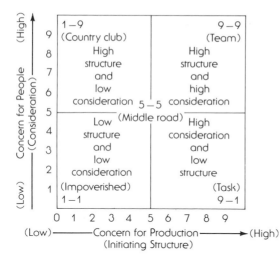

Figure 3.7 The Ohio State studies and the management grid. (Adapted from Paul Hersey and Keith H. Blanchard, Management of Organizational Behavior: Utilizing Human Resources, Englewood Cliffs, N.J.: Prentice-Hall, Inc., 3rd edition, 1977, p. 97.)

committed. It was assumed that such an environment would lead to mutual trust and respect. As a result of everyone having a personal stake in the outcome, there would be no need for an authoritative leader, since external direction and control would become self-direction and self-control.

In essence, the grid that Blake and Mouton developed showed possible leadership styles based on attitudes of managers concerning people and production. Hersey and Blanchard combined the Blake and Mouton grid with the four quadrants of the Ohio State University studies to create a new model. A diagram depicting the merger of the Ohio State University and managerial grid theories of leadership is shown in Figure 3.7. In presenting this merger, Hersey and Blanchard note that there is a fundamental difference between the two frameworks. The authors note that while the Ohio State framework tends to be a behavioral model that examines how leader actions are perceived by others, the Blake-Mouton model tends to be an attitudinal model that measures the predispositions of a manager.

The Leadership Contingency Model

Professor Fred Fiedler has made a significant contribution to the study of leadership as a result of his often-cited contingency model of leadership.[13] In Fiedler's view it did not seem logical to assume that there was one best leadership style that would be effective in all leadership situations. He suggested that a number of leadership behavioral styles may be effective or ineffective depending upon the elements of a particular situation. As a result of more than fifteen years of empirical research, Fred Fiedler developed and tested a model to measure leadership style. Fiedler's work produced a measurement technique whereby persons gave a self-description, as well as a description of his or her least preferred co-worker and his or

---

13. Fred E. Fiedler, *A Theory of Leadership Effectiveness* (New York: McGraw-Hill, 1967), p. 10.

her most preferred co-worker. From these measures, Fiedler derived what he termed *assumed similarity between opposites* (ASo) scores, which showed the differences between the various descriptions. He then characterized *high* ASo persons as being individuals who are concerned about personal relations, have a need to be approved by their co-workers, and feel close to their co-workers. *Low* ASo individuals were characterized as being very independent, less concerned about personal relations, and willing to reject co-workers who cannot complete assigned work. Fiedler's development and validation of a leadership model that explains the situational nature of effective leadership has contributed a great deal to the study of managerial leadership. His work explains why some studies maintain that a directive task-oriented style of leadership is best, while others indicate that a nondirective human-relations style is the best.

Fiedler concluded that there were three major factors that should be considered in any leadership situation.[14] These factors are the following:

1. Lead-member relations. The degree to which the group members liked or trusted the leader and the leader's feelings of being accepted by the group.
2. The task structure. The degree to which the task was well or poorly defined or structured.
3. The amount of power inherent in the position.

According to Fiedler, the most favorable situation for a leader, enabling him or her to effectively influence the group, is one in which the leader is well liked (high degree of leader-member relations), where the task is well defined (high degree of task structure), and where there is a high degree of power inherent in the position. Likewise, the most unfavorable situation for a leader is one in which he or she does not have the trust of the group, where the task is not understood, and where there is little power inherent in the position.

As a result of his work, Fiedler attempted to determine which type of leadership, either task-oriented or relationship-oriented, would be most appropriate for each of the eight possible combinations of the three factors given. His conclusions were that:

1. Task-oriented leaders tend to perform best in group situations that are either very favorable or very unfavorable to the leader.
2. Relationship-oriented leaders tend to perform best in situations that are intermediate in favorableness.

Leadership as a Continuum

Tannenbaum and Schmidt view leadership as involving a variety of styles along a continuum ranging from a style that is highly boss-centered to one that is highly subordinate-centered.[15] According to these authors,

---

14. Fred E. Fiedler, *A Theory of Leadership Effectiveness* (New York: McGraw-Hill, 1967), pp. 143–44.
15. R. Tannenbaum and W.H. Schmidt, "How to Choose a Leadership Pattern," *Harvard Business Review*, 51:3 (May–June, 1973): pp. 321–38.

leadership style is determined by both the situation and the personality of the individual assuming the leadership role. Rather than assuming that there are two styles of leadership—either authoritarian or democratic—these authors believe that there is actually a wide range of styles, any one of which might be appropriate for the situation.

According to Tannenbaum and Schmidt, there are a number of factors that may influence a manager's style along the continuum from boss-centered to subordinate-centered. The most important influential factors are (1) the forces operating in a manager's personality, including his or her personableness, confidence in subordinates, preference in leadership styles, and degree of security in a particular situation; (2) forces in subordinates that will affect managerial behavior; and (3) forces in the situation, such as the organization's values and traditions, team work, the nature of the problem, pressure of time and amount of authority that can be delegated.

In addition, Tannenbaum and Schmidt contend that, because of the nature of leadership styles and the strong pressure both from the organizational environment itself and the social environment within which the organization exists, an interdependency exists between leadership style and environmental forces. Such environmental forces as labor unions, federal constraints, and ecology and consumer movements can force leaders to adapt their leadership styles.

SUMMARY

In this chapter the authors have discussed the role and function of the recreation and leisure service leader. Everyone in the recreation and leisure service field, at one time or another, becomes a leader. Basically, the recreation and leisure service leader works with the human resources of an organization in order to accomplish its goals and objectives.

There are a number of skills that leaders should possess in order to achieve organizational goals. Generally speaking, they should possess knowledge of human relations as well as technical and conceptual knowledge related to the recreation and leisure service field. The degree to which skills from these areas are used will depend upon the level and responsibility of the leader, the power associated with the leader's position, and his or her ability to influence the behavior of employees through personality.

The recreation and leisure service leader fulfills many roles. Roles can be thought of as behaviors that are expected of the manager within the organization. Usually three kinds of roles are played by the manager: interpersonal, informational, and decision making. In addition to fulfilling these roles, leaders are engaged in a number of other processes. Although the leader's level of responsibility within the organization will affect the specific managerial work that he or she performs, in general, all leaders are planners, organizers, motivators, and controllers.

A key factor in the success or failure of the recreation and leisure service leader is managerial leadership style. Leadership style refers to the behavior that the manager exhibits in, primarily, the area of human-resource management. There are numerous theories that explain management style and leadership style. Leadership style usually involves the persuasion of individuals, whereas management style is related to the authority derived from one's management position. It is important to recognize that an individual can be a good leader, but a very poor manager.

Some of the theories that are used to explain managerial leadership styles are: the inheritance theory, the trait theory, and the situational theory of leadership. Many contemporary theories suggest that leadership style should be situationally determined. In other words, the leader's orientation toward completion of tasks and achievement of harmony in human relations should be predicated upon the individual situation. In some cases, the recreation and leisure service leader should be more task-oriented and, in others, more people-oriented.

STUDY QUESTIONS

1. Is the trait theory of leadership more relevant to leisure service organizations than to profit-oriented organizations?
2. What are the main differences among leadership by tradition theories, trait theories, single-dimensional and multi-dimensional theories, and situational theories of leadership?
3. Would a graduate of a university management curriculum be as capable of providing managerial leadership in a leisure services organization (a recreation and parks department, Y.M.C.A., or a commercial recreation enterprise) as a graduate of a university recreation and parks curriculum? Why?
4. What was the main contribution made by Lippitt and White to the study of leadership?
5. The Ohio State Leadership Studies resulted in a new approach to the study of leadership. What was this approach and is it still relevant today?
6. Where did the human-relations approach to leadership have its start?
7. Explain the terms *initiating structure* and *consideration structure*.
8. How did Hersey and Blanchard differentiate between the Ohio State four-quadrant model and the Blake-Mouton model?
9. Explain Fiedler's contingency model and discuss its relevance to a modern, commercial leisure service organization.
10. How is the Tannenbaum and Schmidt continuum similar to or different from the Fiedler contingency model?

CASE STUDY 5

The Committee

Chuck Christopher, in his position as assistant program supervisor of the Canusa Department of Leisure Services, has been asked to chair a committee charged with the responsibility of bringing in recommendations for the reorganization of the department to ensure citizen input. The committee is composed of the following persons:

Chuck Christopher M.S. degree in recreation and park management, minor in management sciences, thesis "Management System Applied to Leisure Service Organizations: A Conceptual Model." Experience includes a variety of jobs during undergraduate and graduate programs. Two four-month internships in a medium-sized city department, one four-month practicum as understudy to director of leisure services in a large urban center. Has completed three months at his first professional position as assistant program director.

Carolyn Baker Newly graduated with B.S. degree in fine arts. No experience in recreation and parks but a good teacher and performer. Most inexperienced member of the committee.

Jean Day A graduate in leisure services, ten years of consistently high-quality work. Skills and training in the area of therapeutic recreation. Always does a good job with assignments, very dedicated to the department and to the profession.

Peter Seniors Peter is currently completing 35 years with the department and is in his last year before retirement. Starting as a parks foreman, he has held a variety of positions and is currently director of Administrative Services. Not known for his forcefulness, Peter is well liked by everybody and is classified as an easy-going, sincere individual. Although he does not have any formal education in recreation, he has been in recreation positions all his adult life.

Fred Forceful Fred, now in his mid-thirties, is rapidly making a name for himself throughout the area and the country. Very aggressive, sometimes too aggressive, his biggest problem is in human relations. In fact, if Fred's powers of delegation were better, and if his human-relations skills were greater, he probably would have been chosen for the prestigious chairmanship that has been assigned to Chuck.

Situation 1

The first meeting of the committee must be called and Chuck is mentally debating the best approach to take. His problem is deciding what type of leadership stance he should take during the first meeting. It appears that he has three choices: (a) call the committee together and present them with an outline of the objectives of the committee and how he feels they can be realized, (b) call the committee together and ask them for their input on how the objectives can be established and subsequently met, (c) call the committee together and attempt to impress upon them the urgency of the task at hand and the tremendous effect that the committee's work will have on the future of leisure services in Blanksville, making the first meeting an inspirational one.

QUESTIONS

1. Which of the three approaches would be the best in this particular situation? Why?
2. Which management style(s) are exemplified by each of these three approaches?
3. Do you think that, considering the persons on the committee, Chuck will make a good chairperson? Why?

Situation 2

After three weeks of operation, Chuck notices that tension is starting to build between Fred and Jean. The trouble appears to be that Fred is telling other people how to do their jobs and is particularly domineering with Jean. He has on occasion suggested that since Jean is having difficulty completing her assignment perhaps a portion of her responsibilities should be assigned to him. In fact, Chuck notes that Fred is becoming involved in everybody's assignments.

QUESTIONS

SHOULD CHUCK, AS CHAIRPERSON:

1. Take Fred aside and explain to him that he is being too dominant, is creating tension within the group—particularly with Jean—and that if he continues the success of the committee will be jeopardized?
2. Sit back and observe the situation on the premise that the group itself will eventually solve the problem in a democratic manner?
3. Ask members of the committee to assess the progress thus far and to make suggestions on how the group can be made more productive?

Situation 3

After six weeks the project is progressing well. Interpersonal relations have improved, and the committee has settled down into a regular work pattern. If you were Chuck would you:

1. Let things progress?
2. Take the view that everything can improve and thus attempt to make the group even more productive by further improving relationships and increasing committee members' objectives?
3. Inform the group of the progress to date and motivate them to continue their good work?
    Which of these three choices should Chuck follow? Why?

Situation 4

It appears that the work of Jean Day and the work of Peter Seniors does not measure up to the quality of work being done by the other three members. While the group as a whole is meeting its objectives, it is only because of the extra work being done by Fred Forceful, Carolyn Baker, and Chuck. The overproduction of these persons is compensating for the work of Jean and Peter.

QUESTIONS

SHOULD CHUCK:

1. Talk privately with Jean and Peter and try to motivate them?
2. At a committee meeting inform all members of the relative contributions being made by each member?
3. Leave the group alone? Why?

Planning

4

It is almost trite now to point out that the only permanent thing in our society is change. Recreation and leisure service organizations, like all organizations, exist in a society that is constantly experiencing tremendous change—changes in our mores and customs; changes in our institutions; changes in economic conditions; and changes in our basic social unit, the family. Probably at no time in our history has there been such uncertainty about the future, and, consequently, probably no time when the ability to plan for the future has been so important.

Recreation and leisure service organizations must learn to respond to these changes if they are to survive. Greater accountability is now demanded of both tax-supported and non-tax-supported recreation and leisure service organizations. Thus, it follows that organizations that can articulate their mission to the public, can explicitly describe their specific objectives, and can achieve these stated objectives have a better chance of receiving public acceptance and support.

Organizations need to develop the skills necessary to clearly define their purposes and to develop techniques to measure their progress towards meeting those purposes. In short, organizations must know the basics of good planning to survive.

PLANNING DEFINED

Planning can be defined as the process of determining goals and deciding how they can be reached. As Koontz and O'Donnell have pointed out, planning is deciding in advance what to do, how to do it, when to do it, and who is to do it.[1] It also involves the establishment of a process whereby the organization's move toward the achievement of goals and objectives can be measured.

Paramount to good planning is the ability to establish and articulate goals and objectives. Without clear objectives, it would be impossible to establish the type of organizational structure needed and gather the type and numbers of human resources necessary to accomplish goals. The process of controlling would also be ineffective since there would be no standards against which to measure performance. Plans serve as the foundation of management, as shown in Figure 4.1.

Achievable goals are an integral part of organizational planning and provide the framework upon which the planning process is built. Goals may be divided into two types: purpose goals and operational and growth goals.

Purpose or Mission Goals

Purpose, or mission, goals may be thought of as those goals that describe the basic mission of an organization. These goals are general and serve as a comprehensive "planning umbrella" for the organization, helping to integrate the efforts of all participating units into a unified corporate effort.

Examples of purpose goals for the National Organization of the Boys' and Girls' Clubs of Canada include the following:[2]

● To play the role of the advocate by lobbying the federal and provincial governments on behalf of the Boys' and Girls' Clubs of Canada.

● To provide general consultative services to clubs requesting assistance or advice in implementing local service.

1.   Harold Koontz and Cyril O'Donnell, *Essentials of Management* (New York: McGraw-Hill, 1978), p. 56.
2.   Boys' and Girls' Clubs of Canada, "The National Survey: A Mandate for Change."

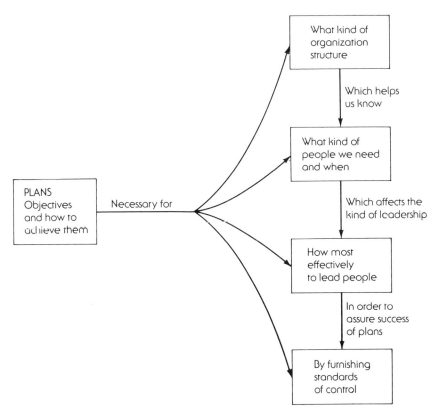

Figure 4.1   Plans as the foundation of management. (From Harold Koontz and Cyril O'Donnell, *Essentials of Management*, **New York:** McGraw-Hill, 1978, p. 57.)

● To develop national standards, goals, and objectives to provide a basic direction to the movement as a whole.

Operational and Growth Goals

Operational or growth goals are those goals that describe the desired future status of the organization within a specified time period, usually within two to five years' time. Such goals are based on the purpose goals and therefore reflect the mission of the organization more specifically. Operational or growth goals give rise to specific action plans or objectives.

Examples of operational and growth goals for a specific voluntary recreation and leisure service organization, such as the Boys' Club, could include the following:

● Broadening and intensifying volunteer participation and involvement.
● Developing manpower capacity.

- Enhancing the image of the Boys' Club nationally and locally.
- Increasing the efficiency and effectiveness of the organization.
- Expanding and diversifying the Boys' Club service to the community.
- Developing working relationships with other human service agencies.
- Increasing financial support for operation through endowments and growth.

Translating Goals into Programs

Operational and growth goals provide a foundation for specific objectives and action steps (programs and activities). Thus, from an original purpose or mission statement, an organization translates its mission into a desired status within a long-range time period (two to five years) and finally translates these goals into specific objectives and action steps for a shorter time period (usually the fiscal year, but up to a 24-month period). Figure 4.2 diagrams this process.

Many recreation and leisure service managers plan and conduct activities and programs with little reflection on how these programs relate to the organization's overall mission or even the organization's growth and operational goals. Such action cannot result in effective planning, since good planning by its very nature would answer the following questions in sequence.

1. *Mission.* What is the organization's reason for being?

2. *Purpose goals.* In what directions does it want to move?

3. *Operational and growth goals.* Where does it want to be at the end of a 2–5 year period?

Figure 4.2   The relationship of operational goals to objectives and action steps. (From Boys Clubs of America, Achieving Excellence through Planning, New York, 1975.)

4. *Objectives.* Where must it be at the end of a shorter period (6–24 months) to reach its operational and growth goals?

5. *Action steps.* What programs and activities must it complete to achieve the objectives in the time frame established?

6. *Budgeting.* What resources (manpower, money, and materials) must be allocated to complete the action steps?[3]

When organizations follow this type of planning, they eliminate many of the pitfalls that result from ineffective, directionless, and haphazard planning. Programs and activities become means rather than ends. In organizational planning (whether that organization is profit- or service-oriented) the mission, goals, and objectives must first be established. Once this is completed, the planning process can progress.

A model that outlines the use of mission, operational, and growth goals is presented in Figure 4.3. In addition, this model introduces two management systems—management by objectives and the program planning budgeting system. Both of these systems, extensively used in progressive organizations, are based on the organization's ability to establish goals and objectives and then measure progress toward them.

MANAGEMENT BY OBJECTIVES

Management by Objectives (MBO) is a results-oriented process. That is, MBO concentrates on the ends achieved rather than the individual or associated activities required to produce them. This does not mean that the use of the MBO process does not involve the identification of a process or set of activities to complete a task, but rather that it focuses primarily on the attainment of objectives. Often individuals expend a great deal of energy and organizational resources to achieve a goal. This expenditure of individual and organizational resources does not mean, however, that an individual has been productive. MBO, then, forces attention on the ends achieved and not the flurry of activity that may accompany them.

MBO, a process first described by Drucker in 1954, permeates the total organization so that each person with accountability for a result has a voice in what that result will be. In addition, each individual knows what part he or she plays in helping to meet the organization's overall objectives. Figure 4.4 illustrates this process.

While in most cases, objective setting should begin at the top, it is not always essential that this occur. Particularly in a service-oriented organization providing recreation and leisure services, objectives may originate from division heads and program supervisors. The extent to which this occurs will depend somewhat on how well all persons in the organization

---

3. Boys' Clubs of America, *Achieving Excellence Through Planning* (New York: 1975), p. 12.

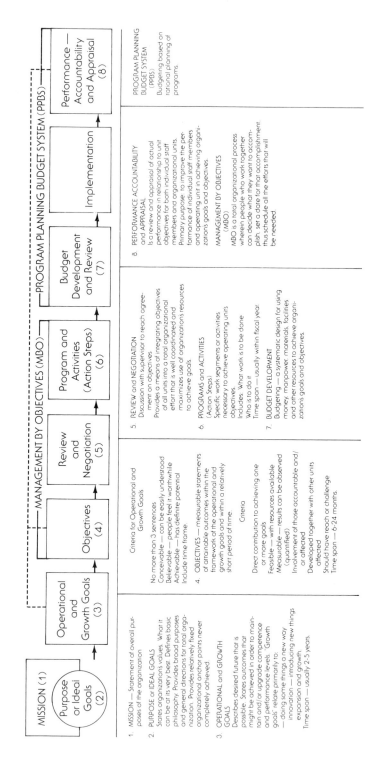

Figure 4.3 The planning process. (Adopted from Boys Clubs of America, Achieving Excellence through Planning, New York, 1975, p. 16.)

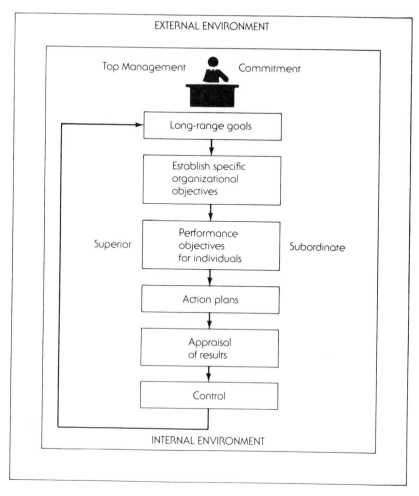

Figure 4.4 The management-by-objectives (MBO) process. (From R. Wayne Mondy, Robert E. Holmes, and Edwin B. Flippo, Management: Concepts and Practices, Boston: Allyn and Bacon, 1980, p. 87.)

understand the overall mission of the agency. However, for purposes of illustration and to complement Figure 4.4, let us follow the system of managing and appraising by objectives.

The Process of MBO

The MBO process in any organization can be broken down into the following steps:

1. Securing the initial support and commitment from top management.

2. Establishing long-term goals and strategic plans (purpose goals and growth goals).

3. Developing specific objectives for the organization as a whole and for each individual unit or department within the organization.

4. Establishing performance objectives and standards for measurement for each individual in the organization.

5. Measuring results achieved against the standards expected.

6. Initiating corrective actions where needed.[4]

We will examine each of these steps in terms of a voluntary recreation and leisure service organization.

Support and commitment from top management. Any planning process can only be successful if it receives the whole-hearted endorsement and support of those persons who will eventually be held accountable for results. Without commitment from the board of directors and the chief executive officer, an MBO system will not succeed. It is vital to secure support and commitment from top management as a primary step.

Establishment of long-term goals and strategic plans. These basic goals help management plan the future direction of the organization. They state what conditions should be present within a two- to five-year period. Three purpose goals that have been generally accepted by the Boys' Clubs of America movement are:

● To strive to achieve equal opportunity and foster respect for human dignity for all youth.

● To initiate and promote services that will enhance the quality of life for all youth.

● To strengthen our role as spokesmen for youth.

When an individual club considers these philosophical statements, at the local level, the result will be the formulation of a number of courses of action to achieve these goals. Examples of such courses of action might be:

● Broadening and intensifying volunteer participation and involvement.

● Developing manpower capability.

● Expanding and diversifying service to the community.

● Developing working relationships with other human service organizations.

● Increasing financial support for operation through endowments and growth.[5]

---

4. R. Wayne Mondy, Robert E. Holmes, and Edwin B. Flippo, *Management: Concepts and Practices* (Boston: Allyn and Bacon, 1980), p. 88.

5. Boys' Clubs of America, *Achieving Excellence Through Planning* (New York: 1975), p. 10.

Development of specific objectives.   The consideration of these general objectives will give rise to the development of operational goals that can be achieved by implementing specific programs and action steps within a given time period. Such programs and actions then become the responsibility of individuals. The objectives must support the overall purpose of the organization and must be expressed as precise and measurable targets. Let us consider the first operational goal and see how it might be refined into objectives and action plans.

An example of an operational goal that relates back to our objective of "broadening and intensifying volunteer participation and involvement" might be:

"By July 1, 1986 (two- to five-year span) achieve broader and more intensified participation and involvement of volunteers on all levels." This fits the criteria for goal development in that it is (1) no more than three sentences long, (2) conceivable, (3) believable, (4) achievable, (5) limited to two- to five year period, and (6) stated in terms of results. Though this operational goal states a desired future direction, it is not yet precise enough to assign responsibility for achievement. More specific, measurable performance goals, or action plans would be required to do this. An example of an action plan for the operational goal just discussed would be the following: "By July 1, 1986, to develop and implement a plan to increase the organization's volunteer board to 24 members and to include representation from the three major ethnic groups in the community, the four major corporations, the school board, parents of members, and prominent alumni of the organization."

This example makes a direct contribution to achieving the goal. In addition, (1) it is feasible; (2) it is measurable; (3) it will have to be completed within the fiscal planning year; (4) it can be assigned to an individual or individuals for action. This objective is of the type developed within an MBO system of management.

The example could be carried further to include the actual action steps that would be necessary to ensure that the objective was accomplished. Such steps might include developing revised criteria for the selection of board members, visiting ethnic groups and major corporations, meeting with the school board, compiling a master list of proposed new board members, and selecting from that list. These steps should be written down, given a date for completion and assigned to a specific individual for implementation. In this way, individuals are held accountable for the action steps that are necessary to reach the operational goal.

Measurement of results achieved.   The next step in the MBO system is to measure and evaluate the results achieved by individuals in terms of whether they have reached the specific objectives for which they have assumed responsibility. This step presupposes that an action plan has been developed and agreed upon by both the subordinate and the manager. When objectives are clearly defined and agreed upon by both persons, then self-evaluation and control are possible.

Initiation of corrective action.   Even an organization with clear-cut objectives, well-defined performance standards, and suitable appraisal procedures may sometimes need corrective action. Corrective action to ensure that the objectives and action plans of the organization are being realized might include such procedures as changes in personnel, restructuring of committees and task forces, allocation of more financial resources, and changes in the objectives themselves.

The Advantages of MBO

It is difficult to imagine that any organization or any individual can operate effectively or efficiently without going through the MBO process, either consciously or unconsciously. We all set objectives; we all measure results. We all take remedial action when the results do not coincide with the original objectives. What varies is the degree of refinement that we assign to the process. We can describe MBO as a conscious, empirical approach to the establishment and achievement of organizational objectives. The benefits of using MBO include the following: improving management at all levels, helping to clarify the organization's purpose and structure, increasing commitment to objectives, and assisting in control.

Improving management.   If one could summarize the overall effect of an MBO program, it would be the improvement of the total management of an organization. Establishing objectives helps managers clarify their own objectives in relation to the overall mission of the organization. An MBO program forces managers at all levels to concentrate on results rather than activities. It also encourages managers to consider alternate ways of attaining results, to consider various organizational structures and to consider personnel and other resources to promote effectiveness. In addition, effective control techniques are made possible by setting clear and measurable standards.

Clarifying organizational purpose and structure.   An MBO system helps individuals within an organization to focus on its goals and objectives. It helps the manager to understand not only where the organization is headed, but, perhaps more importantly, why the organization is headed in one direction rather than another. MBO contributes to organizational goal attainment in a direct manner by helping the manager identify and clarify organizational goals.

Organizational structures within agencies are created so that roles can be identified that collectively assist the organization in achieving its stated objectives. In an MBO program, managers assume accountability for specific results and often analyze the organizational roles that have been created to meet objectives. Thus, there is a continual refinement of the role each individual plays within the organization. Organizational effectiveness and efficiency are increased immeasurably when roles are reviewed, upgraded, revised, and modified on a continual basis by the MBO manager.

Soliciting commitment.   All managers and subordinates in an MBO program have clearly defined directions to reach the objectives for which they are accountable. They also take part in setting these objectives. If employees feel a part of the total planning process, and if they have a voice in setting their own objectives, then it stands to reason there will be more employee commitment than in an organization where direction flows downward.

Assisting in control.   Effective planning involves the development of effective controls. In an MBO program, clear and measurable objectives are formulated. In turn, the establishment of objectives provides a method for evaluating performance against these objectives and a method for correcting any deviations that might occur. The process of measuring and correcting progress is control, and an organization using an MBO approach to management, plans effective controls.

Possible Disadvantages of MBO

Goal setting.   Goals are extremely difficult to establish in organizations whose end product is service. However, it *is* possible to establish measurable goals in human-service organizations. All organizations must know where they are going before they can be successful and an MBO program encourages foresight.

Short-term focus.   Usually, objectives established in MBO programs are set to correspond with the fiscal year. If too much emphasis is placed on these short-term goals, long-range planning may suffer. To prevent this, managers must constantly ensure that all short-range objectives support long-range plans.

Other possible problems.   Some managers may become so involved in quantifying objectives that they attempt to quantify results that defy numerical measurement, or they may tend to downgrade important qualitative services that are difficult to measure. However, even though MBO has some difficulties associated with it as a management system, its positive attributes so far outweigh its drawbacks that it is impossible to conceive of an organization that would not use some type of management-by-objectives-system. Regarding MBO, we have two words of advice for recreation and leisure service managers: Use it!

THE PLANNING PROCESS

Planning is a process. Whether planning occurs within the corporate structure of the Metropolitan Toronto Y.M.C.A., within the corporate structure of the city of Tallahassee, Florida, or within the mind of the reader of this text, the process should be basically the same. Essentially, there are six steps in any planning process, including: (1) the establishment of objectives, (2) the identification of several courses of action to accomplish these objectives, (3) the comparison of these courses to determine which will have the best chance of success, (4) the selection of the best possible course of action, (5) the development of any needed supportive plans, and (6) the instigation of needed action.

Establishing objectives. The logical starting place in any planning process is to know what you want to accomplish. Even though this step seems basic it is probably the most difficult one to complete at either the corporate or individual level. If an organization is able to determine exactly what should be accomplished during the coming year, then it can move on to consider the variety of ways whereby the objectives might be achieved. If, however, the organization is undecided about what should be done, then it will be impossible to instigate any meaningful planning process.

Identifying alternate courses of action. Seldom is there only one way to reach a destination. Similarly, most objectives can be achieved in more than one way, even though all the alternatives may not be readily apparent. Thus, a very important step in the planning process is to carefully articulate all possible courses of action and then, through a process of elimination, reduce the possibilities to those alternatives that appear to hold the most promise for successful completion.

Evaluating alternative courses of action. After a list has been developed of the most promising courses of action to reach a specific objective, the manager must evaluate all the alternatives in light of the original objectives and such variables as human and financial resources, cost and benefits (both immediate and long-term), and risks involved.

Since there are usually numerous possible courses of action to reach any objective, a manager who has become efficient in this process of evaluation will have acquired one of the essential attributes of a good planner. The ability to make decisions at this stage of the planning process is crucial, as is the ability to use objective measurement tools to assist in decision making.

Developing supportive plans. In almost all cases, the decision to adopt a particular plan will necessitate the development of supporting plans that will make the completion of the primary plan possible. If the national council of the Y.M.C.A.s of Canada decides to embark upon a national financial campaign to add additional facilities to their Geneva Park Conference Center, this decision will involve the establishment of many committees and courses of action across the country.

Instigating needed action. The final step, which follows the actual planning process, is the instigation of needed action. Once the plan is operative it ceases to be a plan and becomes a program.

NETWORK ANALYSIS

Just as a goal can be broken down into more specific objectives, any task of reasonable magnitude can also be broken down into smaller tasks or action plans. One of the secrets of planning is the ability to determine the number of separate tasks needed to accomplish a specific objective and to schedule these tasks in their proper sequence.

A method for illustrating the specific tasks necessary to complete a project is network analysis. Perhaps the best known form of network analysis is the Program Evaluation and Review Technique (PERT). Though most recreation and leisure service managers will not become directly involved with PERT, the concepts behind the technique are sound and worth analysis.

PERT was developed by a private management firm in cooperation with the U.S. Navy as an aid to the development of the Polaris submarine program. The management firm was asked to coordinate the thousands of smaller tasks that were required to complete the Polaris project. When a project must be organized that is nonrecurring, large in scope, extremely complex, and involves the coordination of many individuals and firms, PERT is a useful technique that will coordinate all the interdependencies within the network. To understand the concept, a few basic definitions and explanations are necessary.

An *event* is a specific accomplishment that occurs at a particular and recognizable point in time. Events do not require time or resources; they are occurences. The designated symbol for an event is a circle, O.

An *activity* is the work or effort requiring some amount of time to complete a specific event. Activities do require time and resources. The designated symbol for an activity is an arrow, →. The estimated time that it will take to complete each activity (usually in weeks) is shown in numbers beside each arrow.

The *critical path* is the longest time-path charted on a network diagram and represents the earliest possible completion date of the project.

Figure 4.5 shows a simple PERT network that illustrates the activities (→) necessary to complete the project and the completion of these activities (events O). If we count the longest time-path $(3 + 4 + 4 + 6 + 4 = 2)$, we see that the critical path for the project or the earliest completion date is 21 weeks.

Let us demonstrate how a simple PERT network is developed. First, it is important to be able to differentiate between the various subtasks required to complete the project. A project to build a community center might logically be divided into subtasks such as completing the foundation, framing in the building, completing the plumbing, wiring, assembling outside siding, completing the interior decorating, painting the exterior of the building, and assuming the building from the project director.

The next step in designing our network would be to list these subtasks (events) along with their proper sequencing and the estimated time needed to complete each separate task. This step could be accomplished by utilizing charts similar to those in Figures 4.5 and 4.6.

The last step in the process is to construct the network diagram. Possible time paths:

(1) $A \rightarrow B + B \rightarrow C + C \rightarrow D + D \rightarrow G + G \rightarrow I$
    $3 + 4 + 4 + 6 + 4 = 21$
(2) $A \rightarrow B + B \rightarrow C + C \rightarrow E + E \rightarrow G + G \rightarrow I$
    $3 + 4 + 2 + 6 + 4 = 19$
(3) $A \rightarrow B + B \rightarrow C + C \rightarrow F + F \rightarrow H + H \rightarrow I$
    $3 + 4 + 3 + 2 + 4 = 16$

Thus, the critical path is 21 weeks, which represents the longest time path and the earliest possible completion date.

Since the 1950s PERT has served well as a planning and control tool for the management of large-scale complex and first-time projects. In real-life situations, PERT networks involve the coordination of hundreds of contractors, making use of mathematical formulas and computer programs. However, the underlying principles involved—that we should divide projects into subtasks, identify the proper sequencing of events, recognize the relationships among the activities that constitute a project, and use a visual aid to help us to comprehend the project—are sound and a useful aid to planning for recreation and leisure service managers.

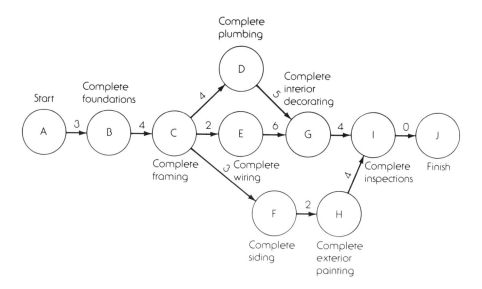

Figure 4.5 The constructed network for building a community center.

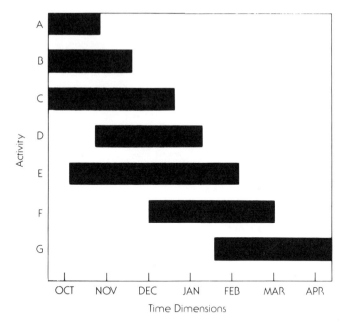

Figure 4.6 A Gantt chart is useful for scheduling all of the subtasks involved in a complex project. Each subtask (A through G) is represented by a bar. The position of the bar shows the expected start time for a subtask. The length of the bar shows the projected time needed to complete a subtask.

TABLE 4.1   Activities and Time Estimates for Building a Community Center

Activities Necessary	Time Estimates
Foundation work	Expected time, 3 weeks.
Framing	Expected time, 4 weeks.
Plumbing, wiring, outside siding	Can be done independently after framing is completed. Expected time: 4,2,3, weeks, respectively.
Interior decorating	Can be done after plumbing and wiring are completed. Expected time, 6 weeks.
Exterior painting	Can be done after outside siding is completed. Expected time, 2 weeks.
Building Inspection	Can be done 4 weeks after interior is finished and the exterior is painted. This completes the project.

TABLE 4.2   Sequencing the Events Involved in Building a Community Center

Event #	Event	Follows	Activity Time
A	Start		0
B	Complete foundation	A	3
C	Complete framing	B	4
D	Complete plumbing	C	4
E	Complete wiring	C	2
F	Complete outside siding	C	3
G	Complete interior decorating	D, E	6
H	Complete exterior painting	F	2
I	Complete inspection	G, H	4
J	Finish	I	0

DECISION MAKING

One of the most important attributes of an effective manager is the ability to make decisions. As Koontz and O'Donnell point out, a plan cannot be said to exist unless a decision has been made regarding commitment of resources and direction. Until a decision is made the only thing that exists is a planning study. A planning study plus a decision results in a plan.

How we plan and how we make decisions greatly influences our lives—both professionally and personally. The process of rational decision-making involves a number of steps, including the development of alternatives, the evaluation of alternatives, the selection of the best course of action, and the evaluation of the decision.

If you as a recreation and leisure service manager decide that there is only one way of accomplishing a particular objective, chances are that there is something wrong with your management skills. As we mentioned in our discussion of the planning process, there are always many solutions to a problem. The ability to develop alternatives is often as important as the ability to choose from among alternatives. Creative thinking, education, and past experience, as well as the ability to involve other people in this process, should help the manager to develop and articulate the different alternatives present in any given situation. Once this step has been accomplished, the manager can proceed to the next step in the decision-making process.

After appropriate alternatives have been developed, the manager must evaluate each in relation to a number of questions. How will this course of action best contribute to the achievement of our objectives? How will this objective interact with both the external and the internal environmental conditions within which our organization operates? What are the qualitative and the quantitative implications of deciding upon this particular course of action? Most decisions of any magnitude have effects that are not apparent at first glance. The skilled decision maker will be able to forecast many of these.

PLANNING TIME USE

Effective managers know how to plan, organize, and schedule their own tasks. It is surprising how much can be accomplished when effort is organized and directed toward a specific goal or set of goals. Successful managers recognize the importance of meticulous planning—planning that starts by analyzing the behavior of managers themselves. Every day, a manager is faced with a series of decisions, both large and small. The decisions that the individual manager makes will gradually shape the organization and will determine the extent to which the organization achieves its goals and the manager succeeds.

Many management decisions relate to how the manager will use his or her time to direct the organization. Conscious planning of time use is called *time management*. Time management is a process of identifying and clarifying factors related to the use of one's time. With respect to the achievement of organizational goals, the recreation and leisure service manager is concerned with using his or her time in such a way as to ensure organizational success. In individuals' personal lives, time management concepts can be used to improve life satisfaction by conscious evaluation and control of time use. Poor time management can result in decisions that produce a sense of frustration, low self-esteem, and stress.

Symptoms of Poor Time Management

There are a number of symptoms of poor time management that can be identified. Some of these symptoms are rushing, indecisiveness, inactivity, missing deadlines, lack of leisure, and a feeling of being overwhelmed.

Rushing.   When an individual is constantly engaged in apparent last-minute crises, or rushing from event to event and activity to activity, he or she is showing signs of poor time management. Hurrying from one activity to another may imply poor planning or procrastination.

Indecisiveness.   People who have difficulty choosing among various alternatives, especially unpleasant ones, can be said to be indecisive. This chronic vacillation often results from poor time management.

Inactivity. Inactivity can be distinguished from productive activity whether at leisure or at work. Inactivity often manifests itself as fatigue or listlessness and results in nonproductive behavior.

Missing deadlines. Individuals who constantly miss deadlines often do so because they haven't planned and otherwise managed their time effectively. Postponing decisions to the last minute is a major reason for missed deadlines.

Lack of leisure. When individuals become so consumed with their work that they don't have time for leisure to balance their work lives, it is often due to poor time management.

Feeling overwhelmed. When an individual finds it difficult or impossible to cope with a large number of concerns, he or she can be said to feel overwhelmed. The effective manager should be able to organize and assume or delegate responsibility for a large task or number of tasks.

Effective Time Management

How does the recreation and leisure service manager effectively manage his or her own time? Basically, the manager must learn to organize work activities in a way that will maximize use of time. This involves *identifying important individual and organizational goals.* To avoid frustration and stress one must have a clear understanding of tasks to be completed. The manager might ask the questions: What do I want to accomplish? What does the organization want to accomplish? Responding to these questions allows the manager to identify and clarify important goals.

The next step in the process of time management is the establishment of priorities. This is a process of decision making; deciding what is important and what is not. In determining priorities, the manager must identify those goals that are essential and will contribute to the attainment of organizational goals and life satisfaction. The manager must also identify those goals that have a reasonable chance of being accomplished. This does not imply that expectations should be lowered, but rather that managers should avoid setting unrealistic goals.

The last step in the process of time management is that of breaking priorities down into manageable steps. Once goals and priorities have been established, the manager is in a position to break each goal into smaller tasks. The smaller and more precise the task, the more possible the attainment of the task becomes. Often an individual will be overwhelmed by a seemingly insurmountable goal, but when the goal or job is broken down into steps it is no longer overwhelming and is seen as being attainable. Managing tasks includes disciplining oneself to work each day for a specific amount of time on goals that have been given a high priority. However, it is important to emphasize results rather than activity. There are many individuals who appear to be quite productive, yet achieve very little. It is important to learn to focus behavior on the accomplishment of high-priority goals. In order to be successful, the manager should take one step toward his or her goals every day. This may involve avoiding new commitments or those commitments that are not related to the achievement of organizational or personal goals.

Good time management should involve the assumption of a proactive posture. It should mean controlling one's life, rather than simply reacting to situations as they occur. It involves planning how to use one's time more effectively to achieve organizational and personal success. Time management may result in a conscious effort to block the use of one's time for nonproductive activities such as daydreaming, watching television, socializing on the phone, engaging in meaningless trivial tasks, and so on. Time management may also involve a conscious effort to allow for events or interruptions that might occur.

North Americans seem to be extremely concerned about time use from two perspectives. The first perspective relates to the work environment. Individuals and organizations are extremely concerned with productivity, and questions such as: How do we become more creative, innovative, efficient, and effective in the pursuit of personal and organizational goals? How do we do the same or more with less and become more productive? Second, in their personal lives, North Americans are becoming more concerned with working in order to play. In other words, they want to arrange their work schedules so that they can pursue leisure and its rewards of happiness and life satisfaction. Further, in their leisure North Americans seem to be trying to pack more activity into less time. This is known as *time deepening*. People tend to participate in activities that have immediate, direct impact, rather than those that have benefits that are delayed. The popularity of raquetball is an example of this phenomenon. These two perspectives (personal and work) illustrate the importance of time management in our lives.

PLANNING FOR PUBLIC PARTICIPATION

It is important that public recreation and leisure service organizations involve their constituents in the planning and decision-making processes that affect the distribution of resources. In these times of financial constraints and increased concern for accountability in government services, it is necessary to accurately reflect the interests of those served. It is not enough to involve individuals or groups on a random, sporadic basis; systematic planning is needed to ensure public involvement on a continuous and permanent basis. Few recreation and leisure service organizations have established a formal plan or guidelines to encourage this.

By systematically planning for participation in the decision-making process, organizations can increase their accountability and hence, their effectiveness and efficiency. There are several reasons why this is the case. First, when those served by an organization feel they are contributing to the decision-making process, they have a sense of ownership that often results in feelings of good will, pride, and interest in the organization. The cultivation of this relationship, a partnership between the organization and its consumers, may culminate in the establishment of a cooperative exchange wherein the goals of the organization can be achieved and the needs of the public met. Second, involving the consumer in the decision-making process reduces the amount of guesswork that takes place in recreation and leisure service organizations. For example, we often plan activities with the assumption that some programs will be well attended while others will not. This cafeteria approach to program planning is not efficient, and wastes organizational resources. It would be more effective to establish an ongoing process of participation in the development of programs to ensure that the programs offered will have a greater chance of succeeding.

What is Planning for Participation?

Planning for participation implies a long-term, continuous, and systematic commitment. It requires the allocation of organizational resources to promote citizen input. It is based on the assumption that planning must involve a broad program of citizen participation as well as an extensive program of education, awareness, and development. In order to succeed, an organization must establish a formal plan or set of guidelines that ensure consumer participation. It cannot be done on a random or sporadic basis, but must be an ongoing and permanent process.

Planning for participation must be a cooperative effort. It must help individuals, interest groups, and other agencies develop a deeper understanding of their community, its needs, problems, resources, and other variables that affect the provision of recreation and leisure services. This type of systematic planning is directed toward creating opportunities for cooperation between individuals, and groups, and organizations. Cooperation requires a willingness on the part of recreation and leisure service professionals to listen to the suggestions of members of the community and to recognize their attitudes, goals, and fears.

In planning for participation, what should the recreation and leisure services professional avoid? In many communities, participation in the planning process becomes pseudo-participation, wherein individuals and groups are involved only to be patronized and their concerns placated. Advice is solicited, but usually ignored or not used. Or, the participation process may be used to sell the organization's predetermined plans to its constituents. The withholding or selective dispersion of information for the purpose of controlling responses of the public will also undermine community participation. The withholding of information often leads to a one-way communication process, leaving the public in a dependent, passive role. Last, planning for participation should not ignore the importance of the contributions of elected representatives. Instead, planning strategies adopted should support existing political structures and mechanisms.

A Strategy for Participation

Participation must be organized so that it is a collaborative process that involves politicians, citizens, special-interest groups, developers, and other interested parties. In order to reach each of these audiences, it is important to recognize that a number of vehicles for participation must be created and employed in such a way that different groups will feel comfortable working with them. For example, a neighborhood association might feel more comfortable preparing and presenting a formal brief, whereas a group of single parents might prefer an open-ended discussion session. By using different vehicles for participation, an agency can increase both the quantity and the quality of participation.

There are a number of processes and tools that can be used to encourage and assist citizen involvement in planning and decision-making. Many of these are used by planning agencies as well as recreation and leisure sevice delivery systems. However, few are employed as a part of a long-term, systematic planning process. The extent to which any of these vehicles can be employed by a given recreation and leisure service organization will depend on the overall planning strategy, as well as the unique conditions found in communities or other political jurisdictions (for example, a park district).

Delphi technique.   The Delphi technique is usually based upon a series of questionnaires and attempts to obtain the opinions of individuals relative to a given subject. The individuals involved in this type of communicative approach are anonymous. The Delphi technique can be used to improve the quality of decision making, although it can be a very time-consuming way of obtaining information.

Nominal group technique.   The nominal group technique employs a highly structured format wherein ideas are ranked by the individuals participating. Initially, group members write down their ideas. Each member then shares one of his or her ideas with the other group members, and these ideas are recorded on a displayed chart. Remaining ideas of group members are similarly shared and eventually ranked on paper by each group member. The group decision becomes the idea that is ranked most often by group members as preferable.

Task forces.   Task forces are made up of individuals who are concerned about a specific issue or concern. They are intensive, short-term work groups that promote an exchange of information between professionals and constituents. They can be useful sources of information that aid in decision making if they are comprised of individuals who accurately represent various viewpoints related to the concern at hand.

Surveys.   A survey is used to gather information about constituents. It can be conducted with a questionnaire or on a face-to-face basis. Surveys can be used to collect demographic information, opinions, and attitudes. Surveys are often used to assess needs and thereby assist in the planning effort.

Briefs.   A brief is a written document wherein an individual states his or her beliefs, values or opinions concerning a particular issue or concern. Briefs allow participants to articulate their viewpoints formally. A brief reduces speculation, heresay and confusion and provides a basis for discussion.

Citizen advisory groups.   These groups are made up of individuals who are appointed because of their interest or knowledge of a given concern or issue. The citizen advisory group is a traditional form of citizen participation in the recreation and leisure service field. Neighborhood advisory associations, program advisory groups, and facility advisory groups are often established to provide additional opportunities for citizen participation.

Plebiscite.   When direct voter approval is sought in the form of a referendum, it is referred to as a plebiscite. Plebiscites tend to dichotomize an issue, creating a win-lose situation. A tax referendum is the most common form of plebiscite employed by public recreation and leisure service organizations.

The intensity, amount, and longevity of citizen participation will vary according to the situation. In some cases, problems can be readily identified and solved in a short period of time; others require more extensive involvement. Within any system there is no end to issues and problems that can be discussed, dissected, and reviewed. The key to long-term participation is the establishment of a program that is cyclical in nature, having phases of participation. A cyclical process of participation involves three basic steps: building awareness, identifying and analyzing issues, and deciding how resources will be acquired and distributed.

Building awareness.   The initial phase of participation should be organized to stimulate community interest in and awareness of a particular problem, issue or concern. It should provide information concerning the problem and suggest avenues for participation.

Issue identification and goal formulation.   The next part of the participation process is the actual discussion of concerns or issues. It involves fact finding and the accumulation of relevant data and information, followed by an analysis of issues.

Resource allocation. The purpose of this part of the participation process is to determine how organizational resources can be acquired and distributed or redistributed to meet a particular concern. This is the payoff point, and in order for participation to be valuable it must result in change.

Once these steps have been completed for a particular issue, the same cyclical process may start again with another problem.

SUMMARY

Planning is a process for determining future objectives and deciding how these can be achieved. Because change is so pervasive in our society, good planning is essential. Planning begins with the establishment of organizational goals. There are basically two types of goals. The first of these is known as a purpose or mission goal. This type of goal is based on the philosophical position of the organization and articulates its basic purpose. The second type of goal, operational and growth, is more specific and usually describes the desired future status of the organization within a specified time period. The six basic steps of the planning process include the following: (1) the establishment of objectives, (2) the identification of alternate courses of action, (3) the comparison of alternate courses of action, (4) the selection of the best possible course of action, (5) the development of supportive plans, and (6) the initiation of action.

One of the more useful management tools that can be used by the recreation and leisure service organization is known as management by objectives (MBO). The process of management by objectives allows the manager and his subordinates to interact in such a way that individual action fulfills the overall mission of the agency. It involves the following steps: (1) support and commitment from top management, (2) the establishment of long-term goals and strategic plans, (3) development of specific objectives, (4) measurement of results achieved, and (5) the initiation of corrective action. MBO helps managers and subordinates clarify their own objectives in relation to the overall mission of the agency, solicits commitment from employees, assists in the process of control, and helps clarify the organization's goals and objectives.

One of the tools that has been employed by recreation and leisure service systems to aid in planning is network analysis. This method offers a procedure for illustrating specific tasks necessary to complete a project as well as (in most network models) the time necessary to complete each of these tasks. Two important network analyses, Program Evaluation Review Technique (PERT) and Gantt Charts, can be useful to recreation and leisure service organizations in the planning process.

The process of rational planning and decision making will greatly influence the success or failure of the individual manager. Central to the planning and decision-making process is the planning, organization, and scheduling of the managers' personal work agenda. Time management is the conscious planning of time use. It is a process directed toward identifying and clarifying factors related to the use of one's time. The recreation and leisure service manager should be concerned with the way in which his or her time is used, and the way in which subordinates' time is used. Organizational success or failure, as well as individual life satisfaction, can be influenced tremendously by the way in which time is used in the pursuit of goals.

STUDY QUESTIONS

1. What is planning? Why is the ability to establish goals and objectives essential to good planning?

2. Distinguish between purpose goals and operational goals. Provide an example of each.

3. Identify the steps in the corporate planning process. How are mission statements and operational and growth goals related to a management-by-objectives program?

4. The process of management by objectives (MBO) is directed at the achievement of objectives rather than at the activities of work. What does this statement mean?

5. Outline and discuss the basic steps in the MBO process.

6. Briefly describe the advantages and potential problems of MBO. In your opinion, under what circumstances is it most feasible to implement MBO?

7. The program evaluation and review technique (PERT) is a form of network analysis. Identify the principles involved in designing a network analysis for a particular task. In what way is this method an aid to planning?

8. Define time management. Why is time management important and how does it relate to management decision making?

9. Identify six symptoms of poor time management. How many of these are evident in your life?

10. Identify a set of organizational goals for a community recreation and leisure service system. Which of these items can be termed mission statements? Which are operational or growth goals? Does the agency

research use an MBO system for planning? If so, identify a specific set of action statements related to recreation program development.

CASE STUDY 6

Internal Communication

Bob Playfair is the director of the Recreation Services Division for the Canusa Recreation and Parks Department. As a result of the size and the diversification of the Recreation Services Division, Bob oversees six separate areas, each headed by a supervisor.

Allocations for two new parks and playgrounds were approved at the last city council meeting based upon Bob's promise to provide a full-time recreational program at each site, beginning June 1, just six months away. The minutes from the city council meeting have not been distributed to the city officials, and George Branch, newly appointed director of Parks and Recreation is unaware of the council's decision concerning the two new parks.

On his way to the accounting department, George Branch met Jim McAdam, chairman of the Canusa Recreation and Parks Committee. Jim expressed his enthusiasm to George about the two new parks and playgrounds, and then asked, "Are we going to have them in full swing by June 1?" George smiled and said, "I'll give you a full report next week at our committee meeting."

George asked Bob Playfair into his office and the following conversation took place.

George: "Bob, I was talking to Jim McAdam, and he mentioned we will have two new parks and playgrounds."

Bob: "Oh, yes, we were allocated funds at the last city council meeting. Haven't you read the minutes?"

George: "The minutes haven't been printed as yet, but I am most concerned about matters such as this transpiring without my being informed."

Bob: "George, I just got you two more parks; what do you want? As your predecessor, the last director, always said, 'Don't worry me with the details, just keep on making the department grow.'"

QUESTIONS

1. How could the planning aspect of management be applied to this situation?
2. Is communication important in the planning process? Cite an example that explains your response.
3. Could policies and procedures have assisted in this concern of George. If so, how and if not, why?
4. What action should George take now? Think how his decision may affect the efficiency and effectiveness of the Parks and Recreation Department.
5. What is the most important issue in this case?

CASE STUDY 7

Management by Objectives

The Canusa Recreation and Parks Department has decided to implement an integrated goal-setting program for all units within the department. The goal-setting program is to be based upon the management-by-objectives approach. Using this approach, the department and each of its units and subunits will be asked to set clear, measurable objectives for the coming year. Programs, policies, procedures, and budgets will then be designed to accomplish these objectives. Each unit and individual employee will then be evaluated annually, based upon whether the objectives were accomplished.

The Canusa Recreation and Parks Department offers a variety of recreational facilities and programs for all members of the community. The funds come from the city government to the department, and the department uses the funds to operate the facilities and programs within broad guidelines set by local government.

George Branch is the newly appointed director of Parks and Recreation in Canusa. He believes his department is not getting its full share of the general funds from the city, because the department has not done a good job in setting objectives. Therefore, he believes the whole department needs to go on a more structured and systematic management-by-objectives goal-setting program in order to provide more effective services to the community and thereby capitalize on the funding available.

The department is structured into sections and subsections. There are three divisions, each of which is headed by a division director who reports directly to George.

The divisions are:
1. Parks and Property Division
2. Administrative Services
3. Recreation Services

Each of these sections has four to six subsections headed by a supervisor. Each subsection supervisor has four to six employees who report to him.

George has heard at several management-by-objectives seminars that for MBO to work, it must be implemented in a participatory manner. Therefore, he plans on meeting with his subordinates to develop a list of objectives, programs, and policies for the department and for each division. Each division head will then meet with the respective subsection supervisor to do the same. Each subsection supervisor will then meet with subordinates in a similar manner.

By developing the MBO program in this way, George believes everyone will be involved in making really important decisions that will guide the future functioning of the department. However, George has several initial concerns which may make this method difficult to accomplish. These are:

1. It will be rather time-consuming and may require two years to be fully developed and tied to the budgeting process.
2. Division directors and supervisors frequently have meetings and programs that require their attention and may find it difficult to attend all scheduled meetings.
3. Some division directors and supervisors are rather autocratic and may not feel comfortable meeting with subordinates in this participatory approach.
4. There is conflict among some divisions. This is particularly true between the

Recreation Services and the Parks and Property Division. This conflict may prohibit a free and open exchange of ideas in the sessions.

5.   There is a good deal of turnover and shifting of assignments within the entire department. This may make it difficult for individuals to participate in setting objectives.

Yet, even with these concerns, George has decided to go ahead with the goal-setting program. An initial meeting has been scheduled for all divisions to discuss the program and plan its implementation. At this meeting, there will also be a preliminary discussion of department objectives.

The meeting is held, and the following dialogue takes place.

George: Thank you all for coming. I know we all have busy schedules, and this meeting shouldn't take more than one hour. I just want to go over something with you concerning a new method of goal setting.

I've talked to one or two of you about this previously and now want to bring everyone up to date. Basically, I'd like to get this department into a more structured system of goal setting that better reflects our plan of service. As you know, we aren't getting our full share of tax funds, and I think a better goal-setting system will help us do this.

Therefore, I'd like to institute a formal system of management by objectives throughout the department. I'd like to do this on a participatory basis and involve as many people as possible in developing the goals.

Chris Johnson (Revenue Operations): Does this mean involving all 40 employees?

George: Yes, at some point, but not initially. I'd like to start with the division directors and supervisors.

Bob Playfair (Recreation Services): How long do you think this will take?

George: Probably two years in total, but I want to get started within two or three weeks.

Bob: Boy, that will be tough. I'm already up to my neck in work.

Tom Green (Parks and Property): I'm busy too, but the idea sounds great. This will give us a chance to really see what's going on in each division. It will give us a good chance to communicate with each other.

George: You're right, Tom. That's one advantage of MBO. People should open up in the workshop sessions.

Chris: I don't know about that. You know I used to be with Disney World up until three years ago when I joined the department, and I went through this MBO stuff in my section. We started out the same way. Lots of meetings and participation. Spent lots of time and money. Outside consultants, seminars, etc. I guess we got some benefit from it, but you know, it wasn't because we participated. What it came down to was the simple fact that each manager ended up having to write the objectives for his unit. The people in each unit couldn't ever agree as to what the objectives should be.

George: Why was that, Chris? Weren't they willing to compromise? Compromise is required in the process.

Chris: Oh sure, they'd compromise—up to a point. But each person had his own point to push. Each person felt he was more important than the other. Each wanted to maintain his own power. Each manager finally had to come down hard on his subordinates to get the people to accept the objectives. It was a classic case of "group think." Everyone finally went along with the objectives because they felt they had to. The manager, in effect, demanded it. Everyone gave in to the way the manager directed the group instead of standing up for what he or she believed in. But I guess that's the way it has to be, or we would never have gotten any objectives written.

George: No, I don't believe so. Sure, participation takes time, and the process can be subverted. Managers can use groups to bring about a group-think philosophy, but it need not be that way. People can compromise without giving up their principles. Groups can have open exchanges. Groups can be creative. I'm going to ensure that this happens here.

Chris: Well, I hope you're right, but I'm very skeptical. If it was hard for Disney, it will be virtually impossible for us. You know how political our agency is; government as a whole is just too political. MBO is a rational, logical process. Government administration is a political and emotional process. I don't think your concept will work. It'll be "group think" all over again, only worse.

George: Well, what do the rest of you think?

QUESTIONS

1. What does Chris refer to when he describes "group think"? Is this characteristic of planning done by groups in government agencies? In private business?
2. Do you think George's planning approach will be successful or not? Why or why not?
3. Can participatory planning and decision-making work? Why or why not?
4. What specific problems do you see arising if George implements a participatory MBO approach in his department? How might these be overcome?
5. If you were in the room with George, Chris, Tom, and Bob, what would you say now in response to George's final question? What would you recommend and why?

Organizing

5

Our society is made up of many types of organizations: formal and informal, large and small, simple and complex. All organizations have a number of common characteristics. First, and most important, all organizations are made up of people who are striving to achieve a goal or set of goals. In order to achieve these goals, individuals within organizations create structures that define the behavior expected of organizational members. An organization's structure defines positions of authority and responsibility, channels of communication, and mechanisms of control and accountability.

In order for a recreation and leisure service manager to be successful, he or she must have the ability to organize the human, physical, and fiscal resources of the organization. A manager should understand how organizations function, the factors that influence people within organizations, and the organizational structures that best achieve organizational goals. The process of organization is essential wherever people work collaboratively.

DEFINING THE ORGANIZATION

An *organization* is a social structure in which two or more people collaborate to achieve desired ends. The major difference between other types of organizations and recreation and leisure service organizations is in the definition of objectives.

The organizing process consists of three related components: establishing roles, establishing an organizational structure, and directing resources. Establishing roles consists primarily of assigning responsibility and granting authority to individuals within the organizational structure. The second part of the process is establishing an organizational structure within which individuals can communicate with one another. The last part of the process of organizing is directing the resources of the organization so that they contribute to the achievement of organizational goals. Sequentially, the essential elements in the process of organizing are as follows:

- Defining goals and objectives
- Determining the work or task to be accomplished
- Determining and acquiring the resources (human, physical, and fiscal) needed to accomplish organizational goals
- Clustering functions within the organization
- Assigning responsibilities to individuals and granting authority
- Establishing and implementing a structure of control and accountability

In describing the process of organizing recreation and leisure service systems, this chapter will also discuss the formal organization, the informal organization, the chain of command, specialization of labor, the processes of departmentalization, delegation of authority, power and authority, span of control, and various types of organizational structures that can be employed by recreation and leisure service organizations.

The Formal Organization

Almost all North Americans belong to some type of formal organization. It is through formal organizations that much of the progress of this century has been accomplished. The material bounty and excellent human services available to Americans and Canadians has largely occurred as a result of our ability to organize and manage ourselves in an efficient way.

We can think of the *formal organization* as a social unit that has been created to achieve a set of predetermined goals and objectives. In the case of recreation and leisure service agencies, the formal organization is created for the purpose of improving the quality of life for a discrete population (youth, families, community, etc.). This involves understanding exactly what work is to be accomplished, assigning responsibility and authority to individuals to complete such work, and then coordinating the activities between various work units within an organization to achieve the overall goals of the agency. We often think of the formal organization as being rigid and inflexible. However, this is not necessarily the case. Managers who are well organized can create work units that are highly flexible and responsive to the needs of different situations.

In order to establish a formal organization, the manager must first define the roles or tasks that should be assigned to individuals within the organization in order to fulfill its goals and objectives. This can often be a difficult task. Poorly defined roles can lead to severe organizational problems.

Once an individual has been assigned a clearly defined role within the organization, he or she should also be given responsibility and authority commensurate with that role. In today's organizations people work best in professional roles that have a high degree of autonomy and independence. Without adequate authority to carry out an assigned task, their effectiveness can be diminished. Once tasks have been assigned and authority has been delegated, the manager can hold each member of the organization accountable for his or her actions. This, then, is the process of organization: creating roles, delegating authority and establishing a mechanism for accountability.

The formal organization is not created by the manager alone. Nor is it confined to graphic representations of organizational charts. The development of the formal organization should occur as a result of collaboration between the parties receiving services from the organization and members of the organization itself.

The establishment of roles within the formal organization may be accomplished in several ways. One theory suggests that individuals know best what jobs they are most skillful at and how their jobs can be designed to facilitate their work. Another theory suggests that individuals cannot be objective about their own work capabilities because they are motivated primarily by their own personal interests. When asked what they do best they will minimize or maximize their capabilities to correspond to these interests. Somewhere between these two positions, the manager must determine the most appropriate method for establishing roles.

Another important factor to be considered in the process of organizing is the difference between primary and support activities. These are also known as line and staff functions within organizations. Within any organization, these two functions are the basis upon which to build the formal organization. The *primary* functions of an organization will vary according to the type of organization. Human-service organizations in the fields of health, education, social welfare, and recreation and leisure services will obviously have different objectives. A mental health agency's primary functions might include preventive intervention, consultation, and crisis intervention. A municipal park and recreation department might be primarily concerned with organizing and promoting leisure programs and maintaining areas and facilities, such as parks and swimming pools. These central functions are the primary activities of these agencies and serve as a basis for the organization of work activities or tasks. *Support* activities within an organization are those that are needed to produce the primary activities. These may include secretarial-clerical, personnel, and research and development work. It is interesting to note that in many organizations support activities become as important as the primary functions of the organization. When this occurs, the organization (or individuals within the organization) has lost sight of its objectives.

The Informal Organization

The informal organization exists side-by-side with the formal organization. The *informal organization* can be thought of as the unofficial organizational relationships that occur within the organization. The informal organization may include one-to-one relationships between individuals, as well as group relationships that are established among individuals within an organization.

The influence of the informal organization on the work of an organization can be both beneficial and detrimental. One advantage of an informal organization is that it can coordinate the formal work activities of an organization in ways that the formal organization is incapable of, as it is established on paper. This is especially true where lateral communication is needed within an organization. If the chain of command were followed in conveying a message from one department to another, the message might go from the bottom level of organization to the top, in one department, and then from the top level of organization to the bottom in another department (an inverted U). The amount of time and effort involved might be out of proportion to the importance of the communication. The informal organization can cut the time involved by allowing lateral communication, thereby increasing the efficiency of the organization.

The informal organization can also impede the work of an organization. Informally organized groups can be a powerful force within the organization, disrupting its work and challenging the formal organizational structure. They often operate covertly and can undermine the manager's authority. There is a tendency for organizations that have not been carefully structured to be usurped by the informal organization. However, it is possible for those in the formal organization to analyze the informal organization and use it in order to meet the goals and objectives of the formal organization.

Why do informal organizations occur? People have a need to associate with one another. They will develop bonds with other people with similar lifestyles, interests and needs. Individuals need to develop relationships with other people that provide emotional and social support. Many formal organizations become impersonal and do not respond to these types of needs. Therefore, people tend to form associations with others as protection from this sort of isolation.

An important product of the informal organization is the emergence of leaders whose power is based on their ability to influence other people, rather than their positions within the organization. These individuals may wield great power within an organization when people perceive that these individuals can advance their interests effectively.

The grapevine is usually thought of as the unofficial communication system of the informal organization. Every organization has a grapevine. Communication through the grapevine is made through individuals who, although they are not formally assigned communicative roles within the organization, have access to those who are in formal communicative roles. These individuals share their information with friends and colleagues within their informal work groups. The grapevine can be a source of accurate information as well as opinion and unfounded rumors.

The Chain of Command

One of the interesting principles of organizational theory is that of the *scalar chain of authority*. The scalar chain of authority is often thought of as the *chain of command*. This is the way that superiors and subordinates are linked together throughout an organization. The concept of chain of command suggests that authority and responsibility is extended down a ladder-like chain of individuals, from the highest management position to the lower positions within the organization. Ideally, communication flows up and down the ladder in an orderly, sequential manner. The principle of chain of command is important to organizational theory because it clarifies relationships and thus assists in the communication and decision making processes.

In most nonprofit recreation and leisure organizations, the ultimate authority rests with the constituents served by the agency. The public exercises control over these agencies by electing individuals who represent particular social, political, and cultural concerns. These elected representatives are responsible for enacting legislation that provides funding, management, and the organization of human services. In this manner, the public has direct control and influence over the formulation of policy leading to the provision of services. Most recreation and leisure service organizations are authorized to provide services by the legislative process that created them. A private, profit-making organization operates under the guidelines established by various political jurisdictions at the federal, state, and local levels of government. For example, a business, in order to operate within a local community is regulated by the ordinances and regulations governing the operation of profit-making agencies in that community. Its permit to operate is granted by the local city government. A public recreation and leisure service organization exists because legislation has been enacted that gives a local subdivision of government the power to collect taxes, hire staff, organize, manage, acquire facilities, and so on. This is also the case with a nonprofit, tax-exempt organization if it wishes to formally incorporate.

At the top of the chain of command, we usually find a governing board. This group of individuals, often known as a board of directors, board members, or commissioners, is responsible for enacting the formal policy of the organization. A board of directors is responsible for ensuring that the constitution and bylaws of the organization are followed in an appropriate manner. The board decides upon the programs that the organization is to provide, the way in which the financial resources of the organization are to be distributed, as well as who will carry out various functions within the organization.

Three types of boards have emerged that influence the management of public recreation and leisure service organizations: separate and independent boards, semi-independent boards, and advisory boards.

Separate and independent boards.   Separate and independent boards of directors are autonomous units that have the power to create and implement policy. This type of board is most commonly found within public human-service agencies and private agencies.

Semi-independent boards.   Semi-independent boards do not have full powers to govern the operation of a leisure service organization. The authority is often split between two boards or legislative units. For example, a board of directors may be given the power to enact policy, but may not have the ability to levy taxes to support services. This latter power would be held by another legislative unit, which affords a system of checks and balances.

Advisory boards.   Advisory boards provide recommendations to a higher level of authority within an organization. An advisory board may be established as a temporary body, rather than as a permanent part of the organization, and may focus on specific issues and concerns. Some leisure service organizations are required by law to establish advisory boards.

Individuals may be either appointed or elected to boards of directors. They usually serve without pay. Their degree of commitment in time and energy can often influence the success of the organization. Individuals should be sought to serve on boards of directors who are interested in the affairs of the organization, its constituents, and the relationship of the organization to the community. A number of factors should be taken into consideration when considering the make-up of the board. There should be representation from various social, cultural, and economic groups, geographic representation, citizen or client representation, professional representation, as well as representation from community leaders. In addition, an effort should be made to provide a balance of men and women and appropriate age groups on the board.

Committees.   A committee is a group formed to assist the leisure service organization in any of a variety of ways. Committees can directly serve an agency by organizing and providing services. More often, they exist either as advisory or as self-help groups affiliated with the organization. They may serve over a long period of time or may be formed to address problems on a short-term basis. In any case, they are a very important component in the organization of human services, especially committees that encourage self-help as well as emphasizing citizen involvement. The recreation and leisure service manager will often be called upon to assist in the organization of committees. This may involve providing the initial impetus to organize the committee by providing staff assistance, physical resources (i.e., a meeting room), or other support services (secretarial help, supplies, and so on). The manager may work with the group to help it through the process of decision making by facilitating group discussion. The manager may help the group understand problem solving, ways of using the news media, and how to identify and tap into community and organizational resources outside the leisure service agency. The manager should serve as a facilitator of group behavior, acting as an educator, catalyst, resource person, analyst, and critic.

The key to providing effective leadership to committees is twofold. First, behind-the-scenes organization is essential. Leisure service managers should collect necessary data and be familiar with the issues. Nothing will kill committee work quicker than lack of preparation on the part of the professional. Second, the manager should have the ability to conduct an effective committee meeting. Long, tedious meetings lacking focus and dominated by one or two individuals are counterproductive. In conducting an informal meeting, the facilitator should strive to identify a well-defined path to solve problems. Discussion within groups where synergy occurs is much more effective than individual decision making. By keeping the committee's discussion on track and by clearly identifying problems and potential solutions, the group decision-making process will be facilitated. When conducting formal meetings and employing *Robert's Rules of Order*, the facilitator should adhere to the order of business, recognize the will of the majority, protect the rights of the minority, and proceed with one issue at a time.

Specialization of Labor

As indicated previously, important in the establishment of the formal organization is the establishment of roles. These roles must be identified and defined by the manager in order to create work opportunities for individual organization members. The process of dividing work tasks into roles is often referred to as *specialization* or *division of labor*. This is a conventional management principle in the organization process.

The development of the recreation and leisure service profession in our society has been directly tied to the concept of division of labor. As society has become more complex, the need for individuals with highly technical skills has increased. Thus, more professions have evolved. The specialization of labor has enabled the creation of a highly trained, competent group of technicians geared to solve specific human problems. In the human services, mental health workers, educators, social workers, and recreation and leisure professionals are examples of occupations that have evolved as a result of specialization. In industry, the specialization of labor has been most useful in the creation of mass-produced products. The material bounty that has become available in North America during the last century is largely a result of specialization of labor.

How does the concept of specialization of labor specifically relate to the organization of human services? Basically, by identifying the tasks that need to be accomplished, work can be categorized and defined. This in turn allows an organization to recruit, select, and train individuals who are best suited to that defined role or task. The individual is able to focus knowledge, skills, and ability on one area of work, thereby becoming expert in that function. When work is specialized, the organization theoretically is better able to control the use of its resources and, in turn, will increase and improve the quantity and quality of services that it can provide. Many organizations fail because they have not adequately divided their labor in order to increase efficiency. Often overlapping jurisdictions, ill-defined jobs, and confusing assignments lead to waste and inefficiency, resulting in poor quality of services. By specializing the work within an organization, appropriate education and experience can be brought to bear on a specific problem. Thus, an organization makes the best use of its human resources.

The process of specialization also has created problems within human-service organizations. As work becomes more narrowly defined within and between human-service organizations, there is a tendency to deal with individuals served by the organizations in a fragmented way. The mental health people may not consult those professionals providing other services, even though it may be in the best interests of the consumer to be treated in a holistic manner. Further, specialization of labor can lead to routine responses to individual needs on the part of the professional. Routine work behavior may also lead to organizational problems as employees become bored.

Some individuals have the capacity to analyze a particular work assignment and break it into its smallest components, thereby simplifying the process. This is an essential management skill. Without the ability to organize resources within an agency, especially human ones, the manager is far less effective. In addition, it is important to remember that the manager may be the only individual who thoroughly understands the total project. It is his or her responsibility to ensure that, as work is broken into its component parts, the completion of a given task is consistent with the overall goals and objectives of the organization.

Departmentalization

Once an organization has divided its work into separate functions, these tasks usually are clustered together. This is known as the process of *departmentalization*. Departmentalization involves clustering common activities into manageable units in order to ensure that the resources of the organization are used in a coordinated fashion. By clustering individuals with similar responsibilities together, routine tasks are handled more efficiently. Terms that are synonomous with department are "division," "section," "unit," and so forth. In certain human-service agencies, these terms are used interchangeably, and there is no consistency in the application of the nomenclature. Sections, divisions, and units sometimes become components of a department. The term "department" is often used to identify a major level of activity within an organization, and other terms are often used to define descending levels within the organization (if a hierarchical structure is employed).

There are a number of ways in which departmentalization can occur within human-service organizations. The administrative divisions of human-service organizations can be determined by function, facility, population, geographical area, service, project, or a combination of these. The decision to adopt one or more of these approaches to departmentalization will depend upon a number of factors. Perhaps the two most important factors affecting the selection of an approach for departmentalization are the type of service the organization produces and the way in which that service is to be distributed. These two variables, in the broad sense, are the most essential factors is establishing a program for departmentalization. Basically, the human-service manager must ask the questions What services do we produce? and How do we deliver these services to those who need them? Consideration of these two factors invariably leads the human-service manager to the question How do we organize our resources to most effectively and efficiently create and deliver the service? If the creation of the service must occur near the place where it is consumed, then the geographic method of departmentalization will be most efficient. On the other hand, if it is more appropriate to cluster purchasing functions at one centralized point, a functional approach will be most efficient.

Departmentalization by function.   The most conventional and traditional way of departmentalization is by function. Historically, this concept evolved in the private sector. As organizations grew in size and scope, similar functions were clustered into three basic areas: production, sales, and finance. Thus, in business all activities related to the production of a product or a service were clustered into a production department. Activities related to the sale or distribution of a product were clustered into a sales or marketing department. Those work activities related to the financial management and control of the organization were placed in a finance department. Although widely used in the private sector, this approach to departmentalization is not widely employed in public or quasi-public recreation and leisure service organizations. It has, however, greatly influenced concepts of organization, such as line and staff functions. Line functions, as previously indicated, are primary to the organization, and staff functions are supportive work activities. In business line functions are production, sales, and finance.

Departmentalization by facility.   Often, the development of a facility will greatly influence the way in which departmentalization occurs. This is especially true when a certain kind of facility is essential to the provision of a particular service. For example, departmentalization within a recreation center would likely be based upon the design of the physical resource itself. The center might have a swimming pool, racquetball courts, gymnasium, and meeting rooms. The work would be organized according to these components of the center. In this case, the organization would be structured so that a hierarchy would exist within the facility that would enable independent management and supervision. In other words, the basis of departmentalization would be the existence of the facility.

Departmentalization by population group.   A popular approach to organization of work within recreation and leisure service organizations is by population group. Population groups are most often defined by age, although frequently they can also be organized by ethnic group, economic status, or by special conditions, such as physical or mental capabilities. Departmentalization by population group in recreation and leisure service organizations is most evident by the clustering of services for children, teenagers, and the elderly.

Departmentalization by service.   Often, a recreation and leisure service organization will cluster its work activities by the services it produces. For example, parks and recreation are two different types of services. The major advantage of clustering by service unit is that it allows for specialization of the employees. The expertise of the individuals associated with a work unit is likely to be used more intensely. Human skills and equipment can be specialized to meet the requirements that are necessary to produce highly complex services. One of the problems associated with this approach, however, is the greater need for control over independent service units. Also, the more service units there are, the more need there is for coordination as well as control. Another problem associated with this type of approach to departmentalization is the cost of duplicating support for each of the units.

Departmentalization by project.   Departmentalization by project is perhaps the newest approach to clustering work. This approach involves the organizing of teams or task forces on an ad hoc basis to complete a particular task. When the need arises to solve a particular problem, diverse resources are combined into a unit for the limited period necessary to solve it. The focus of a project team is short-term. This holistic approach allows the pooling of talent within an organization. The disadvantage of this approach is that it may disrupt other functions of an organization if individuals in key positions are removed for an extended period of time.

None of the different types of departmentalization is best for all situations. A recreation and leisure service organization should use a variety of approaches depending upon its needs and environmental conditions. Some organizations may blend several approaches into a unified structure. Individuals may be asked to be a part of a department organized by service as well as a department organized by facility. Some consideration in the process of organization must be given to clustering activities so resources can be coordinated, communication facilitated, control established, and evaluation undertaken.

Delegation of Authority

One of the important factors in successful organization is the delegation of authority. Delegation of authority implies that the manager is willing to give up a part of his or her responsibility in a certain area in order to achieve organizational goals more effectively. In order to be effective, a manager must be willing and able to share responsibility by trusting other individuals within the organization to perform important tasks.

When a manager delegates responsibility, he or she is basically engaging in three activities: assigning responsibility, creating and granting authority, and creating accountability. In assigning responsibility, the manager reaches a mutual agreement with the employee as to the tasks that he or she will be responsible for performing. In creating and granting of authority, the manager should work with the employee to determine what resources—human, fiscal, and physical—the individual should have control over. The manager should not simply delineate the work activities of the subordinate but should ensure that the subordinate understands the implications of exercising authority within given situations. The last part of the delegation process is that of creating accountability. Accountability implies taking responsibility for one's actions regarding the work assigned. Without an accountability mechanism, the delegation process is ineffective. The manager should not give an employee responsibility without at the same time holding him or her accountable. Without the accountability mechanism, responsibility for decision making, allocation of resources, and supervision of personnel reverts back to the manager, as the next higher level of authority.

Delegating or sharing responsibility is often a very difficult activity in which to engage. Managers may lack the patience and foresight that is necessary to provide an individual with the training necessary to assume more responsibility. There are some key responsibilities that the manager has in the delegation process. These include promoting ideas of others, letting others make decisions, letting others learn from their mistakes, trusting those who have been delegated authority, and developing measures of accountability.

Promoting ideas of others. We know from management literature that team management creates greater commitment and more effective decision making in new and unstable situations. Consequently, allowing the ideas of others to be implemented builds commitment, and provides an organization with alternate solutions on which to base decision making.

Letting others make decisions.   One of the most difficult things in any management situation is allowing other people to make critical decisions. North American managers tend to be highly individualistic and control-oriented. To allow others to make decisions is a key factor in the delegation process.

Letting others learn from their mistakes.   We often don't allow people the time necessary to grow. Inevitably an employee in a new role will make mistakes in the decision-making and supervisory processes. Allowing employees to learn from their mistakes is essential to effective delegation. A mistake-free environment is one in which the risk factor has been minimized. However, few organizations move ahead without assuming certain risks, which, in turn, may involve making mistakes. It has been said, "If you aren't making any mistakes, you aren't trying anything that hasn't been done before." People learn as much, or more, from their failures as they do from their successes.

Trusting those who have been delegated authority.   Mutual confidence, trust, and respect are key factors in the delegation process. When an individual has been given responsibility and authority and is held accountable for his or her actions, there is an implied trust factor in the process. Without trust, the delegation process cannot take place.

Developing measures of accountability.   In order to judge the effectiveness of members of the organization, measures of accountability must be developed. This ensures that there is a clear understanding between the leisure service manager and his or her subordinates as to what constitutes satisfactory performance. One of the quickest ways to undermine the delegation process is to delegate responsibilities without clearly delineating the outcomes by which the subordinate's efforts will be measured.

There are a number of problems associated with the process of delegation. Delegation of authority should not be used by the manager to assign only routine or uninteresting tasks and work activities. Individuals should be delegated responsibility because of their expertise, interest, and competence in a given area and they should be allowed to exercise autonomy in decision making. It is important that work be delegated in a way that allows independence of action. A manager can subvert the delegation process by using it to avoid responsibility for making decisions that are difficult or that involve ethical considerations. Managers should not delegate responsibilities in areas that involve ethical decisions that may result in unpleasant consequences with the thought in mind that the employee may be used as a scapegoat and sacrificed if resignations are called for.

Power and Authority

The exercise of power is a key element in the success or failure of a manager within both the formal and informal organizational structure. Power can be thought of as the ability of one person to influence the behavior of another. The work of an organization is accomplished primarily through its human resources. The ability of the manager to direct individuals in a coordinated and organized fashion is related to his or her ability to exercise power.

Individual managerial power has several sources. One source of managerial power is personality. We often speak of this power based on personality as charisma. Charisma can be thought of as the ability to attract or appeal to others. In the informal organization, the exercise of personal power is the major source of authority. The second source of individual power is the manager's position within the hierarchy of the organization. With the assumption of a position, a person is given certain responsibilities and is granted the right to exercise authority. Authority can be thought of as a right to make decisions, to direct resources, and to command. When authority is granted to a manager, it is done in order to enable that person to move the organization toward its goals and objectives.

Another important source of individual power within organizations is the knowledge or expertise of the individual. Because recreation and leisure service professions are specialized, expertise in the solving of specific problems is highly valued. Individuals in the formal organization who have extensive knowledge of the workings of the organization may have power and influence beyond that usually associated with their positions.

The acquisition and exercise of power is essential to effective management. In fact, successful managers have a stronger desire to acquire power than to be liked by other individuals in the organization. The power coveted by successful managers is not necessarily dictatorial or self-enhancing, but is usually associated with influencing people toward the achievement of organizational goals.

Span of Control

Span of control refers to the number of subordinates that a manager can effectively supervise. Much has been written about this topic in the management literature. Span of control must be determined according to the dictates of a given situation. There can be no universal application of a ratio that suggests an ideal number of individuals that can be supervised effectively. When an organizational structure has been established, usually levels or spheres of responsibility and authority are created. These levels or spheres of responsibility involve the management of other people. If an organization is arranged vertically, there will usually be more levels with fewer people being supervised. If the organizational structure is horizontal or flat, more individuals will be supervised. Tall, or vertical, structures have a small span of control, and flat, or horizontal, structures have a large span of control.

There are a number of factors that may influence the span of control or the number of subordinates a manager can supervise. These variables are diverse and must be individually applied within each organization in order to generate a satisfactory plan for span of control. Each individual manager will have different capabilities and the environment in which a manager operates will also vary. The following are guidelines that can be considered in developing a plan for supervising subordinates.

The skill of the manager.　Perhaps the most important factor in the process of determining the number of subordinates that a manager can adequately supervise is his or her experience, personality, education, attitudes, and management skills. Certain managers have more energy, more flexibility, and more resourcefulness, which increases their supervisory capability.

The skill of subordinates.　The education, experience, personality, and attitudes of subordinates will determine the amount of supervision that will be required for them to carry out their assigned activities.

Type of environment.　Environment can be viewed as existing on a continuum from highly stable to highly unstable. Very stable environments require less supervision than those that are unstable. A stable environment is characterized by relatively few disruptions in the environment in terms of shifts in personnel, changes in tasks, and so on. Unstable environments are highly fluid, with frequent changes.

Type of work activities.　Certain work activities are routine in nature; others are nonroutine and require a high degree of autonomy and independence in decision making. Each requires a different type of supervision. Hence, the span of control will be influenced by the nature of the task. Generally speaking, tasks that are routine in nature require more supervision than nonroutine tasks.

Span of control can directly affect employee morale and motivation, as well as communication and decision making. Close supervision of employees resulting from a limited·span of control can have either a positive or a negative effect on morale. Some individuals are encouraged by the close attention of their superior, whereas others may be intimidated by too much supervision. Consequently, in one situation, close supervision might be welcome and might improve employee morale, whereas in the other situation the reverse might be the case.

The levels or spheres of responsibility within an organization may be directly related to the span of control. The more layers there are within an organization, the more complex the process of communication will be. The fewer the layers within the organization, the more quickly communication takes place. The form in which communication takes place may also be affected by span of control. In situations with fewer layers of organization and a larger span of control, communication tends to take place on a face-to-face basis. In the opposite situation (a smaller span of control), communication tends to be in written form. The larger the span of control, the more likely it is that decisions will be made by individuals directly involved in the provision of services.

ORGANIZATIONAL STRUCTURES

Crucial to the effectiveness and efficiency of any organization is the structure that it establishes to attain its goals. The organizational designs of most private and public agencies follow the traditional bureaucratic model of organization without due consideration of the effects of this or other designs on the creation and delivery of goods and services. Individuals are too often content to rely on the most widely used forms of organizational design without considering the alternate structures that are available. Little is understood about the effects of particular designs on the achievement of organizational objectives. Also lacking is a clear understanding of the differences between organizational designs and the various environmental conditions in which the organizational designs should be used.

This part of the chapter summarizes and integrates the findings of contemporary research and management practice with regard to the structuring of organizations. Different models of organizational design for government and business are presented. Also included is a conceptual model of the variables that can be used in designing an organizational structure and how such variables are affected by environmental conditions.

Historical Development of Organizational Structures

The development of organizational structures occurred in three different eras: the classical, neoclassical and modern.

The classical era. The *classical* era viewed the design of the formal organization as involving a universal set of organizational principles. These principles were based on the assumption that rules of organizational design could be applied to all organizations in all environments. This was thought to be a rational model in which the authority flowed from the top down. It was based on the principles of unity of command, equal authority and responsibility, span of control, delegation of routine matters, and division of labor.

Classical organizational principles are widely found in public agencies that apply the public administration model of bureaucracy. The bureaucratic model of organization evolved in order to provide direct control of government services by the public. As such, it provides a rational way of involving the public, within the rigid framework of classical organizational principles. In the private sector, classical organizational principles are used to organize basic work activities (production, marketing and finance). Application of classical organizational principles allows a manager or a board of directors to directly control these operations. Figures 5.1 and 5.2 are examples of classical design.

There were several problems that evolved during the classical era that were related to the use of the bureaucratic organizational structure. First, there was a failure to recognize the personal needs of people who made up the organization, and, as a result, people developed compensatory informal organizational structures. Second, the classical organizational principles were thought to be universal truths. It has been shown empirically that these principles are not applicable to all environments.

The neoclassical era.   The second period, the *neoclassical* era, corrected some of the limitations of the classical era. Recognizing the importance of people within the organization, the neoclassical era tried to humanize various of its elements. The neoclassical era was concerned with improving the effectiveness of the organizational process, in particular the creation and distribution of goods and services. Some of the issues affecting organizations that were addressed in this period were *centralization* versus *decentralization* and *flat* versus *tall* structures.

In an effort to reduce the effects of vertical growth in the organizational structure, the neoclassical model of *decentralization* was invoked. This model attempted to disperse decision-making authority within the organization and, hence, bring decisions affecting the distribution of resources closer to the people responsible for them. Closely related to the concept of decentralization is the arrangement of positions within an organization. Tall structures have a small span of control; they allow strict discipline and close supervision over subordinates. Flat structures have larger spans of control that force general supervision and delegation of decision making. Flat structures are associated with decentralized organizational structures; tall structures are associated with classical bureaucracy. The neoclassical era did not produce any structures of its own, but modified classical organizational principles.

The modern era.   The *modern* era is based on empirical studies. These studies suggest that different structures exist in addition to those of the classical and neoclassical eras. The modern era recognizes that different environments require different structures—this is the situational approach. This approach assumes that there is no one best way to design an organization. The best organizational design would depend upon the type of technology, the rate of technological change, and the overall stability of the environment. Among the innovative designs which have emerged during this era are Likert's linking-pin modular organization (project and matrix organization), the federation method of organization, and freeform

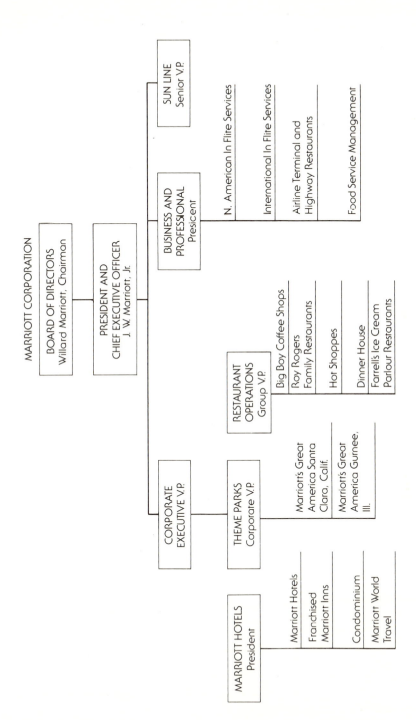

Figure 5.1 The Marriott Corporation, an example of an organization chart of a diverse corporation that provides recreation and leisure services for a profit.

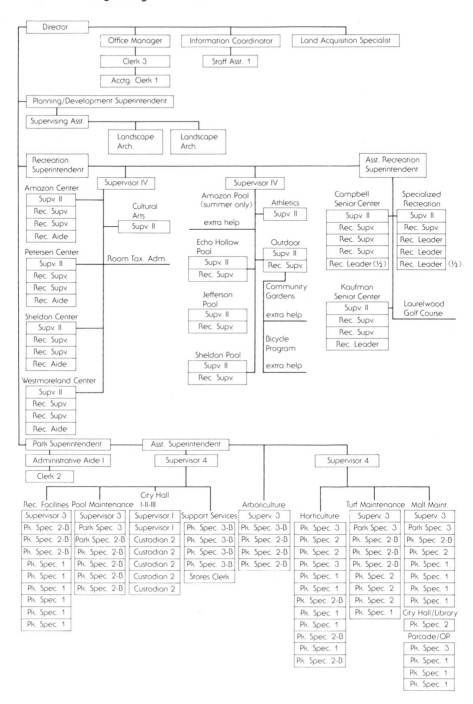

Figure 5.2 Organization chart from the Parks and Recreation Department of Eugene, Oregon.

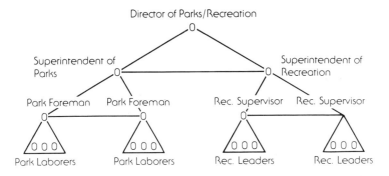

Figure 5.3 Linking-pin method of organization.

organization. There are still other organizational designs that can be considered, and, although they are not included in this discussion, their importance and applicability to public or private organizations should not be discounted. The structures chosen for this discussion represent the most common forms of modern organization that can, in the opinion of the authors, be practiced in leisure service organizations.

Likert's linking-pin model.   Likert's linking-pin theory is based upon a principle that every individual within an organization functions as a linking pin for the work group above and below him or her.[1] Every member is a group leader in a lower subgroup and a group member in an upper subgroup. It is based on group-to-group relationships, as opposed to person-to-person relationships. This structure gives organizations an upward direction; communication, supervisory influence, and goal attainment are forced upwards. The classical, hierarchial structure fosters a downward orientation. The linking-pin structure also provides opportunities for participation in planning and decision making and fosters open communication and commitments that produce binding decisions. This model is based upon the logic that if a person is a member of two groups, he will be loyal to both groups and will exchange information and accept decisions more readily in both groups. It has been shown that ability to exert an upward influence affects morale, motivation, productivity, and performance (see Figure 5.3).

Modular organization.   Another design to emerge during the modern era is known as *project* or *modular organization.*[2] An extension of systems theory, this approach to organizing services finds the manager organizing each of the tasks of a specific project into functional units. Modular

1. Rensis Likert, *New Patterns of Management* (Toronto: McGraw-Hill, 1961), p. 6.
2. G. Rice and D. Bishoprich, *Complex Models of Organizational Applications* (New York: Century and Crofts, 1971), p. 181.

organizations allow the manager to identify the tasks that make up a particular job and to deliberately construct a system that will produce a specific set of outcomes. Modular organizations usually comprise a number of units whose activities are coordinated by an established hierarchy. Functional units can vary in size and composition, depending upon the project to be accomplished. The role of the manager is to decentralize the work of the organization by placing authority to complete a given unit of work. This specialization allows an increase in flexibility by allowing different structures to be used for each work unit. Two types of modular organization—project and matrix—warrant discussion. The *project* type of organization consists of giving an individual or group enough support services to complete a given task. The *matrix* type of organization finds individuals operating with dual responsibilities. The individual is responsible for his or her permanent or traditional responsibility, as well as the completion of tasks for the project team.

The federation model.   The *federation* model of organization allows specialized groups to freely associate with one another within a flexible organizational framework.[3] It is a method whereby specialized groups with independent modes of operation and interests can combine with each other to pursue a common set of goals. In this way, each group within a federation may contribute its talents, abilities, and skills to a larger concern. Organized within a loose, democratic structure, specialized groups are autonomous units that have little authority over other specialized groups within the federation. Each group is thought to be an equal partner within the federation. The federation serves as a basis upon which groups meet to discuss common problems, issues, and concerns. The role of the manager in this type of organizational structure is to serve as a facilitator, catalyst, and enabler to the group.

The freeform model.   The *freeform* model of organization is based upon the principle that the purpose of an organization is to facilitate the management of change.[4] Structural arrangements in this type of organization are highly adaptable and flexible. There is no rigid role definition, and the internal structure is not fixed. There is no one way of organizing. The structure is fixed to particular needs at a particular time. Usually, the departmentalized functional structure is replaced by self-contained centers that encourage participation, individual initiative, open communication, and sensitivity. These organizations may make extensive use of computer information systems and are staffed by young, dynamic managers who are high risk-takers. The freeform structure is highly adaptable for technological and operational change. It readily takes advantage of external change and new techniques.

---

3. G. Rice and D. Bishoprich, *Complex Models of Organizational Applications* (New York: Century and Crofts, 1971), p. 65.
4. D. McFarland, *Management Principles and Practices,* 3rd ed. (New York: Macmillan, 1970), pp. 384–86.

Research on Organizational Design

A number of variables have been identified that can affect organizational design. One of the most important of these is stability of the environment. Burns and Stalker viewed the environment as ranging from stable to unstable.[5] They were able to determine empirically that, in a stable environment, a rigidly organized *mechanistic* structure was most effective, and in an unstable environment a flexible, *organic* structure was most effective. Characteristics of the mechanistic structure include the following: well defined rules, procedures, and functions; vertical interaction; decision making at upper levels; authority based on position; and a closed system. What Burns and Stalker refer to as the mechanistic structure closely resembles the classical organizational design. Characteristics of the organic structures are: rules, procedures, and functions not clearly defined; lateral interaction; decision making at lower levels; authority based on knowledge; and an open system with close monitoring of the environment. Organic structures are referred to as closely resembling a freeform organizational design. Organizations can be seen as existing on a continuum. Figure 5.4 illustrates this concept.

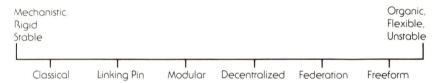

Figure 5.4 Distribution of organizational structure.

Certain functions within government and business have become routine. For example, maintenance may be seen as being better organized in a mechanistic structure, since many forms of maintenance are very predictable and can be organized into a systematic program. The marketing of goods or services may be highly individualized and unpredictable, and the manager may require a high degree of flexibility in developing a strategy to sell the product. Certain organizational functions, such as marketing, are performed within an organic structure.

Another study of particular significance in the designing of organizational structures was reported by Woodward.[6] Studying three types of production technology—unit, mass, and continuous production—she found that the type of technology (process) used by the organization dictates the type of organizational design employed. According to this study, factors that vary include: the span of control of the chief executives;

---

5. T. Burns and G. Stalker, *The Management of Innovation* (Chicago: Quadrangle, 1961), p. 14.
6. J. Woodward, *Management and Technology* (London: Her Majesty's Stationery Office 1958), p. 3.

ENVIRONMENTAL CONDITIONS	ORGANIZATIONAL DESIGN SELECTED	TECHNOLOGY EMPLOYED
• Type of environment • Rate of environmental change	• Bureaucracy • Decentralization • Linking pin • Systems • Federation • Freeform	• Type of technology (process) used • Rate of technological change

Figure 5.5 The interactive process of environment, technology, and organizational design.

the span of control of first-line supervisors; and the ratio of direct to indirect workers. This concept also relates well to the leisure service organizations, which has two basic processes (technologies) related to the development of services. One process would be the prescriptive approach to development of services, and the other process would be the cafeteria approach.[7] Woodward's study indicates that these two technologies would require different organizational designs.

Lawrence and Lorsch have discovered, through empirical study, that in large organizations it might be necessary to organize different functions in different ways.[8] One function may be best organized in terms of the classical type of design, while another function may be better organized using a design that leans more toward the freeform end of the continuum. They found that organizations that are in relatively stable technical, market, economic, and scientific environments can use classical integrative techniques and, thus, are more successful using the classical bureaucratic structures. Organizations that operate in an unstable environment must rely more upon use of modern integrative techniques, such as group-centered decision making, mutual adjustment through network communications, and integrative teams, in order to coordinate highly differentiated functions. They also found that successful organizations are those that recognize that different organizational designs are appropriate for different functions and employ the appropriate method to integrate these functions.

Factors to Consider when Selecting an Organizational Design

Developing a design for a particular organization is an interactive process. Figure 5.5 portrays the components that are involved in this process. Initially, the environmental conditions and the type of technology (process) employed must be analyzed.

---

7. J. Murphy, *Recreation and Leisure Service: A Humanistic Perspective* (Dubuque, Iowa: W. C. Brown & Co., 1975), p. 87.

8. P. Lawrence and J. Lorsch, "Differentiation and Integration in Complex Organizations." *Admin. Sci. Quart.* 12:1(1967): 1–47.

Environmental stability. The first factor to be considered by a leisure service manager developing an organizational design is the stability of the environment itself. The manager should be cognizant of the factors that may affect stability of an environment, such as population growth, rising expectations, changing popular culture, and the decline of traditional institutions.

Technology and organizational design. The second factor to be considered by the manager when designing an organizational structure is the type of technology employed. Recreation and leisure service organizations sponsored by government are concerned with the creation of a service rather than a product. As a result, there are different structural needs in a service-oriented organization than in a profit-oriented one. Different public agencies using different technologies (prescriptive and cafeteria approach) would probably adopt different organizational designs, just as different production technologies have had to use different designs for organizational structures. Each situation is different and each organization must be designed on the basis of those factors unique to its operation.

Structural Variables

Pugh, et al., have identified six major structural variables that can be manipulated when developing an organizational design. They are specialization, standardization, formalization, centralization, configuration, and flexibility.[9] *Specialization* involves the division of labor so that tasks within the organization are distributed or concentrated in a number of positions. The extent to which an organization has specialized may be determined by the number of positions relative to the size of the organization. In order to be consistent, organizations *standardize* their rules and regulations. This allows an organization to maintain stability. *Formalization* occurs when an organization has carefully documented its philosophy, principles, policies, and procedures. *Centralization* is determined by locating positions in an organization that have authority to make decisions. Centralized organizations concentrate decision making; decentralized organizations disperse decision making. The *configuration* of an organization refers to the placement of positions. Some organizations are linear, some are hierarchial, some follow little or no form at all. The last factor, *flexibility*, refers to an organization's ability to make changes rapidly within the environment. Table 5.1 illustrates how these six structural variables differ from one organizational structure to another.

Gibson, et al., have delineated a sequential process model that can be used in designing an organizational structure.[10] This five-step process first

---

9. D. Pugh, D. Hudson, G. Hinnings, and C. Turner, "Dimensions of Organizational Structure." *Admin. Sci. Quart.* 13:1(1968): 65–105.

10. J. Gibson, J. Ivancevich, and J. Donnelly, *Organizations: Structure, Process and Behaviour* (Dallas: Business Publications, Inc., 1973), p. 544.

TABLE 5.1   Characteristics of Organizational Structures

Type of Organizational Structure	Amount of Specialization	Amount of Standardization	Amount of Formalization	Amount of Centralization	Type of Configuration	Amount of Flexibility
Classical						
Bureaucratic	High	High, methods delineated clearly	High	High, top of organization	Hierarchial, pyramidal, "tall"	Low
Decentralized	High	Low	High	Low, dispersed	Hierarchial wide span of control, "flat"	Medium
Modular						
Project	Varies	Low	Varies	Varies	Hierarchial	High
Matrix	Varies	Low	Varies	Varies	Integrated functions	High
Linking pin	Varies	High	High	Low, decision making in group units	Hierarchial group	Low
Federation	High	Low	Low	Low, decision making controlled by federated groups	Flat, a relationship of equals	High
Freeform	Low	Low	Low	Low	Varies	High

involves the identification of the environments in terms of products and technology, determining what goods and services the organization is trying to produce and what the processes (technology) are of producing them. The second step is to identify the relationships among the subenvironments. Following this, the manager would determine the extent to which the work groups are diverse in terms of rate of change, certainty, and feedback. The next step would be to design each work group of the organization as dictated by the environment within which the work group must operate. The final step would be to design the integrative techniques that are consistent with the degree of work group differentiation and the dominant environment.

SUMMARY

An organization exists when two or more people work together to achieve a set of goals. There are two types of organizations—the formal and the informal. The formal organization is a social unit that has been created to achieve a predetermined set of goals and objectives. The informal organization is made up of the unofficial organizational relationships. Both the informal and the formal organizations influence the work of the organization.

Within recreation and leisure service systems, there are a number of organizational principles that should be considered by the manager. The scalar chain of command refers to the way in which superiors and subordinates are linked together within an organization. The concept of specialization, or division of labor, refers to the process of dividing work into its smallest components, thereby aiding the process of assigning and controlling work. Once an organization has determined the tasks it is to perform, the tasks are clustered through the process of departmentalization. There are a number of ways that departmentalization can occur within recreation and leisure service organizations, including clustering by function, facility, population group, geographic area, service, project, or a combination of these. The exercise of authority refers to the manager's ability to make decisions and give commands. An important task of the leisure service manager is delegation of authority in order to increase his or her sphere of influence within the organization.

Recreation and leisure service organizations can employ several different organizational structures. Among these are the bureaucratic model of organization, the decentralized model, linking-pin theory, project or modular organization, the federation model, and the freeform model. These designs can be viewed as existing on a continuum. At one end of the continuum are mechanistic, rigid structures, and at the other end are flexible, organic structures. In order to employ one or another of these designs, one must consider a number of variables, including environmental conditions, and the type of technology employed. These in turn affect the structural variables that can be manipulated by leisure service managers in creating an organizational design or structure.

STUDY QUESTIONS

1. Define what is meant by the term organization. What are the characteristics of an organization?
2. Define the formal organization and the informal oranization. What are the differences between these?
3. What types of legislative bodies are found at the top of the chain of command of recreation and leisure service organizations?
4. Describe the process known as the specialization, or division of labor. Why is this important in the organization of work within an agency?
5. How does the specialization of labor relate to the process of departmentalization?
6. Describe the ways in which the functions within recreation and leisure service organizations can be grouped for administration.
7. What is the relationship between power and authority? What are some of the problems that occur in delegating authority?
8. What guidelines can be used in delineating a recreation and leisure service manager's span of control?
9. Identify and define six different types of organizational structures. What are the differences between organic and mechanistic structures?
10. Identify and discuss the factors that the human-service manager should take into consideration when selecting a particular organizational design.

CASE STUDY 8

The Last Straw

"This is the last straw!" said Laurie George as he slammed down the receiver. "Imagine! That young M.B.A. type telling me what to do and having the nerve to tell me that I am not running this operation right! Why I was the boss here when that young whippersnapper was still in one of our wading pools!"

Laurie George had just received a phone call from Peter Adamson, special assistant to the city manager. Peter, fresh out of the graduate school of business, had been hired to advise the city manager on the effectiveness and efficiency of each department. The hiring of Peter was directly related to the rising costs of administration throughout the city. Peter had just phoned Laurie and told him what he had found wrong and how he must correct some of the most obvious mistakes. Laurie was hopping mad.

In addition to telling Laurie what was wrong and how to correct the problems relating to finances, Peter had told Laurie that he did not delegate enough of his authority to his directors of parks and recreation. "Poppycock," thought Laurie, "since I have the ultimate responsibility for everything that happens in this department, I have to be sure things are done right."

QUESTIONS

1. Was Laurie justified in his feelings toward the phone call from Peter Adamson? Why?
2. Can you think of any other reasons why Laurie might be a poor delegator?
3. Is organizational structure based on the delegation of authority? Why?

Staffing

6

The director of a parks and recreation department was faced with considerable turnover of program supervisors in his organization. During the past several months, three of his seven supervisors had resigned to take positions in other organizations. They left when offered opportunities for increased salaries as well as professional advances. All of these individuals were highly competent, and, as a result of their departure, the department was operating at less than peak performance. Such employee turnover, as well as the subsequent search for new employees, is affected by the management process known as staffing.

Properly applied, the staffing process enables the recreation and leisure service manager to systematically locate, place, and retain the right people in appropriate positions. Staffing is a planned process that finds the manager evaluating the abilities of potential employees on the basis of objective, rational criteria that are based upon the needs of the human-service organization. The benefits of finding and placing people suited to the needs of the organization are great, and the problems caused by poor staffing are enormous and costly. The challenge of staffing is to identify the needs of the organization and then to establish a network to locate, recruit, and train individuals who can make a contribution to the organization.

WHAT IS STAFFING?

Staffing is the process by which an organization acquires and maintains the human resources necessary to ensure that it operates in an effective and efficient manner. The ability of a recreation and leisure service organization to recruit, select, train, and evaluate its human resources is essential to its stated and implied mission. For, after all, it is *people* that make organizations go.

The responsibility for staffing an organization is dispersed throughout the entire organization. All individuals within the organization are potential recruiters of new employees. Further, all of an organization's human resources contribute to each other's development. Therefore, the responsibility for staffing is one that all members of the organization must share. Although certain parts of the staffing process may be delegated to certain departments or divisions within an organization, such as a personnel department, the staffing process should be viewed holistically. It is possible, as the Japanese have demonstrated, for all employees to contribute to each other's development, as well as to assist in appraising each other's work in order to improve quality. With this in mind, the essential elements of staffing are as follows:

- Defining and developing job descriptions that reflect the responsibilities to be undertaken by employees.
- Selecting new employees from outside the organization and promoting individuals within the organization through recruitment, screening, interviewing, and testing.
- Appraising employees' performance to ensure that the organization is run in an effective and efficient manner, as well as to provide individuals with recognition, reward, and opportunities for growth.
- Helping employees develop so that they reach their potential and meet the needs of the organization.

Further discussion of staffing as it relates to the recreation and leisure service organization will center on these four elements. Specifically, we will discuss the job description, as well as factors in the selection procedure, including recruitment, screening, interviewing, testing, decision making, and legal dimensions of this process. In addition, we will detail employee development methods such as in-service training, pre-service training and developmental training. Last, the ways in which staff can be appraised and models for evaluation that can be employed by recreation and leisure service organizations will be presented.

THE JOB DESCRIPTION

The establishment of a job description for each position is essential. Job descriptions are useful to point out the attributes of and the qualifications needed for a job prior to selection. It allows individuals to be self-selective in the recruitment process. If prospective employees read a job description and find that their qualifications, skills, or abilities are not consistent with the stated requirements, they will often decide not to apply.

Once individuals are hired by a leisure service organization, job descriptions can be useful to define their required duties and scope of responsibilities. The job description can also be a useful standard for employee evaluations.

Job descriptions are perhaps more useful for routine jobs than for complex jobs. In a routine job where the tasks are repetitive and narrowly defined, the job description can accurately reflect the actual work of the employee. However, for more complex tasks that call for independence and autonomy in decision making, the job description must be written in broader, more flexible terms. Some would suggest that the broader a job description is, the vaguer it becomes. Therefore, the probability that a broad job description will accurately reflect the detailed nature of the work is reduced. This does not mean that job descriptions that are broad in nature do not give individuals some general guidelines for performing their jobs, however.

What is involved in writing a job description? Basically, a job description includes information about the duties and qualifications associated with a given job. Often a job description will also specify superior and subordinate relationships and such factors as the physical conditions or materials necessary to implement a job. Therefore, most job descriptions include the following:

Job title. The title of a job is useful in identifying the level of responsibility. Although the nomenclature in the recreation and leisure service field is not consistent, the job title usually distinguishes nonadministrative jobs from administrative or managerial jobs.

General description. The general description of a job points out the area of jurisdiction that accompanies it. In addition, the general description might note the job's level of responsibility within an organization. For example, the director of a recreation and leisure service organization might be referred to in the general description as the chief executive officer of the organization.

Duties to be performed.   This part of the job description may be written in a general or specific manner, and indicates the scope and nature of the work to be performed. This is the heart of the job description.

Superior and subordinate relationships.   The job description will often stipulate the employee's superior(s) as well as those subordinates who are to be supervised by the employee. The job description might state, for example, that the employee will supervise a number of full-time and part-time employees.

Physical or other resources.   The job description will often spell out the fiscal, physical, or technical resources to be supervised or managed by the employee. This is often specified where departmentalization is based on available facilities. For example, a job description might state that a swimming pool supervisor will hold responsibility for managing materials and supplies related to the job.

Qualifications and skills.   The job description will also detail the qualifications and skills necessary for a particular position. This may include educational background, experience, and abilities necessary to effectively perform a given job.

Figure 6.1 is a sample job description for the position of program supervisor for senior citizens. The title of the position denotes the general area of responsibility, that is, programming for senior citizens. The general description portion of the sample job description points out the broad responsibilities: directing a wide variety of services geared for older adults. The general description states that this individual would be responsible for the operation of a physical resource, the senior center. With regard to superior-subordinate relationships, the description points out that the individual is responsible to the director of the organization and will supervise permanent, part-time, and seasonal staff. The duties set forth are somewhat more specific and include the services to be provided, relationships with the community, physical appearance of the center, and financial matters. It may be noted that item number 11 (performing other tasks when necessary) keeps the position open, ensuring flexibility. Last, the qualifications and skills area points out the need for a degree in recreation or gerontology and two years experience, as well as other combinations of education and experience that can be substituted.

As can be seen in this sample job description, there is enough general information given to provide the individual with an understanding of the broad areas of responsibility (chain of command and qualifications), and enough specific information to direct the person's work within the physical resource (the senior center) and the program area of service (recreation, nutrition, health and counseling services for the older adults). Further, the duties indicated in the job description stipulate various administrative aspects of the job (attendance, finance, clean environment, fund-raising, publicity).

General Description

The program supervisor for senior citizens does skilled work in directing a wide variety of services geared for older adults. Direct operation and control of the senior center is a main function of this position.

Supervision Received

This position comes under the direct guidance of the director.

Supervision Exercised

Supervises permanent staff at the senior center, as well as part-time and seasonal staff related to program offerings for older adults.

Duties

1. Administer a general program of services, including recreation, nutrition, health, and counseling at the senior center.
2. Establish rapport and communication with the older adults of the community.
3. Provide counseling and guidance for the older adults of the community.
4. Maintain attendance, activity, and financial records and make reports.
5. Maintain the clean and attractive environment of the senior center and recommend maintenance and repair work as necessary.
6. Act as a liaison with community groups and individuals concerned with older adults and speak on behalf of the organization on matters concerning older adults.
7. Stimulate and motivate participants to contribute their time and talents in the planning and implementation of programs.
8. Plan and execute fund-raising events.
9. Plan publicity, including press releases for activities.
10. Make recommendations for program improvement.
11. Perform other tasks when necessary.

Qualifications

Baccalaureate degree in recreation or gerontology with at least two years' experience with older adults, one of which was in a supervisory capacity, or three years' experience in recreation or gerontology with at least one year in a supervisory capacity; or four years experience and training in recreation, gerontology, or a closely related field.

Skills

Knowledge of a variety of services for older adults, including theory, practice, and philosophy related to program services for older adults. Ability to supervise others effectively, plan, and implement those plans. Ability to establish and maintain good public relations and good working relations.

Figure 6.1 Sample job description.

Job specifications. Job specifications detail the qualifications necessary to perform the job, as well as the benefits of the job. These are included in the outline of the job description. The job specifications will add information to the general description that can be used in the recruitment process. This might include specific information such as wage or salary, fringe benefits, and the like. In addition, if the job description is used as a recruitment notice, the person or office within the recreation and leisure service organization to whom the applicant's form should be sent is given, as well as the date, or dates when applications will be accepted. Often the job description will also carry the statement to the effect that the organization is an "equal opportunity employer." This is done to notify the applicant that the recruitment and selection process conforms to E.E.O.C. guidelines.

THE SELECTION PROCESS

One of the crucial elements in the staffing process is the selection of individuals to occupy positions within the recreation and leisure service organization. This is a process whereby potential candidates for a position are identified, the candidate's qualifications are determined, and the individuals selected are placed. This is done through recruitment, screening, interviewing, and testing.

Recruitment

The level of sophistication of the recruitment process varies from organization to organization. In larger organizations, or organizations that have personnel departments, recruitment is often organized in a very systematic, sequential manner. In small organizations, the recruitment process may be handled by individuals that are also performing other functions. Whether small or large, recreation and leisure service organizations should establish guidelines for recruitment procedures.

People apply for positions with organizations for a variety of reasons. Certainly, the credibility of the recreation and leisure service agency, its geographic location, the salary or other benefits that it offers, the people within it, and the social and cultural milieu of the community, are all factors that may influence an individual's decision to apply to an organization. Some of these are within the manager's control, others are not. During recruitment a recreation and leisure service organization identifies potential employees and controls some of those variables that may influence an individual's decision to apply for a position.

There are two sources from which individuals can be recruited. They can be recruited from within the organization or outside of the organization. Individuals within the organization who are ready for promotion, as well as those individuals who can move laterally within the organization, are potential candidates. Although employees do not often think of making lateral movements, such moves can act as a source of stimulation and may offer an opportunity for the employee to broaden his or her sphere of influence within the organization. Internal movement of individuals can be useful from several perspectives. It often improves employee morale because individuals see the opportunity for development as well as rewards for demonstrating initiative and hard work. Internal movement can also be useful because it allows an organization the opportunity to assess potential candidates over a long period of time. This is especially true when reviewing such characteristics as personality and the ability to take and give direction. This is contrasted with the short interview process that may serve as the basis for hiring an individual new to the agency. Internal promotion and movement of employees often help organizations retain competent individuals who, if not presented with an opportunity for advancement, would look elsewhere for employment. The major disadvantages of internal recruiting are the possible lack of individuals within the organization with the necessary skills and abilities for a more responsible position, and the inbreeding of staff that can occur when using this system. Where new ideas are essential, the latter concern must be considered. Using external sources can help overcome some of the disadvantages of internal recruiting. Individuals in an organization often view the bringing in of someone from the outside as contributing to the vitality of the organization with new ideas and new approaches to problems.

There are several ways of locating and informing individuals about the opportunities for positions within an organization. The type of position as well as its level of responsibility will dictate the method an organization employs to recruit. Some of the approaches that can be used are as follows:

Educational institutions.   Technical schools, high schools, colleges, and universities can be an important source of potential applicants for a position. Large corporations spend a great deal of time recruiting for new managers on college campuses.

Professional organizations.   Listing positions with professional societies, organizations, and associations can be an excellent method of recruitment. Almost all professional organizations maintain a job bulletin or referral service.

State employment agencies.   All states in the United States have employment agencies that help people find work. These agencies can be especially useful in hiring classified employees or those paid on an hourly basis, such as secretaries, clerks, and maintenance personnel.

Commercial employment agencies.   Commercial employment agencies locate individuals for a fee, which is assessed either to the employee or the employer.

Executive search firms.   Similar to commercial employment agencies, executive search firms specialize in identifying and recruiting top-level managers. The fee for this agency can range from $10,000 to $20,000 per search.

Newspaper and other advertising.   Advertising positions in either the classified or display sections of newspapers, as well as other journals, can be an excellent method of recruitment.

Labor unions.   Labor unions can be useful in recruiting individuals in the trades and other classified areas of employment. In certain occupations, labor unions are the sole source of employees.

Recommendation by an individual's current employer.   An individual's current employer can be an excellent resource. Often, employers satisfied with their employees' performance will comment about their capabilities. This type of referral, although not overt, constitutes a valid recruitment method.

Unsolicited applicants.   Individuals dropping by an organization can be a source of future employees. An expression of interest may be a reflection of the individual's drive and initiative.

Screening

The next step in the process is the screening of applicants and their applications. In the recreation and leisure service professions, there are usually a large number of applications that must be screened. It is not unusual for an agency to have between 25 and 50 applications for a position, especially at the entry level. In Eugene, Oregon a position for a parent liaison worker for the Center on Human Development attracted over 200 applications. This position required a bachelor's degree and experience related to the work to be performed and offered a salary of $12,000 per year. Thus, the initial process of screening can be very demanding. It is extremely difficult, without the opportunity to meet all of the individuals applying for a position, to determine the extent to which they are capable of performing the job.

Many recreation and leisure service organizations, if not served by a personnel department, attempt to establish a systematic procedure of rating applicants to determine those who are minimally qualified for a position. Using the job description found in Figure 6.1 for the program supervisor for senior citizens, an organization might attempt to set up a rating form that lists the qualifications, skills, and knowledge required by the position. For example, the job description in Figure 6.1 calls for an individual who has a bachelor's degree in recreation or gerontology and two years experience with older adults. Categories might be set up that would enable the screeners to assign certain values to education and to years and type of experience when evaluating applicants. Further, the position requires a minimum of a year in a supervisory capacity. Minimum qualifications might be established and individual applications might be reviewed to systematically determine whether minimum qualifications had been met by the applicant.

Sequentially, the organization would first identify applicants with minimum qualifications and then would rate the minimally qualified applicants. In an objective sense, quantitative assessments (i.e., numerical rating) can be made of the number of years of experience and the level of experience of each applicant. The same can be said of the applicant's educational level. From a subjective standpoint, the reviewers can review and evaluate the comments made in letters of recommendation, as well as the other factors that may affect the degree to which an individual can successfully fulfill the job description. Because it is not cost-effective to interview and test each minimally qualified applicant, the raters must strive to narrow the pool of applicants down to those that should be seriously considered for the position. This will obviously have to take into consideration the financial resources of the organization for the purposes of interviewing and testing individual applicants. In most situations, there is an effort made to narrow the field to the top five to ten applicants.

The next part of the screening process usually involves interviewing and testing. These will be discussed in detail later. Reference checks may be made at this time with previous employers and individuals who have written letters of reference for the prospective employee. The agency may want to determine the performance and interpersonal skills shown by the individual in previous jobs. These checks with references should be done in a discreet manner, and careful consideration should be given to the information collected. Questions should be asked such as, Is the source reliable? Can their comments be taken at face value? There are certain situations in which it may be inappropriate to contact an individual's current employer. Contact may jeopardize an individual's job or opportunities for advancement. There are situations where the prospective employee should be contacted subsequent to the interview to determine whether the person is still interested in the position, as well as to clarify various points concerning the job description (salary, benefits, duties, and title).

The goal of the preliminary screening process is to identify the (usually) top three candidates who will be asked to participate in a comprehensive interview and testing program. It is important to keep in mind the financial limitations of the organization at this point in the process. In many recreation and leisure service organizations, the opportunity to bring the three top candidates in for comprehensive interview or testing is not possible. Often, the agency selects the top candidate for the position and, after inviting the individual to the organization for further interviewing and testing, offers the individual the job if the interview process is completed successfully. If the applicant is not successful, the next individual is brought in for the interview process. This procedure continues until an individual is successful or a new recruitment process is initiated. The luxury of bringing several interviewees in at one time has been sharply curtailed in this period of financial restraint. This is especially the case for entry-level and mid-management positions.

This entire screening process should be handled in a professional and forthright manner. Individuals should be treated with a high degree of courtesy. It is important to realize that persons being screened, if not hired this time, may still be candidates for a similar job in the future. The authors feel that if individuals request it, they should be given the reasons that they were rejected in a tactful manner. This information may help a rejected applicant in a future job search.

Interviewing

Interviewing an applicant is the next step in screening. Interviewing is the most widely used and perhaps most important part of the assessment process. It is through interviewing that we learn the candidates' abilities to communicate verbally, to respond to the demands of different questions and situations, and to present themselves in a manner consistent with the needs of the organization. The interview process should be systematic and should not be conducted in a haphazard manner. The individual completing the interview process should be given adequate opportunities to interact with all appropriate parties within the organization, as well as to visit and view facilities and other resources related to the position.

What types of specific information does the recreation and leisure service organization attempt to derive from the interview process? Questions should be asked such as, Does the individual have the knowledge that is reported in the resume? The interview is an opportunity to explore the individual's qualifications. Does the person have the knowledge necessary to perform the job? Another important aspect of the interview process is the opportunity to assess the individual's personality. Is the applicant's management style appropriate? Does he or she appear to get along well with other people? Is the applicant's demeanor and other behavior consistent with the expectations and policies of the organization? Last, some attempt should be made to determine the extent to which the person fits in with others within the organization.

It is important to remember that interviewing is a two-way process; each person that is interviewed is also assessing the recreation and leisure service organization. Ample opportunity should be given to allow each person to conduct their interview of the organization. In top-level management positions, this becomes a critical dimension of the interview process. Most individuals interviewing for a management position will want to assess the degree to which they can succeed within the organization. This type of applicant might want to know such things as the future goals of the organization, opportunities for growth, opportunities for future promotion, interpersonal problems among staff, and the expectations of the organization. In many situations, the job itself is not the only factor that will influence an applicant's decision. The work environment, the economic conditions within the community, and the educational system could all be factors influencing a person's decision to accept or reject a position. It is important to be frank in answering an applicant's queries, because it is a life decision not only affecting the individual's professional career, but the lives of members of his or her family.

Pattern interview. The pattern approach to interviewing involves the development of a set of questions prior to the applicant's actual interview. This is a widely used technique in recreation and leisure service organizations, where large numbers of individuals must be interviewed. This frequently occurs when hiring part-time and seasonal employees and in situations where three or more individuals for a full-time position are brought in to interview. With this interview approach, the candidates' answers to questions are summarized and compared with one another. This encourages consistency, as each individual is evaluated according to similar criteria. This approach is reliable and usually is a predictor of job success or performance. It also minimizes the bias of the individual conducting the interview process. The disadvantage of this method is that it does not allow for exploration of those factors that may be unique to each applicant.

Nondirect interview. The nondirect interview is an approach that emphasizes open-end questions. Questions such as Tell me about your previous work experience or What do you feel are your strengths and weaknesses? might serve as lead questions to open the interview process. There is no planned format that is followed. The value of this approach is that it enables both the recreation and leisure service organization and the interviewee to explore those areas that are of interest to both parties. This method of interviewing allows a deeper understanding of the individual's aspirations, interests, and knowledge. This is the most common approach to interviewing, although, as a predictor of job success, it is not as effective as the pattern interview approach.

Group interview technique. The group interviewing technique is perhaps the least used. The organization brings together three to six candidates at one time for a group interview. Much of the work of leisure service organizations is done in group situations. This method of interviewing allows the organization to view the individual in this context. Questions that are prepared are presented to a member of the group. This individual responds with an answer and other individuals are given an opportunity to react to that response. This enables the interviewer to detect such qualities as sensitivity to others, ability to listen, ability to expand on ideas and to think logically.

Another variation of the group method is the *panel interview* technique. This approach to interviewing involves the establishment of a panel of individuals who collectively interview applicants for the position. This is common in agencies that have a civil-service board. It has a distinct advantage of allowing more individuals to participate in the selection process. This provides more perceptions of the candidates' ability to fit into the organization. The disadvantage of this method is that candidates may feel threatened or ill at ease when interviewing with a large number of people.

Stress interview.   Another approach to interviewing endeavors to place a person in a situation where stress or tension is induced. The primary purpose of the stress interview is to determine how a person will react under duress. Many situations in recreation and leisure service organizations involve the management of conflict. An individual's ability to handle these types of situations can give the interviewer insight into the candidate's personality characteristics that are often not evident in other types of interview situations. This approach is not widely used because it is a poor predictor of job success. Apparently, placing individuals on the defensive in an interview situation constrains the interview process. Nonetheless, one or more questions that gauge a person's tolerance for conflict or tension may be useful in the interview.

There are a number of guidelines that should be followed in conducting interviews. It is important to remember to avoid stereotyping individuals. One should not base an opinion on one characteristic or dimension of the individual's personality. When conducting the interview itself, there are a number of rules to be followed. The interviewer should try to establish a good rapport with the person being interviewed. A sufficient length of time should be allowed for the interview so that all areas related to employment can be explored fully. Perhaps the most important rule of thumb to follow in the interview process is the need to focus the interview on the position itself. Often interviewers become distracted, forgetting that the primary objective is to glean information that will be useful in the hiring decision.

Testing

Testing is becoming increasingly important in selection. Tests provide the manager with empirically verifiable information. Theoretically, various characteristics can be tested, including one's knowledge and skills in a given area, interests, personality, and intelligence. Tests must be employed in a cautious manner, as recent court rulings have found some tests to discriminate against minorities.

Often tests are employed as a screening device to determine whether individuals have acquired the minimum skills and knowledge to perform a certain task. A test for a clerk typist for the state of Oregon, for example, might include items to test proficiency in grammar, basic arithmetic, and spelling. These types of tests serve as fairly accurate predictors of minimum qualifications for success on the job. In agencies where screening procedures are handled by a civil-service commission, test scores are ranked, and a priority list is established. As openings occur within an organization, managers are able to draw individuals from the priority list and interview them to determine their fitness for the position to be filled. In situations where there are a large number of highly ranked candidates, each candidate receives a number, and when his or her number is picked, becomes eligible to interview.

Validity.   If testing procedures are to be employed, two important concerns related to the construction and administration of tests must be addressed. *Validity* is an assessment of a test as predictor of job success. If a test accurately measures future job performance, it is said to be valid. The validity of a test is established by comparing the relationship of successful performance with test scores. If a set of managers are perceived to be successful in performing their duties, and if their test scores are similar, then it would be appropriate to infer that the test is a valid measure of job performance. It should be noted that this is subject to random error. In situations where successful test completion can be tied to quantitative measure, the predictability is much higher. This is extremely difficult in the recreation and leisure service profession, because we provide services instead of producing material objects.

Reliability.   Reliability is the second concern that needs to be addressed in the development and employment of tests. If a test, over a period of time, consistently predicts success, it is said to be *reliable*. Consistence is the key term. An individual should be able to take the test several times and produce similar scores. One of the factors to be considered in testing is that individuals who have already taken the test become test wise; knowledge of the test items and familiarity with the testing procedure can produce higher scores. There are other variables that can influence the degree to which the test reflects the ability of the individual taking it. For example, if the test procedures are administered differently from one test to another, it can affect the outcome. The state of mind of the person being tested can also affect the score; fatigue and boredom can lower scores. All of these factors must be taken into consideration if tests are major selection criteria.

There are numerous ways to classify tests. There are *individual tests* in which one individual is tested at a time. This type of test is thought to reduce misunderstanding of directions and testing procedures. *Group tests* are given to two or more individuals at a time. Although cost-effective, they are not as definitive as individual tests. Another type of test is one that measures the ability of a person to answer test questions within a specified period of time. This is known as a *speed test*. This can be contrasted with a *power test* wherein the individual is provided a series of subtests that become increasingly difficult. The objective is to measure a person's knowledge and capability instead of speed. *Aptitude tests* are another type of measurement. These types of tests measure an individual's potential ability for a particular type of job. Aptitude tests also are used as predictors of success. Last, *achievement tests* measure both ability and potential ability. These approaches to testing are often combined to produce the four basic types of tests used by human-service organizations. They are intelligence, personality, interest, and skill tests.

Intelligence tests.   Intelligence tests, once widely used in private industry, have been deemphasized during the past decade. Legislation has made the use of such tests subject to careful scrutiny to avoid discrimination. Caution should be exercised in employing intelligence tests in hiring. There are a number of tests such as the Stanford-Binet Intelligence Scale, the Miller Analogies Test, the Wechsler Adult Intelligence Scale, and the Otis Self-Administering Test of Mental Ability that can be employed by recreation and leisure service organizations. Intelligence tests provide an operational definition of intelligence. For example, the Stanford-Binet Intelligence Scale determines a mental age for the individual. In this test, an IQ (intelligence quotient) of 100 is considered average.

Personality tests.   Personality tests are used to assess psychological make-up. These types of tests measure such traits as introversion/extroversion, exclusion/inclusion, dominance/submissiveness, and dependence/independence. There are a number of personality tests that have been used by recreation and leisure service organizations. Among the more common ones are the Minnesota Multiphasic Personality Inventory, the Gordon Personal Profile and Inventory, and the Firo-B. Numerous tests have also been developed to ascertain an individual's managerial leadership style. There are, for example, tests available to determine one's managerial leadership style as it relates to Fiedler's contingency model of leadership effectiveness, the Blake and Mouton management grid, and Reddin's 3-D theory of management effectiveness. These types of tests are common in the screening process. The biggest problem with personality tests is the problem of test reliability. Responses to these types of tests can be faked, and, as a result, they do not necessarily measure what they are intended to measure.

Interest tests.   Interest tests attempt to determine areas in which an individual expresses interest. Since job interest is related to job satisfaction, these types of tests can be useful in this area. The Strong Vocational Interest Blank and the Kudel Preference Record are two examples of interest tests. These tests, like personality tests, can be easily faked. Use of interest tests is not as common as the use of personality and intelligence tests.

Skill and knowledge tests.   Another type of test that is widely used is the skill, or knowledge, test. There are specific occupational skills for which tests can be developed to measure competence. These are commonly used for positions requiring such skills as typing, filing, and bookkeeping. When hiring a secretary, for example, it is common to determine the number of words per minute that the applicant can type. Also, there are knowledge tests that are developed by agencies and professional associations to assess the competence of an individual or certify capability within professional areas of responsibility. A recreation and leisure service worker might be tested in areas such as history, professional nomenclature, philosophy, and the applied or engineered skills of that occupation. Holding certification in a specific occupation may be a prerequisite for holding a job in that field.

Making the Decision to Hire

Once information from various processes has been acquired, the next step in the staffing process is deciding whether to hire. This can be an extremely difficult task for the recreation and leisure service manager. Seldom does one individual stand out so that the choice is obvious. Often, there are two or three individuals whose qualifications, references, and testing are nearly equal. It is a difficult task to select the individual who will best meet the needs of the organization. Further, although the selection process may have involved several members of the organization, ultimately one person will be responsible for making the decision to hire. It is wise for the individual responsible for the final decision to try to work toward consensus with those employees who will be affected by the hiring. With equally qualified candidates, one candidate's ability to fit into the organization may be the deciding factor in hiring.

One should not base selection on only one element of the selection process. All of the information collected should be taken into consideration, not only, for example, the interview. An employer who has taken time to carefully investigate a candidate's background, has expended funds for testing, and personally interviewed potential candidates should use all of these in the decision-making process.

What about those applicants that are not hired? It is appropriate to contact those candidates who have been interviewed to explain the organization's decision. Individuals who are seriously considered for one position with the organization but are not hired may be considered for future positions. If they feel that they have been treated fairly and in a courteous manner, they usually will be open to future employment opportunities with the organization. If personal contact with each candidate that is not hired is impossible, a letter should be sent explaining the organization's decision.

Once the decision is made to hire someone even though organizational members may have had different opinions as to who should have been hired, all parties should coalesce behind the decision and offer support to the incoming staff member. Differing opinions within the organization should not carry over to the work environment once the new person has arrived. Equally important, the new employee's rank and status in the selection process should not be a factor in later job relationships, especially if he or she was not the first choice. The organization's top-rated choice may decline the job offer, requiring the organization to hire its second or third choice. In this circumstance, the organization should make an effort to ensure that the incoming employee is made to feel welcome and essential to the organization.

Compensation. Compensation can be negotiated in the hiring process. Although many recreation and leisure service organizations have fixed packages of compensation that are negotiated periodically, there can be some flexibility in the application of these systems as a method of encouraging an individual to join an organization. Some latitude is necessary in order to recruit individuals, especially at top management positions. However, caution must be exercised when determining a package so that it is consistent with the pay ranges and responsibilities of the position.

Compensation is usually based on a determination of the relative worth of each job within the organization. Usually, the more responsibility attached to a job, the greater the compensation. Compensation can also be affected by external factors, such as the local economy, local, state, and federal governments. Further, a lack of trained professionals might prompt a higher rate of compensation as an incentive to attract such qualified individuals.

There are two types of compensation. The first type is financial incentives—either a wage or a salary. An employee who is paid hourly receives a wage, whereas an individual whose compensation is based on a longer period of time (a month or year) receives a salary. Professional positions in the recreation and leisure service fields are almost always salaried. Other types of financial incentives have been established in organizations, primarily in business. Profit sharing, financial bonuses, and financial compensation based on the merit of suggested ideas are other forms.

Fringe benefits.   The other type of compensation, fringe benefits, has become increasingly important within organizations. For the employee, benefits are made available that might otherwise be unaffordable. Offering benefits as part of its payment package may ultimately represent a savings to the organization. There are numerous types of fringe benefits. Some of these are mandated by law, such as unemployment insurance and disability compensation. Others are offered at the discretion of the organization, such as health and dental insurance, retirement, low-interest loans, life insurance, vacations, and sick leave. The cost of these types of benefits may exceed 25 percent of the financial compensation paid to an employee.

Legal Factors Influencing the Selection Process

During the past several decades, federal legislation has played an increasingly important role in the selection process. Today's recreation and leisure service agencies, as well as other organizations, are responsible for complying with federal laws that prohibit discrimination in a variety of areas. In addition, there are numerous local and state laws affecting recruitment and selection, of which the recreation and leisure service manager must be aware. Some confusion arises as a result of contradictory legislation and the fact that different legislative acts are enforced by different agencies. Inconsistency in information and a lack of coherent guidelines make this is a potentially frustrating area for recreation and leisure service managers. Nonetheless, it is the responsibility of the manager to ensure that agency practices comply with the law.

There are a number of federal laws that directly affect the selection and recruitment process in recreation and leisure service organizations. These laws have developed from concerns expressed by those within the recreation and leisure service movement. To many they are viewed as progressive legislation that has substantially increased the quality of life for all Americans. Some of the most important laws are as follows:

Equal Pay Act of 1963. The Equal Pay Act of 1963 was designed to prohibit wage discrimination based on sex. Organizations are required to pay the same wages to women who are performing the same work responsibilities as men. If a female employee has the same skill level and knowledge base and performs the same tasks as a male, the pay must be the same. When first enacted, this law applied only to nonsupervisory employees. However, in 1972, the act was extended to include individuals in administrative and professional positions. This act is administered by the Wage and Hour Division of the United States Department of Labor.

Civil Rights Act of 1964. The Civil Rights Act of 1964 has directly influenced the staffing process of all organizations. The Civil Rights Act prohibits discrimination on the basis of race, color, or national origin. Specifically, Title VII of the act prohibits discrimination in selection, promotion, and other areas of employment. There have been a number of court decisions that have strengthened the Civil Rights Act as it relates to the staffing process. Three court cases have provided further interpretation and clarification. The federal courts have ruled that organizations cannot discriminate against women in the hiring process because they have young children. In *Phillips* vs. *Martin Marietta*, the courts ruled that the Martin Marietta Corporation engaged in discriminatory hiring practices because of the ages of Phillips' children. The courts have also ruled on the use of intelligence scores. In the *Myart* vs. *Motorola* case, the courts held that intelligence tests could only be used if they were a predictor of job success. In this case a black applicant was denied a job because of a low score on an intelligence test that was not related to the performance of the job itself. In support of this the Supreme Court ruled in *Griggs et al.* vs. *Duke Power Company* that tests taken prior to employment must be job-related.

The E.E.O.C. In order to enforce the Civil Rights Act in the area of employment, the Equal Employment Opportunity Commission (E.E.O.C.) was established. This agency helps organizations comply with the law and investigates alleged discrimination within organizations. The E.E.O.C. has established guidelines in the areas of recruitment, advertising, testing, application forms, etc. to help prevent discrimination in employment. Further, the E.E.O.C. has established guidelines to help organizations increase the number of minority and female employees within their agencies. These types of programs are known as affirmative action programs.

Age Discrimination Act of 1967.   The Age Discrimination Act of 1967, amended in 1978, prohibits discrimination on the basis of age and specifically provides protection for individuals in the 40- to 70-year-old age range. Individuals are protected from discrimination in employment in selection, retention, promotion, compensation and other areas. The Age Discrimination Act is enforced by the Wage and Hour Division of the United States Department of Labor.

The Equal Employment Opportunity Act of 1972.   As indicated, the E.E.O.C. was established to enforce the Civil Rights Act of 1964. This 1972 legislation significantly strengthened the enforcement power of the E.E.O.C. The Commission was empowered to initiate suits against agencies that did not comply with the law. In addition, the act extended coverage of the law to state and local government employees, as well as to those in educational institutions. Further, it stipulated that all organizations with 15 or more employees would be subject to E.E.O.C. guidelines, rather than organizations with 25 or more employees, as had previously been the case.

Affirmative Action Plan.   As indicated previously, organizations, by and large, must establish an affirmative action plan. This applies to all federal agencies, as well as those agencies that contract or subcontract work for the federal government or receive some type of federal assistance. In addition, as mentioned, it also applies to private profit or nonprofit agencies with 15 or more employees. The recent Bakke decision dealing with the establishment of a quota for minorities (in this case admission to the University of California, Davis, Medical School) has caused some concern about the extent to which organizations should aggressively pursue their affirmative action programs. Nonetheless, most organizations of 200 or more employees must establish a program for affirmative action.

Basically, an affirmative action program must conform to a number of guidelines. These guidelines affect such things as employment advertising, application forms and recruitment practices. Specifically, each organization must maintain a record system that accurately reflects its employment practices for the previous three years. On an annual basis, E.E.O.C. requires that the agency file a report that indicates the number of employees who are male, female, white, black, Spanish American, American Indian, and so on. The guidelines suggest that these data should be categorized as to the type of job (administrator, professional, technician, protective-service workers, paraprofessionals, clerical, skilled craft workers, service or maintenance) and the type of appointment made by the agency (probationary, provisional, emergency, exempt, or temporary). Employment advertisement, according to the guidelines, must be nondiscriminatory in nature and must not indicate preferences as to sex, race, age, religion, or color. Application forms must be job-specific; that is, they must be related to the job requirements. The same is the case with test and interview procedures. Such factors as arrest records, photographs, and names of family members can no longer be required by employers. The selection procedure cannot use either marital status or family situation as criteria for selection or advancement.

The affirmative action plan must include a statement with regard to the organization's policy toward discrimination. Specific objectives must be stated, such as the intention to provide for the employment of women and other minorities. In addition, the organization must specify an individual to manage the plan. In large organizations, this person is known as the affirmative action officer. This individual often oversees the development and implementation of the plan, handles grievances, and reviews recruitment documents and strategies.

STAFF APPRAISAL

An integral part of the staffing process, performance appraisal involves subjective and objective analysis of the extent to which an individual completes assigned tasks in an effective and efficient manner. Both the results achieved and the methods used by the individual should be evaluated. The performance appraisal process should be tied, in a broad sense, to the contribution of the individual to the goals of the organization. This is often forgotten in the appraisal process, as there is a tendency to base appraisal on personality and other tangential variables.

There are numerous problems associated with the appraisal process. Often, individuals in superior positions find it difficult to evaluate their subordinates. Managers may be afraid to categorize people as high or low performers. This occurs because appraisals usually have a negative connotation, rather than being viewed as a vehicle for development. The manager may fear that a poor evaluation will be a demotivating factor. Staff members fear criticism. Another problem associated with the appraisal process is the lack of objective performance measures. Because most appraisals are subjective, their usefulness is often questioned by staff, as well as by managers.

In recent years, the nature of performance appraisal has changed. First and foremost, there has been an attempt to objectify the appraisal process. In the past, there was a heavy reliance on the personality traits of the individual for appraisal purposes. These trait-appraisal systems identified and measured a number of personal characteristics, such as integrity, dependability, relationships with people, and punctuality. The problem with rating these types of traits is that they often have little or no relationship to the person's ability to perform the job successfully. Newer systems tend to focus on the identification of objective standards against which performance can be assessed. Objectives for employees are stated in terms that can be measured, making the appraisal process quantifiable. Another important change in the appraisal process has been the adoption of bottom–up measures. In the past, the majority of appraisal systems utilized a top-down approach; that is, an individual in a supervisory position would be responsible for evaluating those persons in positions below them. Newer appraisal systems emphasize peer evaluation as well as the evaluation of superiors by their subordinates. For example, many Japanese corporations have employed a concept known as the *quality circle*. In this kind of appraisal, individual work teams sit down to analyze their work performance with an eye toward improving the quantity and quality of their work. The Sunnyvale, California, Park and Recreation Department employs a system of evaluation that enables individuals to periodically rate their supervisor's performance.

Effective Performance Appraisal

Distilling research findings in the area of performance appraisal, Porter, Lawler, and Hackman suggest a number of characteristics of an effective performance appraisal system. These are as follows:

1. Measures are used that are inclusive of all the behaviors and results that should be performed.
2. The measures used are tied to behavior and, as far as possible, are objective in nature.
3. Moderately difficult goals and standards for future performance are set.
4. Measures are used that can be influenced by an individual's behavior.
5. Appraisals are done on a time cycle that approximates the time it takes the measures to reflect the behavior of persons being evaluated.
6. Persons being evaluated have an opportunity to participate in the appraisal process.
7. The appraisal system interacts effectively with the reward system.[1]

These points can serve as a basis for developing performance appraisal guidelines within recreation and leisure service organizations.

Methods of Performance Appraisal

There are a number of methods of performance appraisal that can be used by recreation and leisure service organizations. Caution should be exercised in adopting appraisal systems that have been developed by other organizations. Each organization is unique in its mission and is affected by the unique characteristics of the community it serves. Therefore, it is recommended that each agency establish its own performance appraisal system. If this is not possible, the agency may want to adapt scales and mechanisms that have been successfully employed in similar agencies.

---

1. Lyman W. Porter, Edward E. Lawler, and J. Richard Hackman, *Behavior in Organizations* (New York: McGraw-Hill, 1975), p. 339.

Some of the methods that can be employed by recreation and leisure service organizations are as follows:

Peer appraisal.   As indicated, one of the more recent forms of appraisal is known as the peer-rating or quality-circle method of evaluation. Using this approach, workers who have equal status work in groups or in the "buddy" system and engage in a mutual evaluation process. This removes the stigma of evaluation by a superior and promotes cooperation, as each individual has a stake in the success or failure of the others.

Management by objectives.   Management by objectives is based upon the management system established by Peter Drucker in 1954. Increasingly it is being used in recreation and leisure service organizations as a method of planning and controlling. As an instrument of employee appraisal, it allows the manager and subordinates to establish mutually agreed upon objectives. At various time intervals, a joint appraisal of the subordinates' performance in terms of these objectives is undertaken. A management-by-objectives system also enables individual goals to be linked with broader organizational goals, thereby tying the work of the individual to the needs of the organization.

Rating traits.   Rating traits is a standard approach to employee appraisal that has been used by many organizations. The manager identifies a number of traits considered to be essential to the job. These might include the ability to work with others, dependability, cheerfulness, quality of work, and so on. Once this list has been developed, a rating scale is established that might range, for example, from poor to outstanding. Individuals are then rated according to how well they demonstrate each trait. Sometimes the numerical scores are added, providing a total score for each individual's performance.

Rank order.   Rank order is similar to the rating trait method. The significant difference is that with the rank order method individuals in similar positions or job classifications are rated against one another. Individuals are placed in rank order with their peers, according to their performance.

Critical incident.   The critical incident approach to appraisal finds the manager systematically recording perceptions of subordinates' performance over a period of time. The obvious disadvantages of this approach are the lack of a standard and the fact that personal impressions may be unreliable.

Forced choice.   The forced choice method of appraisal is not commonly used in recreation and leisure service organizations. This form of appraisal involves the development of a set of statements that reflect both unacceptable and acceptable performance of individuals. The manager then rates each subordinate by selecting the statements that best describe and that least describe the subordinate. The statements are worded in such a way that the manager does not know which statements imply good performance and which statements imply unacceptable behavior. This system has the distinct advantage of discouraging bias on the part of the manager as a result of the personal relationship between the manager and the subordinate.

STAFF DEVELOPMENT

The development of staff is essential in the management of recreation and leisure service organizations. In order for an organization to run at peak efficiency, staff members must be given the opportunity to grow. Our knowledge base in the recreation and leisure field is constantly expanding. For example, it is said that the half-life of management knowledge is about seven years. The way that services are organized and delivered is in a constant state of flux, and individual cultural attitudes, values, and norms change constantly. To cope with the process of change, the development of employees should be an important aspect of staffing.

It is a paradox that recreation and leisure service organizations are committed to the development of people, yet few opportunities for growth are available to their employees. Business does a far better job of organizing employee development programs in a systematic manner. Businesses recognize the importance of keeping staff appraised of changes in the market place and technological changes, as well as changes in management concepts. Perhaps the lack of employee development programs within recreation and leisure service organizations is related to a lack of resources, or perhaps it can be traced to the mismanagement of existing resources. It is not enough to suggest that attendance at conferences, workshops, or seminars will meet the needs of organizational members for development. Each organization should try to develop a comprehensive program that includes a variety of strategies.

It has been said that one of the most serious problems facing recreation and leisure service professionals is that of burnout. This stress-oriented problem occurs because of a lack of supervisory support, as well as the intensity and amount of interaction that takes place between the recreation and leisure service worker and those he or she serves. Coping with stress, as well as demonstrating empathy for the problems associated with this demanding job, can be, in many cases, best handled through the staff development process. Staff development should be seen as not only an opportunity to learn new skills and information, but also as an opportunity to help solve organizational problems.

Methods of Staff Development

The purpose of staff development is to help an individual learn. It is the process whereby an organization enhances employee learning that results in a change in or maintenance of employee behavior. It is important to remember that this change in behavior, in order to be effective, must contribute to the goals of the organization. In a broad sense, there are three types of staff development, or training—orientation, in-service, and developmental.

Orientation training.   Orientation training occurs before an individual begins an actual work assignment. Its purpose is to acquaint the individual with the organization's philosophy, policy, staff, and the assigned work that the person will perform.

In-service training.   In-service training occurs after a person has been with the organization for a period of time. The purpose of in-service training is to reinforce selected skills or attitudes or to provide information regarding changes in operations (perhaps a new piece of equipment, facility, or operational procedure).

Developmental training.   Developmental training is aimed at helping the individual grow, both personally or professionally. It is not necessarily tied to the improvement of a specific job-related skill; instead it focuses on the growth of the individual in ways that are beneficial to the organization. In other words, the basic purpose of this process is to promote personal growth while at the same time contributing to the achievement of organizational goals.

Developing Individual Plans

In order for the development process to work effectively, it must be individualized. The manager should work with each staff member to organize a plan of development that is tailored to that person's needs. There are a number of steps that must take place. First, each employee should understand the tasks and responsibilities that are expected of him or her. These must be defined both in terms of the results to be achieved and the process to be employed. The employee should also have a clear understanding of the goals of the organization. Second, there must be an appraisal of ability and performance. This can be done by both the manager and the subordinate. The appraisal should be understood and accepted by both parties. The next step in the process should be development of the individual plan itself. Initially, a plan should focus on one or two areas. For example, if communication with other people had been identified as an area in which the individual would like to grow, a plan would be developed for this one need. The training program might include opportunities for role playing, simulation, and other opportunities to develop competence in interpersonal communications.

Within the developmental program, it is important to acknowledge the employees' growth. This can be done through the formal reward system or it can occur more intrinsically. Cultivation of the intrinsic reward mechanism (individuals reward themselves, by, for example, feeling a sense of accomplishment) must occur, however. Employees cannot be financially rewarded every time they learn something new or grow in ways that benefit the organization. Rather, growth itself should be viewed as a reward.

There are several problems associated with staff development. First, managers often do not assume the responsibility for training their subordinates. This occurs especially in organizations that lack systematic plans for development and fail to integrate each manager into the process. When plans for the development of employees is left up to individual managers, training often becomes haphazard. A comprehensive program should be established that involves all managers and their subordinates in meaningful ways. One of the ways that this can occur is to require each manager to develop personal growth agreements with subordinates. Another problem that occurs in staff development is the failure to focus upon organizational goals. This is especially true in recreation and leisure service organizations, where much of the development process involves simply encouraging people to attend conferences, workshops, and seminars. The knowledge gained at such events may not be channeled back to the organization in a systematic and useful way. Last, problems in staff development may occur if employees receive training and then are not correspondingly challenged in their jobs. As people change and grow, their jobs should be redesigned and their work reorganized to reflect this change.

SUMMARY

Staffing concerns the way in which a recreation and leisure service organization acquires and maintains its human resources. There are several interrelated components in the staffing process: developing job descriptions, selecting new employees and promoting individuals within the organization, appraising performance, and contributing to employee development.

The development of a job description assists in the selection process and helps individuals understand the role that they are to perform within the organization. A job description outlines such things as the duties and qualifications for a position and defines superior and subordinate relationships. Some job descriptions may also spell out the physical conditions or material for which an individual is responsible.

The recruitment, screening, interviewing, and testing of potential employees and those being considered for promotions is the selection process. Recruitment involves finding individuals to apply for positions available within the leisure service organization. Screening determines which of the individuals identified in the recruitment process is qualified for a position within the organization. Testing offers a way to discriminate between individual applicants. Interviewing is the process whereby individuals meet with members of the organization so that a choice can be made between job candidates. A number of federal laws have been enacted that affect the selection process. These laws prohibit discrimintion in hiring and compensation on the basis of age, sex, race or ethnic origin.

The appraisal of staff involves a subjective and objective analysis of individual performance. Some of the appraisal systems that have been employed in recreation and leisure service organizations include peer appraisal, management by objectives, rating traits, rank order, critical incident, and forced choice. Appraisal systems have become more result oriented in the past decades.

Last, the development of staff focuses on the enhancement of employee learning. This results in the change or maintenance of selected employee behaviors. There are three types of training programs that can be employed by recreation and leisure service organizations: orientation, in-service, and developmental training. Personalized development programs mutually agreed upon by a manager and subordinates are essential. To be effective, these should address both the needs of the individual and the needs of the organization.

STUDY QUESTIONS

1. Define staffing. What are the elements of the staffing process?
2. What is a job description? What components should be included in a job description?
3. Name two sources of employees for positions within human-service organizations. Name nine approaches for the recruitment of job candidates.
4. What is the purpose of the screening process?
5. Name four interview techniques. Who interviews whom in the interview process?
6. Contrast test reliability and validity. Identify and define four different types of tests that can be used by human-service organizations. What problems might be associated with the use of each?
7. Name four federal laws that directly influence the selection process. What is an affirmative action plan?
8. Identify six methods of performance appraisal.
9. Why is staff development essential in human-service organizations?
10. Identify three different types of staff development.

CASE STUDY 9

The Selection Committee

"We have a number of questions before us, ladies and gentlemen," said John Peterson, chairman of the selection committee established to recommend a replacement for the retiring director of Recreation and Parks. "We have received 32 applications, screened to three. You should all have a summary that we prepared of these three applications."

Summary of applications received:

Candidate one. Bob Playfair, age 29, education M.S. in recreation and park management, graduate N.R.P.A. executive development program, five years' professional experience in Canusa, vice president Professional Recreation and Park Association. Married, three children. Interviewed and rated 7 out of 10 by the committee.

Candidate two. George Gantt, age 36, education M.B.A., specialization in fiscal management, ten years' professional experience in business, currently employed as vice president of finance, Canusa Sporting Goods Inc., a chain of three sporting goods stores operating in Canusa and two nearby cities. Single. Interview rating of 9 by the committee.

Candidate three. George Branch, age 55, education B.S. in recreation and park management, 20 years of professional experience, ten years with the Canusa Y.M.C.A., five years as director of parks and recreation for Burlington, population 50,000, and five years with the Canusa Recreation and Parks Department as director of Recreation Services, president of the area professional association, and graduate of the national executive development program for recreation and park managers. Married, two children. Interview rating of 9 by the committee.

"First, should we make an appointment internally, or should we go outside the department and seek candidates? Second, if we go outside the department, what kinds of qualifications should the person whom we employ possess? Third, if we make an internal appointment, is there anybody qualified to assume the position? If we address ourselves initially to these three questions, I believe we can come up with a plan of action. Any comments?"

After considerable discussion it was decided that, although Bob Playfair had indicated an interest in the position, he was relatively young, and the internal friction that might result if he was given the position militated against an appointment. The decision, therefore, was between George Gantt and George Branch, and committee members were asked to speak in regard to these two candidates. The final decision, after lengthy debate, went to George Branch, and it was decided to recommend his appointment to Council effective January 1.

QUESTIONS

1. Of the three candidates, do you have any choices for the position? Why?
2. Is age important in a selection of this kind?

3. Would a graduate degree in business administration (M.B.A.) be a more appropriate degree for this position than the degree held by George? Why?
4. What kinds of educational background would be best for the person assuming this new position? Why?
5. What role does experience play in preparing a candidate for a position such as this?

Directing Human Resources

7

Recently assuming a position as director of a community recreation agency, a young manager reviews the performance appraisals of his subordinates. He finds that one employee is characterized as being effective, cheerful, prompt, industrious and interested in his job, whereas another employee of similar age, background, and experience is characterized as being chronically late or absent, performing his job marginally, and being disinterested in his work. What can account for the differences between these two employees, in terms of disposition and performance? It is likely that one employee is in a job that he finds challenging and that meets his needs; the other is in a job that he finds routine, tedious, and lacking opportunities for growth. It appears that one employee is motivated and the other is not.

Motivation is the key that unlocks human potential. It is the process whereby the capabilities of the individual are used to benefit both the individual and the organization. It is a process that can be initiated by the recreation and leisure service

manager. Motivational techniques can promote organizational harmony; the lack of a motivating environment can
foster resentment, hostility, and poor employee performance.
A motivating environment stems from the manager's knowledge of people's needs and the way in which various
techniques can be employed to help meet these needs, while
pursuing the goals of the organization.

WHY DO PEOPLE WORK?

Why do people work? At face value it would seem that the answer to this question is a simple one: Individuals work in order to subsist. However, the reason that people work is more complex and depends on a variety of cultural factors. In North America, the "Protestant work ethic" tradition of our forefathers produced a culture in which work was embraced for spiritual reasons. Work was the central focus in the life and value structure of people in our early culture. Today, work is shaped by many factors, and the reasons that influence individuals to work are numerous.

Humans have a large capacity for activity. This activity can be manifested in a number of different ways. When it is organized and results in the creation of products or services for which individuals are paid, it is known as work. Definitions of work are culturally based; what constitutes work in one society may be different from what constitutes work in another society. The way in which work is manifested may also vary from culture to culture. In North American society, religious precepts have historically been the primary cultural determinant of work. Currently, however, we view work more in terms of citizenship. For example, a good citizen is one who is employed and thereby is perceived as contributing in a positive sense to the general welfare of society.

Smith has written that work is a primary factor shaping man's life both now and in previous times.[1] He suggests that fundamental cultural values and norms have been primarily defined by the work in which people have engaged. According to Smith, throughout the history of mankind, work has had a more influential role in shaping man's behavior than other factors, such as food or sex. Recognizing the impact of other variables such as religion and education, Smith suggests that work is the central factor shaping human behavior.

There are a variety of incentives that motivate people to work. These can range from the satisfaction that is derived from engaging in the work itself to the lifestyle that one is able to enjoy as a result of a certain level of compensation. The extent to which motivating factors are present in

---

1. K. U. Smith, *Behavior, Organization and Work: A New Approach to Industrial Science* (Madison, Wisconsin: College Printing and Typing, 1965).

the job environment will influence an individual's behavior. When these factors are absent, or are present in a form that does not meet individual needs, employees will do one of two things. Either they will concentrate their activity away from the work environment (perhaps toward leisure concerns) or they will engage in disruptive behavior owing to the monotony of the job. Some of the factors that may motivate people to work are financial rewards, status, recognition, relationships, intrinsic rewards, and growth.

Financial rewards.   Financial rewards for work include both the direct wage or salary paid to the individual and fringe benefits. Money is a major motivator of behavior in that it provides the means to satisfy not only the basic needs of the individual (food, clothing, shelter), but also those needs that are related to leisure interests and family welfare. The direct relationship between financial rewards and employee behavior is imprecise.

Status.   The status that one holds as a result of engaging in a job and being a part of an organization is a factor that influences individuals to work. Certain occupations enjoy a higher level of status in society than others. Individuals are attracted to such occupations because of their high status. Being a part of an organization that enjoys high status is also attractive. The status that persons enjoy in their primary work groups is an important factor motivating work behavior.

Recognition.   The acknowledgment of achievement for effort is recognition. Although recognition is related to status, acknowledgement of an individual's achievements does not necessarily result in increased status. The source of the recognition often determines whether it will influence work behavior significantly. For some individuals, the recognition of the peer group is critical. For others, recognition from the supervisor is important. In recreation and leisure service organizations, the recognition that is accorded the individual from professional societies may be as influential as other types of recognition.

Relationships.   The interpersonal relationships that are formed within an organization can influence individuals to work. Japanese corporations recognize the importance of the cultivation of friendships in the work environment and encourage these as a part of their management strategy.

Intrinsic rewards.   The type of work that a person engages in can be a strong motivator. Further, the way in which an individual accomplishes assigned tasks can influence his or her desire to work. For example, individuals who are allowed to feel a sense of completion are more likely to be motivated to work. Individuals who are motivated to work are not just active, but feel a sense of achievement and involvement as a result of being goal-oriented. In the recreation and leisure service professions, service to others may be a strong motivator.

Growth.   When individuals have an opportunity to learn and to acquire new skills, they are motivated to work. This is a highly individualized experience. What constitutes a growth experience for one individual will not necessarily be one for another. When individuals experience a sense of growth, as opposed to feelings of stagnation, they are more motivated to remain within a work environment.

Motivation Defined

There are different views of motivation. Some theorists suggest that motivation is an act that is imposed on subordinates by the manager. That is, the manager motivates people. Others suggest that it is difficult, if not impossible, to motivate a person. Those who hold this view would suggest that persons cannot be motivated; individuals can only motivate themselves. Taking the latter view, the role of the manager becomes one of creating or developing an environment in which the individual is self-motivated. This might involve removing barriers, establishing reward systems, and establishing methods of recognition.

One of the ideas that managers have clung to over the past several decades is the *carrot and stick theory*. This approach to motivation, still practiced by many managers, rests on the assumption that individuals need to be threatened, cajoled, or bribed in order to perform. It is based on the idea that people will avoid putting forth an honest day's work effort if given the opportunity. It is now known, however, that this is not the case; avoidance of work is related more to poor job design (e.g., routine, repetitive tasks). The recreation and leisure service manager today should be conscious of alternative strategies to motivate individuals, as well as the importance of the variables that affect individual work performance.

To paraphrase Peter Drucker, the one and only responsibility of managers is to ensure that employees do what they get paid to do.[2] In order for this to occur, the manager must structure an environment wherein the capabilities of individual employees are allowed to unfold. This occurs through the process of motivation. We can think of *motivation* as the process whereby an environment is created that enables individuals to be stimulated to take action that fulfills the goals of the organization.

Is motivating the recreation and leisure service worker different from motivating an individual who is in another occupation? Although motivating principles are universal and can be applied in all situations, it is the way these principles are applied in each situation that will often determine the success or failure of the manager in motivating employees. There are

2.   Peter Drucker, *Managing in Turbulent Times* (New York: Harper and Row, 1980), p. 24.

distinctions between profit and nonprofit recreation and leisure service organizations that will affect the motivation process. The primary motive of the nonprofit recreation and leisure service organizations is that of service. Those who benefit from the operation of the organization are those receiving the services, and not the owners of the organization. Further, the measures of performance tend to be qualitative (improvement of mental health and provision of satisfying leisure experiences), rather than quantitative (sales revenue, profit). In addition, employees of recreation and leisure service agencies are hired to act in independent ways. There is often a continuous reassignment of tasks, rather than a high degree of task differentiation with precise delineation of responsibilities. A higher value is placed on human-relations skills than on technical knowledge or skills. The commitment of individuals within the organization is not directed toward the organization itself, but toward the ideals of the profession. In recreation and leisure service organizations, the pattern of authority, control, and communication also varies from that of other organizations. Centers of authority and control are derived more from individual expertise than from a hierarchical chain of command. In this way responsibility is often shared and is not limited to those in management positions. Because of this sharing of responsibility, the communications network is more open and expansive. Communications systems in other types of organizations tend to be more controlled. Recreation and leisure service organizations also tend to emphasize group problem solving, even though decisions are made hierarchically.

What type of work environment must exist in order for motivation of employees to take place within recreation and leisure service organizations? A work environment should exist that allows people to assume responsibility, engage in problem solving and decision making, and to act in an independent manner, once the direction of the organization has been determined. Decision making and problem solving by consensus are also desirable. Employees in recreation and leisure service organizations are more likely to be motivated by the rewards associated with client satisfaction than by financial rewards. Recreation and leisure service workers should have a voice in what constitutes their tasks and how decisions are made about the direction of the organization, and should be given autonomy to carry out their functions. In the latter case, recreation and leisure service workers should have the freedom to determine specifically how their work is structured.

The challenge to the recreation and leisure service manager to create an environment wherein these types of motivating factors are available is tremendous. Many managers cling to outdated notions of management that emphasize authoritarian leadership, unilateral decision making, and incentives based on financial reward. It is important to note, however, that managers are influenced by the social and cultural values that predominated during their formative development. Discussing the differences in what motivates people in different times, Mondy et al. present this scenario:

"You either do it my way or you're fired!" This type of motivation may have worked at the turn of the century, but today many employees would tell their supervisor to "Take this job and--------!" Today's new breed of employees does not respond to "traditional" values that might have motivated them 20 or 30 years ago. Employees in today's organizations are better educated, more highly skilled, and work with more advanced technology. They have significantly higher expectations, which creates difficult challenges for managers.[3]

This scenario illustrates the effect upon motivation of differences in values between persons of different ages. There are also differences between the attributes of recreation and leisure service agencies and other organizations that affect motivation. With this in mind, the recreation and leisure service manager must ask, How can I ensure the existence of an environment that motivates my employees to perform in a satisfactory manner? Such an environment does not exist without planning, support, and an understanding of the needs and behavior of one's employees. There are a variety of strategies that can be used together to create opportunities for motivation. Motivation should be viewed as a responsibility of all of the members of the organization, since the members have an impact on one another. Although managers often recognize the value and importance of motivation within the organization, they may not organize a systematic approach to achieve it. Thoughtful attention to the theories of motivation, as well as the process of motivation, will make the work of an organization much more effective.

The Motivation Cycle

Humans, whether active in the work environment or not, are affected by needs and drives that produce goal-oriented behavior. This is known as the motivation cycle, common to all organisms. It suggests that, as an organism has a deficiency or need, it acts to alleviate the deficiency. Individuals employed by recreation and leisure service organizations have a variety of needs, some of which can be met by the organization, others of which cannot. To satisfy these needs, an individual will become active and put forth effort. If this activity is structured by the organization in such a way that the goals of the organization are also met, organizational effectiveness will result. In defining the components of the motivation cycle, Luthans provides the following definitions for need, drive and goal.

1. *Need.* The best one word definition of a need is deficiency. In the homeostatic sense, needs are created whenever there is a physiological or psychological imbalance.

2. *Drive.* With a few exceptions, drives or motives (the two terms will be used interchangeably) are set up to alleviate needs. A drive can be

---

3.   R. Wayne Mondy, Robert E. Holmes, and Edwin B. Flippo, *Management: Concepts and Practices* (Boston: Allyn and Bacon, 1980), p. 262.

simply defined as a deficiency with direction. Drives are action oriented and provide an energizing thrust towards goal accomplishment.

3. *Goals.* At the end of the motivation cycle is the motivation goal. The goal in the motivation cycle can be defined as anything that will alleviate or reduce a drive. Thus, attaining a goal will tend to restore psychological and physiological balance and cut off the drive.[4]

There are a variety of needs and motives that can be addressed by the manager in the work environment. McClalland has suggested that humans have three primary motives—the need for achievement, power, and affiliation.[5] The need for achievement can be thought of as the individual's desire to perform competitively in a superior manner. Individuals with a high need for achievement are often more capable of self-direction. The need for *power* can be thought of as the extent to which an individual controls or influences the behavior of others. The use of power in organizations is extremely important. The manager who can influence others to achieve the goals of the organization in such a way that the employee's personal needs are also met is an asset. Another basic need is that of *affiliation.* Individuals tend to have a desire for establishing relationships with others and receiving affection.

Reinforcement

The key to the successful motivation of employees is to provide reinforcement. Most individuals will respond in a favorable way to a manager who offers them support and recognition for their efforts. We often think of reinforcement as giving an individual a pat on the back or providing strokes. Stroking can be done in many different ways, however it should be tailored to each individual's needs.

Recognition of the inherent value or worth of the individual is central to effective motivation. Each person within a recreation and leisure service organization likes to feel that he or she is an important part of that agency's efforts. By reinforcing either the work of individuals or their personal disposition, feelings of self-worth can be enhanced. It is important to recognize that not all jobs have been designed to permit the individual to derive satisfaction from the work itself. Consider the case of a secretary who may do an excellent job, but does not find the work itself challenging. Such a person may be motivated more by reinforcement than by the work itself. By letting that person know that he or she is competent, well liked and appreciated, the manager can increase the probability that the individual will continue to function effectively.

Our knowledge of behavior reinforcement comes from psychological

4.   Fred Luthans, *Organizational Behavior,* 2nd ed. (New York: McGraw-Hill, 1977), p. 313.

5.   D.C. McClalland and David H. Burnham, "Power is the Great Motivator," *Harvard Business Review,* 54 (March–April, 1976):103.

theories relating to instrumental conditioning. Instrumental conditioning requires an active participant, as opposed to classical conditioning, which produces involuntary responses. From instrumental conditioning, researchers have derived principles of learning that have enabled psychologists to develop models for behavior. These models are based on the use of positive or negative reinforcement in order to produce or eliminate given behaviors. For example, if an individual were consistently late to work, one might offer the incentive of additional time off for each week that the individual arrived at work promptly. This is an example of positive reinforcement used to modify the individual's behavior. It is interesting to note that some studies have determined that the threat of discipline (or negative reinforcement) is not viewed as a motivator by employees. Withdrawal of attention or rewards may produce the employee behavior desired; however, it may also be resented and have other negative effects.

It is important to remember that for learned behavior to be effective in terms of the needs of the organization, it must be demonstrated appropriately by the individual. People can learn new types of behavior, but without an opportunity to demonstrate them the process falls short. Thus, the creation of environments that enable employees to demonstrate learned behavior is critical. Another important factor related to the learning process is the fact that reinforcement is most effective when it occurs on an *intermittent* basis. Intermittent does not imply inconsistent reinforcement. If the manager constantly tells an individual that he or she is doing a superior job, the individual begins to question the sincerity of the manager and the reinforcement is ineffective as a motivator. The manager should be selective in providing reinforcement, depending upon the situation and the needs of the individual. The type of reinforcement that is given can also be varied.

VIEWS OF HUMAN NATURE

The way in which human behavior is perceived is very important in the motivating process. If the manager views individuals as being inherently lazy, incompetent, immature, and lacking in self-discipline, this perception will influence his or her treatment of employees. The manager with this perception and managerial leadership style would tend to be discipline- and control-oriented. Further, the manager might believe that the best way to motivate such individuals is through disciplinary measures. However, a manager who views individuals as being capable of being self-disciplined, industrious, and competent might attempt to motivate employees by facilitating this behavior. In the management literature there are two models that have been developed to help managers understand the way that their perceptions of individuals affect their management behavior. These models are McGregor's theory X and theory Y and Argyris's maturity-immaturity continuum.

Theory X and Theory Y

In 1957, McGregor offered his now famous ideas about human nature.[6] He suggested that many of our past conceptions of human nature were inappropriate. McGregor felt that the potential of humans as creative beings was not being fully employed. He felt that under proper conditions, human energy could be employed in a more efficient and effective manner to benefit mankind. Basically, he believed that there were two assumptions that one could make about human behavior. He called these assumptions theory X and theory Y. Conventional organizations, according to Mc-Gregor, were structured on the premise of *theory X* assumptions. These assumptions are as follows:

1. The average person inherently dislikes work and will avoid it if possible.
2. Because of the dislike of work, most people must be coerced, controlled, directed, and threatened with punishment to get them to perform effectively.
3. The average person lacks ambition, avoids responsibility, and seeks security and economic reward above all else.
4. Most people lack creative ability and are resistant to change.
5. Since most people are self-centered, they are not concerned with the goals of the organization.[7]

McGregor felt that the majority of organizations operating today were built on the theory X assumption. Theory X assumptions led to a coercive style of motivation. People were seen as being lazy and uninterested in work. Further, they were viewed as opportunistic—taking advantage of the organization and primarily motivated by financial incentives. These assumptions, if accepted by a manager, led to one of two styles of management. The manager either demonstrated a very hard management style, emphasizing strict discipline and tight control, or was softer, cajoling employees. According to McGregor, practice of theory X management led to undesirable behavior on the part of the employee. Force was met with force. Reacting to the hard management style, employees responded with acts of sabotage and low productivity. The soft theory X approach to management led to milder resentment, characterized by job dissatisfaction and absenteeism.

As an alternative to the control-oriented posture of theory X management, McGregor offered the alternative *theory Y*. The manager accepting the assumptions inherent in this theory views the individual as exercising self-control and self-direction. Theory Y assumptions are as follows:

6. Douglas McGregor, "The Human Side of Enterprise," in *Adventures in Thought and Action* (Proceedings of the Fifth Anniversary Convocation of the School of Industrial Management, Massachusetts Institute of Technology, 1957), pp. 23–30.
7. Douglas McGregor, *The Human Side of Enterprise* (New York: McGraw-Hill, 1970), pp. 33–34.

1. The expenditure of physical and mental effort in work is as natural as play or rest.
2. People will exercise self-direction and self-control in the service of objectives to which they are committed.
3. Commitment to objectives is a function of rewards associated with achievement.
4. The average person learns, under proper conditions, not only to accept but seek responsibility.
5. The capacity to exercise a relatively high degree of imagination, ingenuity and creativity in the solution of organizational problems is widely, not narrowly, distributed in the population.[8]

Theory Y assumptions find the manager having an increased faith and trust in employees and believing that individuals can and will be committed to an organization. Under theory Y assumptions, management practices would change dramatically. Managers would be able to do away with time clocks, establish flexible work schedules, and encourage employees to participate in decisions affecting both the employee and the organization. A key factor in the theory Y management concept is the idea that individuals can exercise self-direction and self-control if they are committed. In recreation and leisure service organizations, for example, individuals tend to be committed to the ideals inherent in the provision of the service. Thus, according to theory Y precepts, they can and will work with other individuals within an organizational structure who are committed to the same ideals.

Interestingly, the Japanese have placed a great deal of importance on the commitment of employees to the organization and vice versa. This is demonstrated, on the organization's part, by lifetime employment of employees. In turn, employees are committed to the organization above and beyond the dedication necessary to receive financial remuneration and complete the basic work tasks assigned. Japanese organizations also demonstrate commitment in their decision-making process. Employees collectively assume the primary responsibility for quality of products and services. This is administered through the organization of peer groups that attempt to comment on ways to increase employee effectiveness and efficiency.

The essence of theory Y management is the belief that employees will go "the extra mile" if they are made to feel that their contributions are worthwhile and meaningful. Sacrifice on the part of employees can occur if rewarded by the organization. The rewards need not necessarily be financial ones, but rather opportunities for recognition, status, growth, and commitment from the organization.

---

8. Douglas McGregor, *The Human Side of Enterprise* (New York: McGraw-Hill, 1970), pp. 33–34.

Maturity-Immaturity Continuum

Argyris's maturity–immaturity continuum provides another model for analyzing the human nature and applying the concepts of the continuum to the management of people in recreation and leisure service organizations.[9] First, Argyris suggests that individuals start out as immature beings and then mature, if given the opportunity. Second, he points out that an immature person will behave passively, whereas a mature individual will behave in an active manner. The immature person is dependent upon others; the mature individual will operate independently. In attempting to understand this component of Argyris's model, it is helpful to consider the growth of a child. Babies are very dependent upon their parents; as children grow older, they become more and more independent. The third component of Argyris's model suggests that immature individuals behave in few ways, and mature individuals are capable of behaving in many different ways. Fourth, the immature person demonstrates erratic, shallow interests, whereas the mature person has deeper interests. Fifth, the time perspective of the individual is also influenced by level of maturity. Immature individuals have a short-term perspective, whereas mature persons have a long-term perspective. Sixth, mature persons according to Argyris, find themselves in superordinate positions, whereas immature persons remain in subordinate roles. Last, Argyris suggests that immature individuals lack self-awareness, whereas mature individuals can exercise self-control and self-awareness.

Managers who view people as being essentially immature, as many managers do, use corresponding managerial leadership style and motivation techniques that tend to be control-oriented. For managers who view individuals as being mature, a more open managerial style is possible. Most organizations, through the application of conventional management practices, keep employees in an immature state. For the purpose of control, they do not want individuals to behave in a mature manner. This is evident in the creation of roles that are narrowly defined, as well as management policies that do not allow for self-control. If employees are denied an opportunity to make decisions, to develop their work agenda, or to have a say in the establishment of organizational policy, they will remain in a dependent, subordinate position.

It is essential in recreation and leisure service organizations, because of the type of work that is done, to provide for the maturing of employees. If this is not done, there may be conflict within the organization between managers and their subordinates. Individuals who are highly educated and ideologically committed may become frustrated and anxious if kept in a highly dependent state. As previously indicated, the need for recreation and leisure service professionals to operate in an autonomous, independent fashion is essential. Only when managers recognize that the organization must be structured to promote growth and independence will

---

9.   Chris Argyris, *Personality and Organization* (New York: Harper and Brothers, 1957), p. 50.

individuals prosper. Since employees may be at different levels of maturity, a variety of strategies should be employed to enable all employees to grow.

MOTIVATION THEORIES

There are a number of theories of motivation that can be useful to the recreation and leisure service manager. These can be divided into two categories: content and process theories of motivation. *Content theories* of motivation focus on the elements within the work environment that are motivating to employees. Maslow's theory of motivation and Herzberg's motivation-hygiene theory are two content theories that are concerned with employee needs that can be met within the work environment. We will discuss these two content theories, as well as two *process theories* of motivation: Vroom's expectancy theory and the Porter and Lawler theory of motivation. Process theories center on the variables that exist in the motivation process itself.

Maslow's Theory of Motivation

In 1943, in an article appearing in *Psychological Review,* Maslow presented his theory of human motivation.[10] His theory suggested that humans have a basic set of needs. Maslow categorized these as physiological needs and needs for safety, love, esteem, and self-actualization. Maslow's paradigm has served as a basis for other motivation theories and is often referred to, not only by management theorists, but also by those in the recreation and leisure service professions.

Physiological needs are at the base of Maslow's paradigm. The basic need that the body has to maintain a level of homeostasis is one type of physiological need; that is, a need to gain food in order to function efficiently. Maslow also suggested that physiological needs include other factors, such as sexual desire, and various sensory feelings such as tasting, touching, and stroking. The second level of needs, according to Maslow, are those that can be categorized as relating to one's *safety.* Environments that provide a predictable level of safety and are nonthreatening to the individual are seen as desirable. When an individual achieves a state of stability, free from danger, both physical and social, this need has been met. The next type of need described by Maslow is the desire for *love and affection,* as well as the need to be a part of a group or organization. People not only have a need to be liked by others but also a need to feel that they are a part of a group. The need for *self-respect* or self-esteem is the next level in Maslow's paradigm. This refers to the need that individuals have to

---

10. Abraham H. Maslow, "A Theory of Human Motivation," *Psychological Review,* 50 (1943): 370–96.

gain the respect or recognition of others. It also relates to the ability of the individual to develop a sense of self-confidence. Persons who do not have self-respect are said to lack a sense of personal adequacy. The last type of need described in Maslow's hierarchy is the need for *self-actualization*. This need is highly individualized. It refers to an individual's desire for self-fulfillment and can be demonstrated in creative ways. The painter, the performing artist, and the athlete may find self-actualization through the expression of their talents.

Maslow suggests that these needs are hierarchically arranged. As an individual fulfills one basic need (for example, the need for food) he or she then progresses to the next higher level of need (for example, the desire for safety). Maslow suggests that human behavior will be monopolized by the drive to fulfill the need that is currently dominant. However, needs that have been fulfilled are often forgotten or denied, according to Maslow.

Although Maslow's theory has been widely read and interpreted and applied by management theorists in the recreation and leisure service professions, there is little evidence to support Maslow's theory. The notion that physiological needs will always predominate over others may be a fallacy. For example, a struggling artist may put the need for self-actualization above all other needs, including the need for safety, love, and food. In the management area, the major contribution of Maslow's hierarchical concept of needs is that it alerts the manager to the fact that individuals have many and diverse needs. A number of management theorists have linked Maslow's hierarchy to the work environment. They have suggested, for example, that one's need for self-respect is encouraged through titles and other status symbols. Security needs are available in the form of workman's compensation, sick leave, and guaranteed pay increases. The needs for love and affection and belonging to a group are satisfied through membership in both the formal and informal components of an organization.

Herzberg's Motivation-Hygiene Theory

One of the more widely cited motivation theories is Herzberg's motivation-hygiene theory.[11] Building on Maslow's hierarchy of needs, Herzberg suggested that Maslow's needs could be categorized into two areas: hygienes and motivators. *Hygiene factors* refer to such things as salary, supervision, company policy, interpersonal relations, and working conditions. According to Herzberg, these factors can be related to Maslow's lower-order needs. *Motivators* focus on the higher-order needs in Maslow's hierarchy and refer to the ability of an individual to have a sense of achievement, recognition, responsibility, and advancement. Herzberg also

---

11. Frederick Herzberg, Bernard Mausner, and Barbara Bloch Snyderman, *The Motivation to Work* (New York: John Wiley and Sons, 1959), p. 141.

maintained that an individual's work, in and of itself, could be a strong motivating force.

Herzberg suggested that an individual was not necessarily motivated by the provision of such factors as an adequate wage, fringe benefits, and good supervision. He felt that the presence of these hygiene factors did not necessarily satisfy an individual. The provision of these types of rewards prevented job dissatisfaction, without necessarily promoting job satisfaction. Herzberg contended that most managers concentrate primarily on hygienic factors and therefore do not actually motivate individuals. Motivators, on the other hand, when present in the work environment, do provide job satisfaction. These motivators are related to Maslow's higher-order needs. According to Herzberg's theory, individuals are motivated when they have an opportunity for challenge in their work environment. This means that the manager may provide for the individual's basic needs but unless a job is challenging and offers opportunities for recognition, achievement, and growth, an individual will not be motivated.

Wasiniak recently reported an interesting study tied to Herzberg's motivation-hygiene theory. Identifying a set of 20 statements that reflect the degree of motivation of an individual, as presented in Table 7.1, Wasiniak was interested in determining what motivates nonsupervisory employees. Further, he was interested in determining whether supervisors held views concerning motivation that were similar to those of their subordinates. Conducted among human service organization professionals (Social Security Administration employees) the study found that 96 percent of those surveyed were motivated by "the feeling of achievement you get from doing challenging work well." The study also found that 94 percent of those surveyed were motivated by "one's inner need to always try to do a good job." These statements fall within the category of motivators. On the other hand, items dealing with interpersonal relationships ("friendships," "being the leader of a work group") were rated extremely low. These statements fall within the category of hygienes.

There were differences in the perceptions of supervisors as to what motivated their employees. Wasiniak has written:

First line supervisors, as a group, do not have a good understanding of the factors that motivate their employees; they tend to underrate the achievement motive and overrate the recognition motive. They also tend to drastically underrate their employee's desires to help the agency reach its goals.

Supervisors seem to see employees as more externally motivated than they really are, heavily overrating the power of such motivators as peer recognition, the annual performance appraisal, work group membership, and disciplinary action.[12]

This is an interesting dilemma. Often the perception that a manager or supervisor has of an employee's needs is contrary to the employee's

---

12.   Richard E. Wasiniak, "What Really Motivates Workers?" *Management*, (Summer, 1980): p. 16.

TABLE 7.1   What Motivates Human Service Professionals?

Motivators	Employees' Rating		Supervisors' Rating		Contrast
	Rank	Percent Selecting	Rank	Percent Selecting	Percentage Difference
1. The ratings on your next performance appraisal	9	49	9	59	+10
2. Your possibility of an award	16	32	14	37	+5
3. Your personal work-related goals	4	83	5	72	−11
4. Good physical working conditions	15	34	15	33	−1
5. Your feelings of loyalty and friendship for your supervisor	18	18	16	31	+13
6. Your doing interesting work	5	78	8	60	−18
7. The possibility of higher salary	8	51	13	41	−10
8. Your not wanting to let the group down	13	38	10	53	+15
9. Recognition by your peers	12	40	2	79	+39
10. The possibility of promotion	6	71	4	73	+2
11. Feelings of achievement from doing challenging work well	1	96	6	69	−27
12. The possibility of disciplinary action by your supervisor	20	3	17	23	+20
13. Being part of a team	16	32	11	52	+20
14. Your inner need to always try to do a good job	2	94	7	68	−26
15. Strong job security	14	36	18	20	−15
16. Appreciation and recognition from your supervisor	10	42	2	79	+37
17. Your doing work you feel is important	3	88	1	81	−7
18. Your desire to help the agency attain its goals	7	57	20	7	−50
19. The possibility of increased freedom on the job	11	41	12	48	+7
20. Being appointed the leader of a work group	19	10	19	11	+1

Adapted from Richard E. Wasiniak, "What Really Motivates Workers?" *Management*, (Summer, 1980): p. 17

perceptions of his or her own needs. This lack of congruence in perceptions may result in disharmony within the organization. For example, the manager may perceive him- or herself as being employee centered, whereas the employee may perceive the manager as showing a lack of understanding. This points up the need for the recreation and leisure service manager to strive to accurately determine what motivates an employee.

Herzberg's motivation-hygiene theory has been criticized by some. The basic concerns that have been expressed have focused on the research methodology used by Herzberg in testing his theory. The criticism has centered on the fact that the employment of a different research methodology produced results that varied from those produced by Herzberg's primary method of research, the critical incident. The major difference in results is that subsequent studies found no distinctions between those statements that produce job satisfaction and those that are seen as leading to job dissatisfaction.[13]

Vroom's Expectancy Theory of Motivation

Vroom's model of motivation was developed after close analysis of the Maslow and Herzberg theories of motivation. Vroom was critical of Herzberg's model because he felt that the content of a job might have more to do with job satisfaction, and hence motivation, than Herzberg had stated. Vroom, in turn, developed his own model for work motivation. His model was based upon research that he had conducted relative to worker performance and satisfaction.[14]

The Vroom model of motivation is based on the concepts of valence, expectancy, and the potential outcomes to be derived from the interaction of the first two factors. *Valence* can be defined as the value that an individual places on a particular outcome. *Expectance* is an individual's perception of the probability that a desired outcome will occur. The interaction of expectancy and valence will produce an individual's level of motivation. Both variables must be present in order to ensure a high level of motivation. High expectancy or high valence by themselves do not produce a high level of motivation. For example, if a person perceives that there is little chance (expectancy) for promotion, even though that individual places a high value (valence) on the status derived from the occupation of a high-level position, that individual would not be motivated to attain the position.

Unlike Herzberg's model of motivation, Vroom's theory suggests that individuals can be motivated by different rewards. For example, an individual may place a high value on time, creativity, or financial gain. In Herzberg's theory, financial gains, as well as the fringe benefit of vacation time, would be viewed as hygienes—alleviating job dissatisfaction but not necessarily leading to job satisfaction. In Vroom's theory, if the value associated with the reward is high and the probability that the person can achieve it is also high, job satisfaction is likely, hence the individual will be motivated.

13. Fred Luthans, *Organizational Behavior*, 2nd ed. (New York: McGraw-Hill, 1977), p. 413.
14. Victor Vroom, *Work and Motivation* (New York: John Wiley and Sons, 1964), p. 183.

This means that a person can be highly motivated and find job satisfaction in a job associated with financial gain. Or, an individual might desire to maintain job security at the sacrifice of job promotion.

Before using Vroom's theory of motivation the manager should be aware of the needs of each employee. Each individual's needs and values will affect job performance. Not everyone will strive for self-actualization; each will individually define what constitutes a fulfilling work situation. The manager should help employees to understand the ways in which the recreation and leisure service organization can help them meet their needs. In one case this may involve removing obstacles within the organization that might prevent the successful achievement of desired rewards. In another situation this might involve assisting the employee in a reorientation of goals to correspond with existing organizational resources. In addition, it is important that the manager clearly communicate the relationship between the reward structure and the performance expected of the individual.

Porter and Lawler Model of Motivation

The Porter-Lawler model of motivation is a refinement and extension of Vroom's expectancy theory of motivation.[15] Basically, it suggests that there is a complex relationship between motivation, performance, and satisfaction. In addressing this relationship, Porter and Lawler have developed a conceptual model that identifies six variables that affect motivation and influence employee job satisfaction. These six variables are: the individual's effort, performance, value of rewards, probability of rewards, abilities, and role perceptions.

Effort can be thought of as the amount of energy that an individual puts forth in completing a particular assignment. In the model, effort is not viewed as being similar to performance or accomplishment. According to Porter and Lawler, two variables affect the amount of energy that an individual puts forth: the value of the reward and the probability of the reward. The *value of the reward* is subject to individual interpretation. To one person, working with friends may be more desirable than a promotion. The reverse may be the case for another person. The *probability* of an individual attaining a reward is related to perception of the availability of the reward. The interaction of these two variables culminates in the individual's effort. If a person places a high value on friendship as a reward, and also perceives that he or she can attain friendship, then he or she will put forth a great deal of effort to achieve it.

Porter and Lawler point out that people's values change, and these changes in values will affect the effort put forth. During a person's work lifetime, his or her value structure can change dramatically. A person's

15. Lyman W. Porter and Edward E. Lawler, *Managerial Attitudes and Performance* (Homewood, Illinois: Richard D. Irwin, Inc., 1968), p. 165.

financial needs, for example, might change, affecting what is valued in terms of rewards (perhaps money is valued, instead of free time or friendship). As mentioned, the effort a person puts forth is not necessarily synonymous with performance, however.

The *performance* of an individual is usually measured in terms of the ability of the individual to efficiently and effectively complete a given task. Thus, individuals can put forth a great deal of effort, but not necessarily perform successfully if their actions are not consistent with the goals of the organization. Performance, like effort, is affected by two variables. The first of these variables is the *abilities and traits* of the individual. Individuals' skills and knowledge will affect their ability to perform successfully. There are many people who have good intentions and put forth an honest day's effort, but because they lack the capabilities necessary to perform the job effectively, their performance is not satisfactory. The second variable is that of *role perceptions*. This variable can be thought of as the view that one has of the job. An individual's perception of what is to be done can vary dramatically from person to person. Employees whose role perceptions are congruent with the perceptions of the organization will put forth effort that will be viewed as effective performance.

The Porter and Lawler model also deals with the relationship of job satisfaction to effort and performance. As the reader will recall, the Maslow, Herzberg, and Vroom models of motivation did not deal with the relationship of job satisfaction to performance. Although the Herzberg model discusses job satisfaction, there is little empirical evidence to support the notion that certain job variables lead to job satisfaction, and that other job variables lead to job dissatisfaction. According to Porter and Lawler, satisfaction is directly related to the attainment of rewards. Simply stated, if the rewards that an individual receives meet or exceed his or her expectations, job satisfaction occurs.

ORGANIZATIONAL CLIMATE

It is important to remember that the climate existing within an organization greatly influences motivation, performance, and job satisfaction. Because recreation and leisure service organizations are made up of many different personalities with different needs, aspirations, and expectations, no two organizational climates will be similar. The blending of these personalities in such a way that a positive, supportive environment is created is a key task in the management process. The organizational climate of an agency can be thought of as its psychological disposition. No two agencies will have the same climates, even though their mission and resources are similar.[16] Some of the variables that can affect the organizational climate are as follows:

---

16. Mondy et al., *Management: Concepts and Practices* (Boston: Allyn and Bacon, 1980), p. 262.

Managerial leadership style. Research suggests that managerial leadership style will affect the climate of an organization. Such factors as the manager's concern for people or concern for increasing output will influence the environment. The example set by the manager while performing his or her job will have an affect on the climate as well. Finally, the work atmosphere can be affected by the degree of aloofness or closeness that a manager projects.

Work groups. In most organizations, individuals work as members of a group. The extent to which a group is committed to the mission of the organization and the tasks that it has been assigned will influence the organizational climate. The morale that exists within work groups will also affect the work environment. Work groups that are characterized by supportive interpersonal relationships will have a positive effect on the organizational climate. The way in which work groups perceive their assigned tasks, as worthwhile or as busy work, will also affect the atmosphere of the organization.

Organizational characteristics. The size and complexity of the organization will affect organizational climate. Smaller organizations will have a more intimate atmosphere than larger organizations. Complex organizations tend to have more task differentiation and specialization than smaller organizations. Some organizations codify their policies and procedures and therefore are seen as being more formal and less flexible than smaller organizations. The type of organizational structure employed can also influence the climate. Certain structures allow more flexibility and freedom, whereas others promote control.

Administrative processes. Four processes directly influence the environment of an organization: rewards, communications, conflict resolution, and propensity for risk taking. Achievement can be promoted by directly linking rewards to performance. Communications systems can be open or closed, thereby promoting different forms of interaction within organizations. Some organizations have a high tolerance for conflict, viewing it as a natural part of the interaction within organizations. Other organizations attempt to avoid conflict, viewing it as a negative influence within the organization. Also, some organizations have a high propensity for risk taking, creating an atmosphere of free-wheeling entrepreneurship, and other oganizations are more sedate.

Building a Positive, Supportive Environment

A positive, supportive work environment is characterized by openness, commitment to employee development, good interpersonal relationships, and consideration for each individual as a uniquely contributing member of the organization. Environments that do not have these characteristics are viewed as being closed and potentially threatening to employees. Positive, supportive environments are ones in which a common commitment to both the needs of the individual and the goals of the organization are forged. A spirit of trust, compromise, and cooperation exists between management and workers in supportive organizations. There are numerous variables that can influence the creation of a supportive environment. These variables range from the way in which a job is structured, to the types of interpersonal relationships that exist within the organization, to the types of recognition that are available to the employee. These variables are discussed in detail below:

Trust.   An essential element in the creation of a positive, supportive environment is trust. Trust is developed when decisions are perceived as being in the interest of all individuals within the organization. Further, trust is present when individuals have confidence in each other's abilities to perform tasks effectively and efficiently.

Freedom.   In recreation and leisure service organizations, some freedom to exercise professional judgement is necessary in order to ensure that the organization functions effectively. The recreation and leisure service manager should provide a general framework within which specific job details are left to the discretion of the individual. There is nothing more frustrating than to have someone looking over your shoulder, constantly dictating the work agenda.

Respect for the style of others.   In the creation of a positive work environment, it is important to remember that individuals will approach the work environment in different ways, employing different strategies to accomplish their work. Different personalities and styles can be threatening. An attempt should be made, however, to view the content of decisions objectively. Many organizational problems are associated with the inability of individuals to cope successfully with style differences. Often a manager will be criticized for specific actions when, in fact, the problem can be traced to a lack of acceptance of the manager's style of operation. When there is disagreement between individuals, it should be determined whether it is a result of different styles.

Commitment to similar goals.   The common commitment of individuals to the collective goals of the organization is essential in the establishment of a positive, supportive work environment. If individuals within the organization are moving in separate directions without being united in a common goal, creation of a positive work environment is difficult. Commitment to common organizational goals can be encouraged by discussing the various perceptions that employees have of the mission of the agency and the steps that the agency is taking, or should take, to fulfill its mission.

Commitment to high output goals.   Employees perform according to the expectations of the organization. When expectation levels are high, performance is also high. Most employees prefer to work in a challenging and stimulating work environment. Environments that challenge individuals to give their best promote improved worker performance and higher job satisfaction.

Open communication.   Open and honest communication between individuals is essential in the creation of a positive work environment. Hidden agendas, talking behind people's backs, double talk, and other negative forms of communication undermine the work of the organization. When people are open and honest with one another, the communication process is enhanced and the trust level within the organization is increased.

Sharing information.   Closely related to open communication is the willingness to share information. People have a desire to be informed. Feelings of insecurity, of being left out, and of being unimportant are often associated with negative environments that do not share information. Much of the information that is withheld from people in organizations could easily and justifiably be shared, thus contributing to a better work environment.

Group decision making.   Today, individuals expect to be involved in decisions that affect their lives. A higher degree of commitment can be achieved when the group decision-making process is employed. Although group decision making may take more time, it builds a stronger commitment to the course of action taken by aligning individuals behind similar goals. The Japanese employ this technique extensively in their organizations. They use the term *nemawashi,* which means "root binding."

Interpersonal relationships.   A major reason that people work is to have an opportunity to interact with others. The development of friendships within work environments is a key motivator. Although the maxim that you don't have to like your colleagues in order to work with them successfully is true, it is much easier to work with people that you like.

Team building.   Organizations that make a conscious effort to promote staff unity have more productive work environments. From a strategic standpoint, team building is the process whereby trust, respect, open communication, freedom, goal congruence, and problem solving takes place. Team building can occur in a formal way, focusing on job-related activities, or can be done more informally in a social setting.

Task delineation.   Similar to goal congruence, task delineation suggests that there is a need for individuals to clearly understand what is to be done and have available the means to achieve it. Frustration often occurs when individuals do not understand their jobs or do not have the resources available to complete them. It is the role of the manager to help employees understand their jobs and to remove any barriers that might prevent employees from completing their tasks (by acquiring resources or mediating conflicts, for example).

Opportunities for growth.   Individuals may become excited and enthusiastic about their work environments when actively engaged in the learning process. Employees who are stimulated to grow, as Argyris notes, are maturing. As a result of this maturation process, individuals are better equipped to communicate effectively, engage in positive interpersonal relationships, and understand the goals of the organization and the way in which their jobs relate to these goals.

Work environment.   Although peripheral, the physical environment within the organization can have an effect upon employees. A clean, safe work setting is necessary for a supportive work environment. An unsafe, unclean work environment may be depressing and may create an anxious feeling on the part of the employees.

Recognition.   Employees should receive recognition for their contributions to the organization. Further, each individual's need for self-esteem should be recognized. These two factors are tied together by the fact that employees' self-esteem is enhanced when they feel that they are contributing to the goals of the organization. Recognition comes in many forms, from pay increases to verbal support. All employees, both superiors and subordinates, need recognition. It is important to recognize that the acknowledgement that is given the superior by the subordinate is as important as the recognition given the subordinate by the superior.

Mental attitude.   Individuals can approach life and work in a predominantly positive or negative way. The cultivation and reinforcement of positive mental attitudes is central to the creation of a supportive work environment. Constant complaining, whining, and expressions of inability are detrimental to the work of the organization and reflect a need deficiency within an individual. It is exciting to be a part of an organization in which employees are enthusiastic about their work and work associations.

Active support.   Closely related to recognition is the idea of giving peers active support. Providing active support implies that individuals within the work environment are understanding of the viewpoint, concerns, and needs of others within the organization. Active support also implies giving of one's self to other individuals in order to help them improve their personal performance.

Although this list of factors influencing the work environment is extensive, each of these variables can and should be addressed by managers and subordinates. These variables are interrelated. The more clearly employees understand their jobs, the greater is the probability that they will be recognized for achievement. Group decision making promotes open communication, helps build interpersonal relationships, helps build trust, and produces common commitment to the goals of the organization. To facilitate organizational growth and to build a supportive work environment, each one of these variables could be isolated and discussed at staff meetings. For example, a manager might want to discuss ways in which the organization provides, or could provide, opportunities for personal and professional growth. From this could come a strategy for the organization's training and development.

Participatory Management

Participatory management is an overall management strategy that can be used to create a supportive organizational climate. This management strategy is built on the idea that greater organizational commitment is developed when individuals have a part in decision-making processes that affect them. Participatory management allows individuals to be involved in the establishment of organizational goals, as well as to share the responsibility associated with the achievement of these goals. Essentially, the manager attempts to build a strong mental and emotional commitment to the organization.

Participation in management decisions as a strategy can be employed both formally and informally. There are a number of variables that determine the type and amount of participation that should occur within an organization. The first of these is the type of decision to be made. Decisions regarding routine matters usually do not involve participatory activities. On the other hand, decisions that are more unusual, requiring either commitment on the part of employees or the formulation of novel solutions, will call for participatory involvement. The second variable is the amount of time available to make a decision. In an emergency situation, participatory management may not be effective. Participatory decision making may be best used when making decisions concerning long-term goals. The third variable deals with the costs associated with participatory decision making. The point at which the cost of participation, in terms of work hours and resources, exceeds the benefits should be determined.

Implementing participatory management. In order to implement a program of participatory management, managers and their subordinates must be trained to work effectively within this type of management process. Too often managers assume that an individual will be able to function effectively in a decision-making role, without previous experience. This may not be the case. Efforts must be undertaken to train individuals in group processes, decision-making techniques, and role playing. Another concern regarding participatory decision making is the fact that channels through which continuous involvement can occur are not always clearly identified. Recreation and leisure service agencies often start participatory decision-making programs, but are not fully committed to the concept over a long period of time. As a result, employees become frustrated and confused, since they may lack understanding as to when their input is appropriate and when it is not.

Pseudoparticipation is also a concern when an organization attempts to establish a participatory decision-making program. Programs may be set up that do not genuinely solicit participation from employees, being established to gain employee commitment by pretending to engage in participatory decision making. In this case, management may try to placate employees or use the forum as a vehicle to persuade employees to support management's viewpoint. Also, there is a tendency for management to gather individuals together ostensibly for the purpose of participatory decision making, but in actuality to maintain discussion until the management's point of view is suggested and endorsed.

Advantages and disadvantages of participatory management.   There are a number of advantages and disadvantages to participatory management. Management theorists would suggest that the advantages outweigh the disadvantages. Some of the advantages are detailed below:

1. Employees develop a sense of involvement that results in greater intellectual and emotional commitment.

2. The quality of the decisions that are made is improved. Synergistic decision making in situations where little is known about the problem has proven to be more effective.

3. Change can be introduced in such a way that individuals who participate in decision making are not threatened by it.

4. The organization can draw on its total resources, while at the same time improving employee morale and allowing individuals to make meaningful contributions to the agency.

5. It increases the cooperation that exists between managers and their subordinates. It establishes a formal process of negotiations.

Participatory management has proved to reduce turnover, absenteeism, and tardiness, as well as the grievances that occur between management and subordinates. Further, participatory management has been linked to the improvement of production techniques, thereby increasing organizational efficiency. Some of the disadvantages of participatory management are as follows:

1. The participatory decision-making process is time consuming.

2. Participatory management is not cost effective in all situations.

3. It is easy for pseudoparticipation to occur, thereby creating a sense of false involvement.

4. Employees may come with ideas and support decisions that are untenable, creating an awkward situation for managers.

All in all, participatory management appears to be an effective technique for use in decision making in recreation and leisure service organizations. A balance must be struck, however, between the cost and potential benefits of such a course of action. Further, it must be viewed as a long-term, ongoing process that may involve the establishment of mechanisms (group processes and decision-making techniques) to facilitate it, as well as the training of individuals to use these mechanisms.

SUMMARY

Motivation is the process whereby individuals are stimulated to take action in order to fulfill their needs. The role of the recreation and leisure service manager in this process is to create an environment wherein the individual is motivated. Removing barriers, establishing reward systems, and using methods of recognition are all options that the manager might use to assist individuals in meeting their needs. There are a number of factors that motivate individuals, such as recognition, interpersonal relationships, the work itself, and opportunities for growth.

There are two basic types of motivation theories: content and process. The two predominant content theories are Maslow's theory of motivation and Herzberg's motivation-hygiene theory. Maslow's theory suggests that people's needs are hierarchically ordered in terms of psychological needs, safety needs, love and affection needs, self-esteem needs, and need for self-actualization. Maslow believes that, as needs are met at one level, one moves to the next level of need. Herzberg suggests that people's needs can be divided into two categories: hygienes and motivators. The presence of hygienes will prevent job dissatisfaction, but does not provide job satisfaction. Two process theories have also been presented. Vroom's expectancy theory suggests that motivation is dependent upon the individual's perception of the probability that an outcome will occur (expectancy) and the value associated with the outcome (valence). Porter and Lawler's model of motivation suggests that effort is not necessarily associated with performance. A person may put forth a great deal of effort, but, because of a lack of appropriate skills or knowledge, may not perform effectively.

The creation of a positive, supportive organizational climate is an essential component in the motivation process. There are numerous variables that must be addressed by the recreation and leisure service manager in order to produce such a climate. These variables concern interpersonal relationships, freedom, trust, goal congruence, and group decision making. One of the techniques that can be used to assist in the creation of a positive organizational climate is that of participatory decision making. This technique can be useful in building a strong emotional and mental commitment to an organization.

STUDY QUESTIONS

1. Define work. What variables influence the extent to which a person is motivated in the work environment?

2. Identify and discuss six factors that motivate individuals to work. How can the manager use these to motivate individuals?

3. Define motivation. What is meant by a motivating environment?

4. Discuss how changes in employee attitudes have influenced the motivation process over the last twenty years.

5. How can the manager's view of human nature influence the strategies used in the process of creating a motivating environment?

6. From your own perceptions and experience, how can the work of an individual be reinforced?

7. Compare and contrast content theories of motivation with process theories.

8. What is meant by a positive, supportive work environment? Identify and discuss the variables that may affect this type of environment.

9. What is participatory management? What are the advantages and disadvantages of this management technique?

10. Why is motivation so important in the management of people?

CASE STUDY 10

Let's Get Motivated

It is late one afternoon and Chuck Christopher and Lucy Brown have been talking about their work situation. Lucy is relating to Chuck some problems she is having with several employees. "You know Chuck, I have a number of employees who are not performing very effectively. They don't seem to care about doing their jobs well." Chuck replies, "I have always felt that the best way to get employees to do what I want them to do is to take direct action. In other words, I'd give them a kick in the pants. I feel that unless you let people know exactly what they are supposed to do, how to do it and the consequences if they don't do it, they won't perform effectively. Further, I believe that you have to watch people carefully, I mean, supervise people, to make sure that they get the job done." "Well Chuck," Lucy responds, "I've tried that, and it doesn't work."

Just as Lucy and Chuck are talking, Bud Smith happens to walk by and hear their conversation. He says "I don't know if I agree with either one of you. I don't think you have to kick people to make them work; but, rather, I think that you have to entice them to work hard by promising them promotions and raises if they do a good job. In other words, you have to tell them that if they'll play ball with you, you will take care of them. You can't threaten people and expect them to want to work. I think you have to sort of make them like to work by promising them material rewards."

This conversation bothered both Chuck and Lucy. They decide to make an appointment later in the week with George Branch to discuss their concerns. After relating their concerns to George, they ask George his opinion. He says "Well, you're asking an important question: How do I get my employees to do what I want them to do? How do I motivate them? This is a very difficult question to answer, but it is my opinion that people are not motivated primarily by the use of threats or promises of rewards. I feel that people are best motivated when they can control their work environments, have a sense of achievement, and opportunities for growth and recognition." George asks Lucy and Chuck to think back to work experiences that they have had in the past and:

1. List ten factors that contributed to a work situation in which they were highly motivated and performed very effectively.
2. List ten factors that existed in a situation in which they performed very poorly and were not highly motivated.

Chuck and Lucy think for a minute. Lucy says, "Well, I think that situations in which I have had responsibility and control of my work **were** ones that I liked the best and ones in which I was the most productive. But, I also like the jobs that paid a lot of money! Chuck responds by saying, "Well, I don't really know how to answer these questions. But let me think about it for a few days." Lucy then joins in and says, "Yes, let me think about it too for a few more days."

QUESTIONS

1. How would you respond to George Branch's two questions: What are ten factors that contributed to a work situation in which you were highly motivated and performed very effectively: What are ten factors that existed in a work situation in which you performed very poorly and were not highly motivated?

2. What kind of strategy do you feel would be most effective in motivating employees? Why?

3. What is the purpose of providing a motivating environment? What happens when the environment is not a motivating one?

4. Is motivation a two-way process? In other words, can employees actively participate in the motivation process, or even motivate themselves? Or, is it solely up to the employee's superior to provide the motivating environment?

Financial Management   8

As expenditures for such items as personnel, heat, light, transportation and equipment grow, as interest rates and inflation continue to rise and the demand for financial accountability increases, efficient management of financial resources becomes extremely important. The managers of recreation and leisure service organizations should not only be proficient in planning, organizing, and working with human resources, but should be capable of good financial management.

Financial management may be described as "the administration, custody, protection, and control of all revenues received by the leisure service system from all sources as well as the proper expenditure of funds for approved purposes."[1] We often equate the term "financial management" with budgeting. Therefore, it would be appropriate to begin a discussion on financial management with a discussion of budgeting. All

---

1. Jesse A. Reynolds and Marion N. Hormachea, *Public Recreation Administration* (Englewood Cliffs, New Jersey: Prentice-Hall, 1976), p. 248.

managers, regardless of their level within the organization and the type of organization in which they work, will have responsibilities for financial planning and budgeting.

BUDGETING AND RESOURCE MANAGEMENT

When we think of budgeting, we usually think of numbers. However, it is important to recognize that budgeting, whether in the public or private sector, is a process of translating individual and collective choices into numbers. A budget reflects the needs and interests of the individuals served by the recreation and leisure service organization. The private, profit-oriented organization responds to need by acquiring and transforming resources into products and services. The budget of a profit-oriented organization is a reflection of its desire to create products and services that meet needs in such a way that revenues will be greater than expenditures. In the public sector, individuals exchange taxes for programs and services. Although the resource allocation process is political, rather than market oriented, resources are still acquired and transformed into services that meet consumer needs.

The Budget as a Planning Tool

A budget is a proposed program of action for an organization that is expressed in financial terms. A budget can be considered as a financial expression of the services that an organization offers over a specific time period. The actual preparation of a recreation and leisure service budget should occur during and after, not before, program planning. It is only after the program objectives have been set that the manager can start to estimate costs of providing services. Though this sequence appears obvious, it is not always the procedure followed in budgeting. It is common for budgets to be prepared on a purely incremental basis, by taking the current year's expenditures and simply adding a predetermined amount (perhaps 12 percent) to allow for inflation and to estimate anticipated expenditures for the next fiscal year. This is not good budgeting practice. Budgets should be considered as plans detailing the costs involved in the provision of needed services over a specific time period to achieve organizational goals. Budgeting is that part of the total planning process that deals specifically with revenues and expenditures and focuses on the costs involved in providing services. It involves the selection of ends and the selection of means to reach those ends. Although the budget has a number of applications in the overall management of a recreation and leisure service agency, its primary use is as a planning tool. A well-planned budget will not only detail the estimated costs involved in providing a service, but will force the manager, during the preparation of the budget, to engage in planning.

The Budget as a Control Technique

The twin sisters of management are planning and control. A good plan, whether it is concerned with financial or other resources, will have a built-in control system. Control, as it relates to a budget, can be thought of as the process by which the manager monitors and, if necessary, corrects the organization's flow of resources to ensure that the objectives of the budget plan are being achieved.

A well-prepared budget facilitates an organization's control over all facets of the organization. Since a budget outlines the anticipated revenues and expenditures for each department over a specific period of time, it provides a series of check points against which accomplishments can be measured and evaluated. A department that is not operating as anticipated can be detected quickly by comparing its actual revenues and expenses with the financial plan. Deviations from budget expectations will alert managers to take appropriate remedial action.

It should be noted that deviations that occur in budgeting can be either positive or negative. Though good budgeting presupposes good forecasting in terms of both revenues and expenditures, sometimes fluctuations occur, owing to unforseen circumstances. For instance, the endorsement of a citywide learn-to-swim campaign by the school board and a special publicity campaign spearheaded by a local service club might result in increased registration. As a result, both revenue and expenses would be increased. In order to ensure the best possible control, the budget should allow for income variations as well as other possible deviations from the plan.

The Budget as an Official Endorsement

In a tax-supported organization, a budget, once approved, becomes a legal sanction for the organization's fiscal operation and for the services outlined. In Canada and the United States, provincial and state legislation stipulates how fiscal management will be conducted in recreation and leisure service organizations that receive public funds. For both nonprofit and profit-oriented organizations, approval of the budget by a corporate board of directors also gives endorsement to the program plans of the organization.

The Advantages of Budgeting

While the overall advantage of budgeting is the encouragement and enforcement of sound financial planning, there are a number of specific advantages of budgeting that should be mentioned.

1. The budget translates programs and other services into financial terms.
2. The budget provides a mechanism for appraising staff, officials, and other interested parties of the financial operations of the organization.

3. Budgeting provides a means for systematically identifying and evaluating procedures, programs, and other services.
4. The budget provides a record of the financial transactions that take place within the organization itself and with other individuals and organizations.

THE BUDGET PROCESS

The preparation of a budget does not have to be mysterious or overly complex. Budgeting, like planning, is simply a matter of defining where you want to go, how you wish to get there, and who will do the work involved, then placing numerical values on the plan. Generally, the budgeting process can be divided into four stages: development, structure, presentation and approval, and implementation. The budgeting process should be continual; at any point in the entire year, one or more of the stages should be in process. Following is a detailed discussion of each of these stages.

Development

Budget development is a continuous process whereby planning for the following fiscal years begins well in advance of them. If a budget is going to adequately reflect an organization's plans for the future, then as much careful thought and effort must go into budget development as would go into any other type of planning. Almost all recreation and leisure service organizations have one or more individuals whose primary responsibility is budget development, although all personnel will share some of this responsibility.

In most organizations, the procedures involved in developing the annual budget are written down. Such instructions give timetables, classifications, and other explanations that help managers prepare their own sections of the overall organizational budget and help ensure continuity between departments. Thus, one of the first tasks of any recreation and leisure service manager should be to become thoroughly acquainted with the budget manual for the organization.

Budget development should be looked upon as a twelve-month task. Staff meetings and budget meetings with boards, city councils, and heads of departments should be scheduled on an ongoing basis throughout the year. Items should not be included in a budget simply because they were included in previous years. Each item should be justified as though it were in the budget for the first time. If requests for budget funds are weak, without clarity and promise of being productive, then they should be excluded. The budget should be as clear and concise a document as possible. Legislators, city councilmen, and budget officials in voluntary agencies, if they are proficient in their roles, will develop a system of examination to spot inflated or weak budgets.

Once the budget has been prepared and approved, it should be distributed to all units. It should be monitored throughout the year for control purposes and for revision where necessary. Finally, it is worth mentioning again that the manager who follows planning procedures when developing the budget will usually end up with a budget that has the support of staff and that reflects organizational objectives.

Budget Structure

The budget structure will vary according to the type of budget procedure under which an organization operates. The budget structure usually consists of the following components: budget message, budget summary, budget narrative, and budget detail. The *budget message* is a section of the written document (budget) presented to the individual or group with the authority to approve or disapprove the request. The message describes the budget in terms of the major points, changes, new programs, or new items that have been added from the previous year. The *budget narrative* gives a synopsis of what is included in the budget, along with the program objectives to be accomplished if the requested funds are allocated. Graphs and figures may be incorporated within the budget design to help the reader understand what is being proposed. The *budget detail* sets forth the individual items within the budget and the amount to be spent on each. In some budgets, the detail is very specific, delineating the exact number of paper clips to be purchased, for example. The *budget summary* offers an overview of the major accounts within the budget. Less specific information is provided in this section of the document. Projected expenditures in major account areas, rather than the specific information included in the budget detail or budget narrative, is included.

A section that is sometimes included in the budget format is a priority cut list. This section is optional and, if included, would usually be inserted directly after the budget message. The priority cut list details those items not included in the budget that could contribute greatly to fulfilling the organization's objectives. These items would be presented in the order that they should be considered if further financial resources could be made available.

Budget Presentation and Approval

Once the budget design has been refined to the satisfaction of the designated recreation and leisure service officials, the budget presentation is prepared. Although the presentation is only a component of the total budgetary process, it is a key component that offers a means to summarize the budget and highlight new programs or changes, as well as a means to answer any questions of the governing board. The manager might use graphic as well as verbal methods to present the budget. The purpose is to communicate in such a way that the objectives of the program are understood and endorsed by those reviewing the budget. The focus of the presentation should be on the benefits derived from programs, as well as their costs. Preparation and knowledge of detail is the key to a successful presentation.

More important to budget approval than the actual budget presentation itself is the reputation that the organization has developed. Appropriations should be based on the quality of services offered during the year, rather than solely on the type of presentation the organization has made. The adoption of a budget will proceed more smoothly if:

1. The organization builds up its community and political supports and involves them in budget planning as much as possible. Care must be taken to ensure that participants are aware that you will use their input.
2. You are a good politician and manager yourself and, thus, you make it possible for the organization to develop a good reputation and win the confidence of the governing bodies by following sound budgeting practices.
3. The budget is carefully planned, based on organizational goals.
4. The budget is prepared so that every expenditure can be justified.
5. The budget is followed carefully each year, once it has been approved, so your organization builds a reputation for sound financial management.

Implementation

The final stage in the development of a budget is implementation. Upon approval, it is necessary to implement procedures that make sure the document is administered properly. Specifically, procedures are needed to disperse, record, and account for financial resources. Often this process is aided by using a computer. The role of the recreation and leisure service manager in the implementation procedure is threefold. First, the manager should ensure that funds are expended on those items for which they were designated. Second, the manager should ensure that expenditures parallel budget estimates. And last, the manager should ensure that expenditures and collections of revenues are transacted within the procedures and policies established by the organization.

Problems Associated with Budget Procedures

A number of problems are associated with the budgetary procedure:

1. Often it is difficult for an organization to foresee all of the costs that may be incurred during the upcoming fiscal year. In many organizations, a miscellaneous, or "slush" fund is established to deal with such unanticipated expenses. A ceiling should be placed on expenditures that can be paid out of this fund, and care should be taken to see that such a fund is used for the appropriate purposes.

2. Budgets are financial plans that are based on organizational priorities. Sometimes priorities change as a result of unforeseen circumstances.
3. Determining appropriate fees and charges poses a number of difficulties as mentioned earlier. Whether programs should be costed out and a break-even analysis performed is often questioned.

TYPES OF BUDGETS

Two types of budgets are commonly included in the overall budget of the recreation and leisure service organization. These are capital and operational budgets.

Capital budgets.   A capital budget specifies monies that are designated for the improvement, expansion, or initiation of programs, facilities or additional fixed assets. It also details the sources from which these capital investments can be obtained. Capital investments represent a relatively permanent commitment and involve long-term fiscal decisions.

Operational budget.   An operational budget is an action plan that specifies the monies that are used to pay for personnel, maintenance, materials, promotions, and so on. Operating budgets deal with short-term fiscal decisions and represent daily or temporary needs.

METHODS OF BUDGETING

There are a number of different methods of budgeting that can be used by the manager. They include: line-item budgeting, object-classification budgeting, program budgeting, program planning budgeting system (PPBS), and zero-based budgeting (ZBB).

Line-item budgeting.   Line-item budgeting was the most common budgeting system used by recreation and leisure service organizations until the early 1960s. It was a product of municipal or social reform in the early 1900s. During this period there was a need to clarify what revenues were being used for in municipal government. Line-item budgets were established in order to delineate specific costs for budget items within a fiscal year. These budgets today usually set forth the amount of money to be spent on each item and are primarily used as a control mechanism. The line-item budget implies that monies will be spent only for those items specified and that expenditures will follow exactly the estimates made. Usually it has strict procedures for enforcing the conditions prescribed in the budget document. It is relatively simple to review the status of various items or accounts within this type of budget. Obviously, it is easy to read and therefore is easily understood. The major disadvantage of line-item budgeting is the inability to calculate costs for specific programs or activities.

Object-classification budgeting.   A major derivative of line-item budgeting is object-classification budgeting. This approach to budgeting involves the clustering of various items into a number of categories. These categories are much broader than those found in line-item budgets. In addition, the categories are consistent among most organizations. Object-classification budgeting focuses on the amounts of money to be spent in relationship to the quantity of items to be received or purchased. This approach to budgeting is built on a system of accounts organized in a hierarchical manner to reflect organizational expenditures. The budget includes the amount of funds necessary to purchase a given number of items and, thus, provides information for both planning and control. Major categories in most object classification systems are personnel services, contractual services, current charges, purchases of supplies and equipment, and debt payments. Under each major account, subaccount classifications may be established to meet the accounting needs of the particular recreation and leisure service department. An example of an object-classification system is as follows:

Account Number/Name

1,000 Services—personnel: involves salaries and wages.

2,000 Services—contractual: involves work performed, services rendered, or materials supplied on a contractual basis.

3,000 Commodities: supplies and materials.

4,000 Current charges: includes rent, insurance, licenses, etc.

5,000 Current obligations: fixed expenses such as interest, taxes, or loans.

6,000 Properties: cost of equipment, buildings or land.

7,000 Debt payment.[2]

Object-classification budgets offer a convenient way of viewing the major categories in which money is spent. They do not relate expenditures to specific programs, thus they make the evaluation of specific program costs difficult. Often organizations will extend the object-classification system of budgeting by establishing an additional hierarchy or level of classifications. This usually involves the separation of such functions as administration, program, and maintenance. This additional hierarchical categorization is known as *functional classification.*

Program budgeting.   Program budgeting emerged in the 1960s. It offers a way of identifying program objectives, benefits, and costs. A program budget essentially identifies the unit cost for each program or service and the total budget costs of the organization. The key to this type of budgeting is the isolation, identification, and analysis of specific work

2.   Richard Kraus and Joseph Curtis, *Creative Administration in Recreation and Parks* (St. Louis: C. V. Mosby Co., 1977), p. 151.

programs that, in turn, are broken down into unit costs (e.g., each lesson, each park per day, each class of a series) for the various work programs. For example, a program budget would show the estimated number of units and the average cost of each unit.

Program budgeting provides information that can be easily interpreted, giving the reader a clear indication of the specific costs of a given program or work unit. This type of budgeting is often used in situations where the cost of the activity is paid for by the user.

Program budgeting has an analytical base that forces choices among the competing demands for expenditures. These choices call for the development of objectives by the recreation and leisure service administrator and by other decision-making officials. This form of budgeting also helps to facilitate decisions concerning the allocation of resources. In addition, program budgeting allows the establishment of a realistic fee structure based on the actual cost of the service.

Planning and budgeting have sometimes had a tendency to run along parallel lines with coordination resulting through informal consultation and review. The program budget forces the development of a bond between planning and budgeting for operating programs, capital budgets, and projections of both revenues and expenditures.

PPBS.   The program planning budgeting system (PPBS) is one of the most popular methods of program budgeting. It is used to generate systematic decisions based on a set of objectives and other required information. The focal point of this type of budgeting process is the assessment of the costs and benefits of different spending plans. It attempts to delineate expenditure aggregates. Specifics of these aggregates are generated only as an understanding of the complete budget or of possible alternatives among competing programs is developed. Such a process draws attention to a planned group of data that allows easier comparisons among alternate spending proposals. The purpose of PPBS is not to serve as a substitute for, but rather as an aid to, human judgment. In other words, decision makers use the data generated by this technique to make better decisions. PPBS revolves around four basic practices:

1. Budget alternatives must be exact and reflect public objectives rather than self-serving agency activities and operations.
2. Multiyear costs and effects of programs are estimated, not just cost estimates for the subsequent year.
3. Structured inquiry for achieving public needs is required and necessary.
4. Evaluation is carried out to determine the benefits of the organization's expenditures. This is done in order to assess the costs and trade-offs between alternatives, as well as to ascertain whether programs have achieved stated objectives.

In a PPBS system, classifications essentially deal with the basic mission of the recreation and leisure service agency. These classifications are joined to the process of policy implementation and decision making through the allocation of resources. This appraisal of alternatives and the subsequent selection of activities to be authorized are what characterizes PPBS.

This type of budgeting is sometimes described as budgeting up the ladder. The PPBS budget process should stimulate the continuous analysis of problems among competing needs and programs. This being the case, all of the activities in the PPBS budget process will combine to form departmental aims that should be consistent with organizational goals. PPBS will also translate aims into programs and performance. Once established, PPBS assists in the execution of programs that have been authorized and the evaluation of performance as it relates to established goals.

The PPBS form of budgeting concentrates on the development of alternate possibilities for achieving stated objectives. It is an intelligent approach that relates resources to aims and has proven to be a sound instrument for sharpening administrative judgment in planning and decision making. This system of budgeting also concentrates heavily on the end result, rather than the means by which it is accomplished. An example of PPBS budgeting is offered in Figure 8.1.

Zero-based budgeting. ZBB, or zero-based budgeting, divides programs into packages composed of goals, activities, and resources and then calculates the costs for each package. Each program budget is started at a zero base, and all packages are justified with the corresponding costs calculated. This eliminates the common practice of just adding an incremental amount on to the previous year's actual budget. Each program or item is reviewed from the ground up and is considered anew each year in light of its relative priority. The fact that a particular program or activity has existed for many years does not justify its continuation. Some of the specific advantages of the ZBB budgeting process are as follows:

1. Organizations that are faced with a decreasing tax base and increasing demands for services can use zero-based budgeting as a systematic, rational approach to decision making.
2. ZBB allows for the reallocation or elimination of activities inconsistent with program needs or agency philosophies. It rules out the possibility of duplication of services, clarifies resource responsibility, and defines lines of authority and responsibility.
3. This type of budgeting does not operate on past precedents. Each budget item is placed on trial and competes for funds each year.
4. ZBB accounts for indirect costs and gives an accurate indication of total program costs. Areas of potential cost savings may be discovered as organizations gather more information about the nature of their organizations and where money is being spent.

There are some disadvantages to the zero-based budgeting approach:

1. Zero-based budgeting is a very time-consuming process.

2. ZBB involves too much paperwork, an almost unmanageable amount.
3. The possible development of too many decision-making packages may make it impossible to make rational choices.
4. ZBB places too much emphasis on the ends and not enough on the means.
5. Individuals employed in the organization may lack the skill or knowledge necessary to implement zero-based bugeting.
6. It may be questionable whether the results obtained using ZBB are really different than the results obtained from other traditional budgetary forms. ZBB, if implemented ineffectively, may result in merely a rehashing of programs currently in existence, resulting in incremental changes at best.
7. Organization and program objectives are often ambiguous, thereby making it difficult to allocate resources rationally. To overcome this, objectives must be stated clearly and defined so that decisions that support these objectives can be implemented.

Despite the disadvantages stated above, zero-based budgeting is gaining ground in the recreation and leisure service field. The following steps are necessary to successfully design a zero-based budget for approval and implementation:

1. Develop a program structure which clearly delineates all operations, personnel, and supportive operations.
2. Design a chart of accounts which would include codes for functions, objects, facilities and programs.
3. Prepare a summary budget which would indicate current units and objects of expense.
4. Justify the decision package with program descriptions, benefits, alternatives, objectives and direct costs.
5. Show various funding levels in terms of preferred, minimum or reduced levels.
6. Determine the priorities of the decision package spending levels.
7. Consolidate decision packages through higher administrative echelons.
8. Prepare the budget document with supportive displays of program cost, priorities, savings and other possibilities.[3]

In order to rank decision packages, the following process should be used:

1. Assemble the decision-making team. Users, politicians, staff, and nonusers may all be involved in this process.
2. Participants should fill out the decision package forms.

3. George Hjelte and Jay Shivers, *Public Administration of Recreational Services* (Philadelphia: Lea and Febiger, 1972), p. 492.

RESOURCE ALLOCATION ANALYSIS

Program Number and Title: 616   Tennis Activities

Program Management: Marty Ruberry
Recreation Administrative Supervisor

Program Mission: Provide recreation tennis activities and
facility maintenance at the Sunnyvale Municipal Tennis
Center and City-wide tennis instruction.

Fiscal Year	Work Hours	Total Cost	Equivalent Unit Cost
Actual			
1975-76	--	--	--
1976-77	1,090	28,373	26.03
1977-78	1,203	34,937	29.05
1978-79	1,741	55,411	31.83
Estimated			
1979-80	1,887	52,649	27.90
Proposed			
1980-81	1,726	69,159	40.07
Projected			
1981-82	1,726	82,862	48.01
1982-83	1,726	89,490	51.85
1983-84	1,726	96,652	56.00
1984-85	1,726	104,385	60.48
1985-86	1,726	112,737	65.32
1986-87	1,726	121,753	70.54
1987-88	1,726	131,496	76.19
1988-89	1,726	142,016	82.28
1989-90	1,726	153,378	88.86

SPECIAL NOTES: Addition of 3 courts and upgrading of all
lighting at the Sunnyvale Municipal Tennis Center were
completed in fiscal year 1979-80.

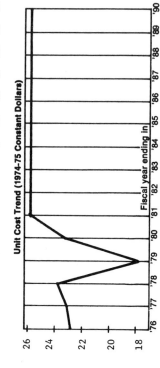

Production Trend

DATA WILL BE CHARTED NEXT YEAR

Fiscal year ending in
'76 '77 '78 '79 '80 '81 '82 '83 '84 '85 '86 '87 '88 '89 '90

Unit Cost Trend (1974-75 Constant Dollars)

Fiscal year ending in
'76 '77 '78 '79 '80 '81 '82 '83 '84 '85 '86 '87 '88 '89 '90

PROGRAM SERVICE OBJECTIVES

616 TENNIS ACTIVITIES

Program Wide Objective:
PROVIDE 13 TENNIS COURTS IN SUPERIOR CONDITION AT THE
SUNNYVALE MUNICIPAL TENNIS CENTER, WITH RELATED TENNIS
LESSONS AND SERVICES, ON A 100% FEE SUPPORTED BASIS.

Objective: 616A MAINTAIN THE TENNIS COURT TURF AREAS, GROUND COVER,
TREES, COURTS AND BUILDINGS AT A "SATISFACTORY"
LEVEL OF HEALTH/CONDITION.

Task	Type of Units	Units	Unit Cost	Hours	Task Cost
61601 MOW LAWNS	ACRES	92	24.70	161.0	2272.01
61602 EDGE LAWNS	LINEAL YARDS	42016	.02	72.0	928.40
61604 FERTILIZE AND AERIFY LAWNS	ACRES	2	200.23	41.0	400.45
61607 CONTROL WEEDS IN TURF	ACRES	2	200.23	41.0	400.46
61610 MAINTAIN COURTS	COURTS	13	836.13	608.0	10869.63
61611 MAINTAIN SHRUBS & TREES	SHRUBS AND TREES MAINT.	147	13.15	147.0	1932.60
61613 MAINTAIN GROUND COVER	SQUARE FEET	153	12.70	153.0	2006.87
61625 MAINTAIN IRRIGATION EQUIPMENT	REPAIRS	20	12.08	20.0	241.54
61640 MAINTAIN BUILDINGS	OCCASIONS	305	29.74	483.0	9071.50
					28,123.47

Objective: 616B PROVIDE UTILITY SERVICES AT THE SUNNYVALE
MUNICIPAL TENNIS CENTER.

Task	Type of Units	Units	Unit Cost	Hours	Task Cost
61631 PROVIDE SMTC PG&E	KILOWATTS USED	89583	.07	.0	5912.50
61632 PROVIDE SMTC WATER	100 CUBIC FEET USED	3970	.37	.0	1485.00
					7,397.50

Objective: 616Z OVERSEE THE SUNNYVALE MUNICIPAL TENNIS CENTER'S
RECREATION TENNIS OPERATION AND THE TENNIS PRO'S
LICENSE AGREEMENT WITH THE CITY SUCH THAT ALL
CONTRACTUAL OBLIGATIONS ARE COMPLIED WITH.

Task	Type of Units	Units	Unit Cost	Hours	Task Cost
61691 PROVIDE ADMINISTRATION	PARTICIPANT HOURS	60000	.56	.0	33638.00
					33,638.00

TOTAL For TENNIS ACTIVITIES   69,158.97

Figure 8.1   An example of a program budget.

3. Brainstorming within the team should occur in order to establish the criteria by which the decision makers might rank the packages. Examples of criteria that might be used are attendance, numbers served, user satisfaction, and cost.

4. Next, the criteria must be weighted. This could be done by the use of a five-point Likert-type scale. The decision-making team would be asked to vote on the relative importance of different criteria so that a weighting factor may be assigned to the criteria.

5. The decision-making team would then be asked to vote, on a scale of one to ten, on how well the decision package meets the selected criteria. The mean score of the votes would then be obtained and the average score recorded.

6. The next step in the ZBB process is to rank the various packages by their cumulative scores. This is done by multiplying the criteria weighting by the average package score to get the cumulative score.

7. A package cut-off point would then be established. A price must be associated with each package ranked until the total budget is used up, then a line would be drawn to establish the cut-off point for programs. See Figure 8.2 below and on the next page.

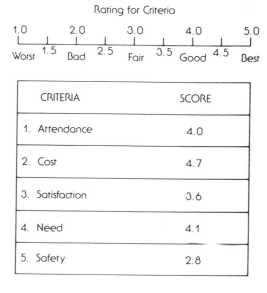

Figure 8.2 Zero-based budgeting: rating for criteria and sample decision package.

PACKAGE NAME:	AUTHORIZATION:	RANK:

Purchase of a kiln and
potter's wheel

STATEMENT OF PURPOSE: To purchase and install a kiln and potter's wheel in the craft room so that boys and girls may pursue their interests and skills. Clay and paints are presently lying idle in the craft room.

DESCRIPTION OF ACTIONS (OPERATIONS):

- Compare prices among three suppliers for purchase and installation costs
- Classes will be offered for beginner, intermediate and advanced levels. Club members will utilize room and equipment after school hours and during the early evening hours.
- Senior citizens and other community members may use the facility during the mornings and early afternoons or other such times that the room is available. A fee of $20.00 per session (ten weeks) will be charged in addition to the cost of supplies used.

ACHIEVEMENTS FROM ACTIONS:

- Enhances the variety of programs offered by the club.
- Boys and girls can remain in their club to meet needs.
- Promotes the club in the community by bringing youth and adults together to share a common interest.

CONSEQUENCES OF NOT APPROVING PACKAGE:

- Youth would have to look to other sources to provide for their needs. For many, transportation and cost of service would be a hindrance.
- Craft room is not being used to capacity; supplies would continue to lie idle.

QUANTITATIVE PACKAGE MEASURES:	FY 1981	FY 1982
Capital Outlay (Equipment)		$2,869.00

QUALITATIVE PACKAGE MEASURES:

Clients served
Creativity enhanced

ALTERNATIVES (DIFFERENT LEVELS OF EFFORT) AND COST:

Level 1 (80%)
Level 2 (100%)
Level 3 (180%)

ALTERNATIVES (DIFFERENT WAYS OF PERFORMING THE SAME FUNCTION) AND CONSEQUENCES:

Conduct classes using supplies on hand and send finished pieces out to be fired.
Not as feasible because
a) Cost per items will exceed cost of kiln within two years.
b) Boys and girls will be required to pay this price, thus eliminating many interested members.
Rent a kiln and potter's wheel; however, cost in the long run will exceed purchase and installation of the equipment.
Bus members to the community center for classes—transportation costs and a driver will be required, staff would be required to accompany members.

COMMENTS:

SOURCES OF REVENUE

Nonprofit and profit-oriented organizations have significantly different sources of revenues. Profit organizations receive revenues primarily from sales of products and services. Nonprofit, service-oriented organizations receive revenues from various sources. They may, for example, establish a fee structure to offset the cost of providing programs, or they may receive revenues from foundations and gifts. Public recreation and leisure service organizations receive revenues primarily through the appropriation of taxes. Since the majority of revenues of public nonprofit organizations comes from taxes, the public is the major funding source of such revenues.

The primary sources of revenue for recreation and leisure service organizations are discussed below:

Compulsory income. Compulsory income is generated for tax-supported organizations by the government. Examples of compulsory income are taxes, special assessments, and fees from licenses or permits.

Contractual income. Contractual income includes revenues received from various public properties and from public-service enterprises. Examples of contractual income are leases, rentals, and concessions.

Gratuitous income. This type of revenue is usually in the form of donations made to the organization. Examples of gratuitous income are donations of land, tangible properties, or money. In public and private nonprofit organizations, this type of income may be essential. The manager may devote a large amount of time attempting to secure this type of revenue, applying to groups such as United Way, foundations, corporations, or to individuals.

Earned income. Earned income is revenue received by the levying of fees for services rendered. Examples of earned income include court fees charged to a user at a pay-as-you-play tennis facility, membership fees, user charges for a group home for government employees, and monies received for specific services such as citywide clean-up campaigns.[4]

Within these four primary sources of revenue, there are a variety of specific sources of revenue, described below.

---

4.   T. I. Hines, *Revenue Sources Management in Parks and Recreation* (Arlington, Va.: National Recreation and Park Association, 1974), p. 13.

Taxes and Assessments

General property taxes.   The principal support for most local government services is the property tax. The amount of tax placed on a property is determined by the property value, or assessed valuation. The rate of taxation is expressed as mills per dollar, or a tenth of a cent per hundred dollars of the assessed valuation. For municipal parks and recreation services, property taxes are the largest source of revenue. The formula used for expressing property tax is:

$$MILLS \times ASSESSED\ VALUATION = TAX\ PAID$$

Special millage taxes.   Another way in which public organizations gain tax support is by levying a special tax for the support of a particular service. The base of this tax is also the assessed value of property. This tax is expressed in mills or cents per hundred dollars of the assessed valuation.

A special millage tax would be an advantage in a jurisdiction of government where the specific service would obtain more funds through the establishment of such a fund than it would competing with all departments for tax revenues. The amount of special millage tax appropriations is established by charter, approved by the electorate, and the approved amount of tax remains frozen until the charter is amended. This inflexibility can be seen to be a distinct disadvantage of the special millage tax.

Special assessments.   Special assessments are used to assist in the acquisition and upgrading of property. All surrounding properties that will benefit from improvement or construction are assessed and must pay a fee for this benefit. These assessments are paid in cash, provided their cost does not exceed a specified amount. Assessments of amounts over the stated ceiling may go to bond to be paid off in equal annual installments, normally extending over a ten-year period.

Certain problems associated with the use of special assessments are as follows:

1. Poorer neighborhoods do not have an equal opportunity for special assessments.
2. It is difficult and costly to determine which properties in an area will benefit from improvements. Assessments are also graded, with those sites closer to the development being charged more. This type of assessment is extremely time-consuming and for a small development or improvement may not be worthwhile.

Grants, Bequests, and Foundations

Grants-in-aid.   Grants-in-aid are revenues that are received primarily by government units from higher levels of government, usually for specific projects. Grants-in-aid programs are operated by federal, provincial, and state governments and form an important source of funding for recreation and leisure service organizations. The largest single unit of government that is involved in such programs is the federal government. According to Harold Moses, "grants-in-aid assistance from the federal government is nothing more or less than receiving in return the proportionate share of funds taken from the local government unit by the federal government."[5] Federal grant-in-aid monies have, until recently, provided an incentive for state and local governments to plan, acquire, and develop areas and facilities. Recent political changes emphasize the inherent dangers of organizations becoming overly dependent on this type of funding. In cases where organizations have depended solely on such grants, the withdrawal of aid has resulted in serious financial difficulty.

Grants and bequests.   Individuals or organizations may donate money, securities or property for use by recreation and leisure service organizations. This form of revenue usually takes the form of a grant or is left in a will. Some of the best municipal parks in both Canada and the United States have been given to cities through such means. Many voluntary agencies, such as the national organization of the Boys and Girls Clubs of Canada and the national councils of the Y.M.C.A.'s of Canada and the United States rely on grants and bequests for a portion of their revenues.

Foundations.   Another source of funding is made available when a recreation and leisure service organization establishes its own foundation. Funds that are a part of a foundation's financial resources can be invested. Annual profit on the invested resources may be used by the organization to finance its objectives, including personnel, maintenance, and operating costs. The effectiveness of this strategy depends on having an endowment fund large enough to make the annual contribution worthwhile and on investing wisely for the greatest possible return. The Boys and Girls Clubs of Canada, through a foundation arrangement, are able to generate a source of revenue for the provision of national scholarships, professional in-service programs and administrative costs.

Leases and Rental Fees

Revenue is sometimes generated from the rental or leasing of property owned by the organization. Resources such as water can be tapped for electric power; timber and fertile agricultural land can be rented or leased in order to generate additional revenue for the organization.

---

5.   T. I. Hines, *Revenue Sources Management in Parks and Recreation* (Arlington, Va.: National Recreation and Park Association, 1974), p. 13.

Leasebacks. A rather uncommon and costly method of financing capital improvements is the use of a leaseback. According to Hjelte and Shivers, leasebacks are used to "build facilities by contract with private corporations under the provision that the finished facility will be leased back to the city at an annual rent, over a stated number of years."[6] Such plans, which must first be approved by the city, usually are expensive for the city, since rental must include incurred interest and the corporation's profit, as well as the principal cost of the project. In some cases, however, the leaseback may be the only method that can be used to achieve a desired financial end.

Concessions and Fund Raising

Concessions. Concessions offer users an opportunity to purchase commodities at service locations. Concessions may be contracted out to private business by bids or may be managed by individuals hired expressly for this purpose. Whether nonprofit organizations should participate in profit-oriented undertakings is sometimes questioned, for it encourages private profit from public investment. Private contracts should be short in duration, preferably one to three years, with a cash or surety bond to guarantee performance. Examples of types of concessions are parking, refreshment stands, amusements, equipment stores, and rental of various types of equipment.

Fund-raising events. A number of nonprofit recreation and leisure service organizations engage in annual fund-raising programs in order to secure additional revenue for operating and capital expenditures. When allotments from government are insufficient, fund raising helps to stimulate community awareness and to arouse the interest of community members to participate in organizational activities. It may also help to facilitate the implementation of specific organizational objectives.

Donations can usually be secured from the private sector, employing such techniques as canvassing or mailings to solicit contributions. Special events are another popular method for obtaining funds. Examples of special fund-raising events are bikeathons, car washes, benefit performances, raffles, bazaars, and others.

Fees and Charges

A rather obvious way in which recreation and leisure service organizations produce revenue is by charging participants a portion of, or the total cost of, the service rendered, program participated in, or the equipment

---

6.   Hjelte and Shivers, *Public Administration of Recreational Services* (Philadelphia: Lea and Febiger, 1972), p. 492.

used. Fees and charges may be defined as payment for a given commodity such as food, lessons, or an entrance fee, or payments made for professional services such as consulting.

Recreation and leisure service organizations are primarily concerned with the well-being of their participants and the successful provision of service programs. With the reduction of available revenues and the increasing public demand for accountability, the fees and charges in recreation and leisure service organizations are being reevaluated. Some guidelines to consider in the assessment of fees and charges include the following:

1. *What is affordable?* The clientele served will dictate, to some degree, the amount of fees and charges. A boys' or girls' club, primarily serving children from low economic areas, will not have the same charges as a Y.M.C.A. working primarily with young adults in a suburban, professional community.

2. *What is the total cost of the service?* Some programs as a result of such factors as leadership, supplies, equipment, and transportation are extremely expensive. It can be argued that, in such cases, the recipients of such services should bear a large portion of the cost.

3. *What are the characteristics of the service?* The service offered may be geared to the public in general or it may assume a narrower focus whereby the benefits are reaped only by those who participate. Most often, individual users are expected to pay the full cost of services offered by the private sector, whereas the cost of services in the public sector are supported in part by the community tax system.

4. *What is the mission statement of the organization?* The philosophy or goals of an organization will help determine whether it is appropriate for that organization to charge its clients. If the mission of an organization is to serve all of the community's members through participation in organizational programs, then it is not desirable to expect people to pay an amount of money that would preclude participation.

5. *How much does the program cost when compared with similar programs?*

The type of service offered has a direct relationship to who pays for the service (the individual or the community). In order to differentiate between types of services, Crompton has categorized organizations as follows: Public service, merit service, and private service. Service differences and sources of revenue are concisely shown in Figure 8.3.

A fee or charging structure has four primary functions, namely equity, revenue production, efficiency and income redistribution. Following is a detailed discussion of these four functions.

1. *Equity.* Charging of fees ensures that those who benefit from a service pay for it. People residing outside of the community are often required to pay for community services received.

2. *Revenue production.* Recreation and leisure service agencies cannot

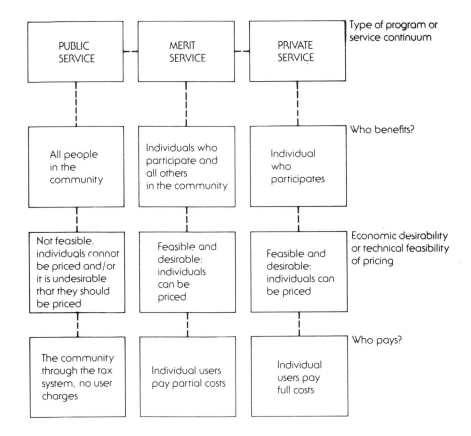

Figure 8.3   Types of organizations and their effects on pricing. (From Dennis R. Howard and John L. Crompton, *Financing, Managing and Marketing Recreation and Park Resources,* Dubuque, Iowa: William C. Brown, 1980, p. 407.)

afford to meet all of the needs, wants, and interests of those they are attempting to serve. Assignment of a user fee helps to offset operational costs and financial constraints. Such a fee structure allows more services to be offered because the needs of the entire community cannot be met by revenue received from one funding source. Fees may also help an organization to finance capital expenditures more easily.

3. *Efficiency.* Inefficiency and overcrowding can be reduced by charging different prices for facilities or services at different times. For example, many raquet clubs charge higher prices for hours that are designated as "prime time." This variable type of pricing helps to distribute usage more evenly, thereby promoting efficiency. Too much demand for the service may result if no price is charged. On the other hand, imposing a fee may have a rationing effect on scarce resources. Only participants who really desire the service will be willing to pay the price.

4. *Income redistribution.* Levying of fees and charges on service recipients
    can be a means of distributing income from higher to lower income
    groups, thereby offsetting the cost of services for lower income groups.

Fees and charges can encourage positive user attitudes. According to
Crompton, "anything at price zero tends to diminish its psychological, as
well as its economic value."[7] Participants often appreciate services more if
they have to pay some amount for them. Fees also help to secure participant
commitment. When a fee is charged, people are more likely to attend a
program regularly.

Charges or fees may be used as incentives to use scarce resources
efficiently. Fines for water pollution could, for example, help to reduce a
manufacturing firm's tendency to dump waste products into the water. A
low fee could also encourage people to attend an activity. In addition, an
established fees and charges system provides some direction for program
execution and planning.

There are also some disadvantages associated with the use of fees and
charges, however. The opportunity to participate in recreation and leisure
services is considered by some to be not only a need, but a right of all
individuals. Therefore, perhaps no fees should be charged at all. Charging
for services may also eliminate some individuals who need services but are
not able to afford them. If fees and charges are assigned to services,
organizations may over emphasize revenue-producing programs to the
detriment of programs offered at no charge. Government tax support may
decline if services are better able to finance themselves through fees.
Additional funds may be needed just to keep pace with last year's level of
services, let alone to continue to grow to meet expanding community
needs. Emphasis may shift from maximum participation to the standards
associated with commercial profit-making organizations.

There are a number of different types of fees and charges, including
admission fees, entrance fees, rental fees, user fees, and special service fees.
In addition, fees and charges may involve revenue from sales of licenses and
permits.

1. *Admission.* Admission fees are charges for an individual entering an
    area or facility, such as a theater. This type of fee is assessed for
    attendance at a performance or exhibit.
2. *Entrance fee.* Entrance fees are charged for admission to an area. For ex-
    ample, theme parks, such as Disney World or Canada's Wonderland
    charge an initial entrance fee. Other fees are often charged for rides
    and performances after entry to the park.
3. *License and permit.* Licenses or permits give an individual legal consent
    to perform an act. Licenses or permits may regulate hunting, fishing,
    driving, and other types of recreational activities.

7.   Borris W. Becker, "The Pricing of Education-Recreational Facilities: An Administrative
     Dilemma." *Journal of Leisure Research*, 7, no. 2 (1975):88.

4. *Rental fees.* A rental fee is a charge that entitles the payer to exclusive use of rented equipment or property, provided that it is returned in the same condition that it was borrowed. Renting roller skates in an arena would be an example of this type of fee.

5. *User fee.* A user fee is the price paid for the privilege of participating in an activity. This type of fee usually implies that usage will be shared with other participants, in contrast to the exclusive rights obtained when a rental fee is paid.

6. *Special service fee.* A special service fee is levied for extraordinary articles or accommodation.

7. *Sales revenue.* Sales revenue is obtained from stores, concessions, restaurants, and the sale of goods and services.

Organizations have different philosophies regarding pricing. Pricing should reflect the organization's mission statement and specific program objectives. It would be impossible to establish one blanket pricing strategy applicable to all programs. Instead, programs should be considered individually to assign a meaningful price. Often, general introductory costs are written off as community expenditures, whereas more specialized programs are paid for by the user.

Bonds

Issuing bonds to help finance capital improvements is one means to obtain revenue that large organizations might consider. A bond may be defined as a "written promise to pay a specified sum of money at a fixed time."[8] Accrued interest in addition to the principal sum is paid at the time of bond maturation.

The building of recreation and leisure service facilities has not kept pace with the growing demands for facilities, purchases of properties, and improvements. Capital budgets often offer meager support to finance such long-term projects. A number of recreation authorities presently use bonds to finance their capital-improvement programs. It is the most prevalent means by which public organizations involve themselves in long-term financing. Bonds must be approved by the electorate, the bond ordinance being the formal legal document allowing for the collection of the principal and interest accumulated at the date the bond falls due.

Definite advantages and disadvantages can be seen in the issuance of bonds to finance government expenditures. Investments in recreational places or spaces result in the creation of valuable property. In the case of land, a permanent value is created with its acquisition; a space which can be used by future generations. Bonds also allow for significant programs of

---

8.   T.I. Hines, *Revenue Sources Management in Parks and Recreation* (Arlington, Va.: National Recreation and Park Association, 1974), p. 47.

capital development to be undertaken in a relatively short time. In addition, they allow for long-term loans that are financed by future generations that will reap the benefits from such an expenditure.

Bonds have drawbacks in that the principal cost of projects financed with bonds is greatly increased due to interest accrued by the time the bond matures. Such payments may become the burden of citizens for a number of years to come. Also, care should be taken not to extend bond repayments beyond the anticipated life of the improvement they were created to finance.

Possible Solutions to Lack of Funds

Not all requests for funds secure approval. If a budget is a financial reflection of the organization's program objectives, then the obvious solution in cases where allotments are below requests is to curtail services. The good manager will anticipate such cutbacks and have alternative procedures ready. Some of the possible solutions are:

1. A reduction of programs.
2. A possible change in the program philosophy of the organization (perhaps from direct programming to facilitation). Such a change must, however, complement the organization's services.
3. Change resulting in more efficiency. Such changes might be accomplished by implementing efficiency models, cost units, or other management techniques.
4. Establishing ties with other community agencies in order to secure funds, offer services jointly, or share facilities.
5. Finding other means of obtaining income. Possible sources are foundations, fund raising, securing government grants, and obtaining contributions from federal fund-raising programs.
6. Increasing or changing the fees and charges systems of the organization.

FINANCIAL ACCOUNTING

It is important for an organization to have some method whereby expenditures and revenues can be recorded. This procedure is known as accounting. Budgeting is concerned with the future use of financial resources; accounting is concerned with past and current fiscal events. Accounting serves as a record of revenue sources and how these funds were used to accomplish organizational objectives within a given time frame. It is a tool used by administrators to keep an eye on the financial flow of the agency so as to control the budget. In addition, these procedures record transactions within the agency and between other agencies.

Why Accounting?

Following are three reasons to use accounting in recreation and leisure service organizations.

1. Accounting allows for standardization and record keeping.
2. Accounting is used for organizational accountability and provides a legal document that identifies how funds have been allocated and dispersed.
3. Correct accounting information provides the organization with data on which decisions can be based. It can also determine the financial situation of the organization.

Accounting Procedures

A complete set of rules exists for business accounting practices; however, considerable concern about the lack of consistency in the accounting procedures of nonprofit organizations has been expressed. As a result, in April, 1978 the Nonprofit Organizations Subcommittee of the Accounting Standards Executive Committee published a report codifying a set of rules for the accounting and disclosure of nonprofit service organizations.

The accounting system, regardless of the nature of the firm consists of the following steps:

1. Gathering evidence of business transactions, through purchase invoices, sales slips, payroll records, and so on.
2. Recording the transactions, as they occur, in a journal.
3. Classifying the information recorded in the journal into special ledgers—for example, purchases on credit into the accounts payable register.
4. Summarizing and arranging the information contained in the various accounts in the form of monthly or annual financial statements.
5. Interpreting the information contained in the financial statements—for example, trends in earnings or relationships between assets and liabilities.[9]

Journals.   As soon as an organization receives monies or makes payments, these transactions should be recorded in a journal so that these entries may be used as a base to balance the books at the end of the month. Many bookkeeping systems utilize three different types of journals.

1. *The receipts journal.* The total income of the organization is recorded in this type of journal.

---

9.   Maurice Archer, *An Introduction to Canadian Business*, 3rd ed., (Toronto: McGraw-Hill, Ryerson Limited, 1978), pp. 256–57.

XYZ COMPANY
BALANCE SHEET
DECEMBER 31, 1981

ASSETS

	1981	1980
GENERAL FUNDS		
Cash and Deposit Receipts	$122,064	$117,079
Accounts Receivable	5,820	5,140
Equipment	11,920	
Pre-paid Rent	2,985	2,644
	$142,789	$124,863

LIABILITIES

	1981	1980
GENERAL FUNDS		
Bank Advance	$_____	$ 45,580
Accounts Payable	10,425	9,860
Loan Payable	80,000	68,350
Notes Payable	9,168	38,268
	$ 99,593	$162,058

OWNERS' EQUITY

	1981	1980
SURPLUS (DEFICIT)	22,630	(60,250)
SPECIAL PROJECT RESERVE	12,706	2,430
	35,336	57,820
RESOURCE DEVELOPMENT FUND	7,860	20,625
	43,196	(37,195)
	$142,789	$124,863

Figure 8.4   Sample of a balance sheet.

2. *The check disbursement journal.* All payments or disbursements made by check are recorded here.
3. *The petty cash journal.* All payments which the organization has made by cash are recorded here.[10]

Ledgers.   From the journal, the financial administrator will post revenues and disbursements in a ledger. A ledger is a file of accounts, each showing the effects on one asset, liability, or element of owner's equity.

The balance sheet.   The balance sheet is a very important financial statement detailing the nature and amount of the organization's assets, liabilities, and owner's equity. The balance sheet is correct when the following equation balances (see Figure 8.4):

---

10. Ministry of Culture and Recreation, *Bookkeeping Procedures for Community Groups* (Toronto: 1981), p. 11.

TOTAL ASSETS = TOTAL LIABILITIES + OWNER'S EQUITY

The income statement. The income statement is considered the most important financial statement. An income statement shows how much profit or loss an organization has experienced over a specific period of time, usually a fiscal year. Care must be taken to list all the revenues and expenses flowing in and out of the organization. Simply stated, all income statements are based on the following premise:

REVENUES − EXPENSES = NET INCOME

Revenues exceeding expenditures result in a profit, whereas expenses exceeding revenues result in a loss (see Figure 8.5).

Petty cash. Petty cash is a cash fund kept on the premises to reimburse employees for small, unexpected, out-of-pocket expenses. Accounting records of all funds disbursed must be kept. Figure 8.6 provides a typical example of a petty cash form used by a recreation and leisure service organization.

The petty cash of an organization should have a stated monetary ceiling and expenditures exceeding this amount should be billed to the organization. The following expenditures should *not* come out of a petty cash fund: payment for personnel services, items regularly warehoused, items exceeding the stated ceiling of the fund, cash advances to employees, or cashing of personal or payroll checks.

XYZ COMPANY
INCOME STATEMENT FOR
YEAR ENDED DECEMBER 31, 1981

	1981	1980
INCOME		
Contributions & Foundations	$280,560	$196,830
Federal Government Support	14,000	16,400
Provincial Grant	7,430	4,980
Membership Fees	1,050	862
Interest	4,120	1,040
Miscellaneous	5,405	5,868
	312,565	225,980
EXPENSES		
Field Services	72,000	48,000
Communications	3,080	1,000
Supplies	34,262	29,065
Interest & Bank Charges	5,920	4,860
Administration	98,980	66,482
	214,242	149,407
Net Income	98,323	76,573
Deficit,Beginning of Year	(60,250)	(78,480)
Surplus (Deficit), End of Year	$ 38,073	$ (1,907)

Figure 8.5 Sample income statement.

PETTY CASH

Date _____ No. _____

EXPENSE:	
DETAILS:	
TOTAL:	

Received, the sum of _____

_____ Signature

Authorized by: _____

Figure 8.6   A sample petty cash form.

Purchasing

Purchasing is the phrase given to all actions associated with the securing of supplies, equipment and services for an organization. Purchasing for a multifaceted organization may take place through centralized or decentralized operations.

Within a centralized purchasing system, the main office purchases the necessary supplies to be distributed accordingly to the local·units of the organization. The decentralized purchasing system requires each local unit to purchase materials necessary for its own operations. Following are detailed some of the advantages and disadvantages associated with each type of purchasing.

Centralized purchasing.   The central organization can buy in bulk and then distribute the materials to their local units, thus allowing for the economies of scale to occur. Costs will be lower, owing to quantity purchasing. Centralized buying encourages a person specialized in purchasing to perform this function, rather than numerous individuals with varying degrees of expertise. This allows for a standardization of procedures and practices. However, centralized purchasing may be a less direct process and consequently more time consuming. Perhaps electronic data processing could eliminate part of this problem, however such sophisticated equipment is only available to large organizations.

Decentralized purchasing.   Local units may know their own needs better than the central organization does. Decentralized purchasing can also promote good community relations if local units purchase supplies from local merchants. This might help to boost the economy of the area in which the service is located. This type of purchasing may allow the local unit to function in a more autonomous and effective fashion. However, decentralized purchasing may require extra purchasing staff to be hired. The savings that could be realized by buying in bulk might be lost and gaps or duplication of materials or services may occur.

Major steps in the purchasing process.   There are several major steps in the purchasing process. Most park and recreation departments follow the procedures listed below:

1. *Receipt of a purchase requisition.* A requisition is a formal order, usually written by an individual authorized to request items, materials, or services to be purchased. In this step, the person(s) in charge of purchasing receives these forms.
2. *Request for a quotation.* A request for a quotation requires the person in charge of purchasing to secure estimates as to the various prices for materials or services to be purchased. This document usually includes information such as items required, prices, delivery date, and terms of payment. Quotations help to provide accurate estimates that can be used in budget preparation.
3. *Issue of purchase order.* The purchase order is a formal contract to purchase a commodity from a supplier, based on the terms specified.
4. *Follow-up.* At the follow-up stage in the purchasing process, the buyer will confirm the delivery date with the vendor. If the date specified is not possible, alternate arrangements should be made.
5. *Receiving report.* A receiving report shows exactly what the organization has received from the vendor. This invoice is used to check off supplies requested as well as used. The receiving report also functions as a receipt for the accounting department.[11]

Received articles are then distributed by the central organization or by departments.

Auditing

Auditing is a type of control check on the organization's accounting system. It is the act of checking accounting records to ensure their validity and accuracy. This practice involves the regular review of journals, ledgers, and accounts such as securities, inventories, and receivables. There are two types of audits an organization may undergo—internal and external:

---

11.   Maurice Archer, *An Introduction to Canadian Business*, 3rd ed., (Toronto: McGraw-Hill, Ryerson Limited, 1978), pp. 256–57.

Internal audit. This type of audit is done by a staff member of the organization itself. Checks of this nature may be carried out periodically throughout the year.

External audit. Public organizations often arrange for a public accounting firm to assess their financial standing. This practice insures that shareholder's or taxpayer's interests have been preserved and monies have been handled with honesty and integrity. External audits have more credibility than those audits done by company members.

SUMMARY

Financial management involves the administration, custody, protection, and control of the fiscal resources of recreation and leisure service delivery systems. Financial management is often equated with the term "budgeting." A budget can be thought of as a financial plan—a way of expressing the program of an organization in financial terms. The budget is also useful in controlling the flow of resources within an organization to ensure that its objectives are achieved. A budget is established for a predetermined period of time, such as a year.

The budget process consists of four steps: development, structuring, presentation and approval, and implementation. Budget development is a continuous process that involves many members of the recreation and leisure service organization. It is a process of collecting information, developing plans, and determining associated costs. A written document is prepared that includes a detailed narrative of the proposed financial expenditures, as well as a summary of major activities. Presentation and approval of a budget is made in conjunction with an appropriate policy-making body. In public recreation and leisure service organizations, the adoption of the budget is often dependent upon the relationship of the agency to its political constituency. Budget implementation involves careful administration of funds in order to ensure that they are expended appropriately.

There are two major types of budgets within the overall organizational budget. Capital budgets detail funds intended for improvement, expansion, or acquisition of areas, facilities, and other fixed assets. The operational budget details the portion of the funds that are to be used for paying personnel, purchasing supplies, equipment, and materials, as well as other financial obligations. Capital budgets usually involve long-term financial transactions, whereas operational budgets are more short-term. Some of the methods of budgeting used in recreation and leisure service agencies are line-item, object-classification, and program, including program planning budgeting system (PPBS) and zero-based budgeting (ZBB).

A recreation and leisure service organization can have a number of sources of revenue, including compulsory, contractual, gratuitous, and earned income. More specifically, revenues can be generated from a variety of sources, including property taxes, grants, bequests, leases and rentals, concessions, special fund-raising activities, and fees and charges. This last type of income has become increasingly important to recreation and leisure service organizations in the public sector.

The procedure of recording expenditures and receiving revenues is known as accounting. Accounting is useful in that it allows standardization of records, provides a tool for fiscal accountability, and provides information for decision making. Most recreation and leisure service delivery systems use the accrual method of accounting. This is a system that contrasts current revenues with expenditures. Other financial concerns related to accounting are the way in which items are purchased, including the processes of requisitioning and bidding.

In these times of financial austerity, the management of the fiscal resources of any recreation and leisure organization is extremely important. Detailed attention should be given to the planning and development of a budget. It must be an honest, accurate reflection of a program's goals. The financial plan must provide procedures to ensure that fiscal resources are collected and distributed in a manner consistent with the mission of the organization and the laws governing its operation.

STUDY QUESTIONS

1. Budgeting can be viewed as a planning tool and as a control technique. Comment.
2. What advantages will a manager enjoy if he employs a budgeting procedure?
3. Outline and discuss the four main steps in the budgeting process.
4. Compare and contrast object-classification budgets and functional-classification budgets.
5. Discuss the differences between line-item budgeting, performance budgeting and program budgeting.
6. What is zero-based budgeting? What are the advantages and disadvantages inherent in ZBB.
7. What are the prime sources of revenue for nonprofit service organizations? Give an example of each.
8. Under what circumstances would it be desirable for a leisure service organization to initiate a fee and charges system? What types of fees and charges could be implemented?
9. Identify the steps involved in an accounting system.
10. Briefly discuss the process of auditing. What are the two types of audits in which an organization may engage?

CASE STUDY 11

The Staff Meeting

George looked up from his notes as Bob Playfair, Tom Green, and Chris Johnson entered his office. "Greetings, gentlemen," he said, "we have only a few problems to settle this week so we should be finished in time to stop off for a quick one at five o'clock. Everything looks okay for next week, so it seems that we have a short agenda for this week's meeting."

George then distributed the notes he had made prior to the meeting and pointed out that there were seven items for discussion, which he had arranged in order of priority as follows:

1.   New filtration plant at Memorial Pool.
2.   New playground equipment for Central Park.
3.   Request for use of skating rink.
4.   Request for use of lighted athletic field.
5.   Preliminary budget estimates.
6.   Request for new organizational chart.
7.   Vandalism after teenage dance.

After everybody had settled in their seats, George opened the meeting by saying, "I have some good news for this afternoon in reference to items one and two. After checking our expenditures to date, it seems that we have enough money to go ahead with the new filtration plant at Memorial, and therefore I have put through a purchase order to have the job completed. Furthermore, it would seem that there will be enough money saved from that staff position we could not fill to purchase new apparatus for Central Park. Quotes for new apparatus should arrive next week and when we meet again next Friday, we can finalize the order in terms of what pieces of equipment we can afford. I would suggest, therefore, that we do not need to discuss these first two items this afternoon and proceed to items three and four."

After 20 minutes of rather repetitious conversation, it was decided to grant approval for both the use of the skating rink and for use of the athletic field on the dates requested. George promised to write to the parties concerned and inform them of the decision. The fees of $25.00 for the field and $45.00 for the arena were agreed upon.

When the group considered item number five, concerning next year's budget, George showed them preliminary figures that had been prepared by himself and Tom Green.

"Basically," reported George, "we have increased our request for the next year's operating budget by an amount equal to 15 percent. I feel that the city manager will recommend an increase of 12 percent to council, and if we are lucky this figure will pass. However, I can't see council giving us less than 10 percent. So, until we hear the definite figures we should count on an increase of somewhere between 10 and 15 percent. Probably 12 percent would be a safe bet."

"Frankly, gentlemen," he said, as he read the memo requesting an up-to-date organization chart, "I don't know quite how we should handle this request from the mayor at this time. I would suggest that we hold a special meeting next week and at that time we can fill in all the names in the boxes and fix the chart so that it looks presentable to council. I have asked my secretary to make the necessary changes in light of the staff turnover during the past year. Don't forget that Chuck Christopher will be starting work on Monday and his position should be shown on the chart that we will finish when we meet next week. I'll have extra copies made up by then and if you think of any changes, phone Sally before our meeting. I hope you like this new chap Christopher," he said to Tom Green. "He was impressive when he worked here during the summer. I just hope he doesn't try to show us too much of this new management theory that they are so hot on now in the universities. I still believe that experience is the best teacher when it comes to common-sense administration."

After another 20 minutes of discussion, it was agreed that the vandalism after the teenage dances was out of hand. George promised to speak with the police department and request a closer watch put on the area. Bob Playfair volunteered to attend the next few dances and try to find out what the problems were.

"Maybe," suggested Tom Green, "you should stop the dances as they seem to be getting out of hand lately.

"Let's give them a few more tries," said George, "and then assess the results in about a month."

"Any further business?" asked George glancing at his watch, which now indicated that it was 5:05. "None? Okay then, let's head over to the hotel for a few minutes before we head home. Incidentally, Bob, I'll bring this new chap Chuck Christopher down to your office after I take him to see Chris and the personnel department on Monday morning. I would like you to get him started right away on that new program we talked about last week. I'll fill him in when he reports to me on Monday and tell him that you'll give him the details. Let's go, fellows, before it gets too late. Meeting adjourned."

QUESTIONS

1. Should bosses socialize with their subordinates as George did with Chris and Bob?
2. What is your opinion on the manner in which George:
   a) prepared for the staff meeting?
   b) conducted the meeting?
   c) ended the meeting?
3. Is George a good delegator?
4. Are there any indications of good or bad fiscal planning in the organization?
5. How does an organization chart relate to the planning process? What is the relation between organizing and planning? Which comes first?
6. Is experience the best teacher when it comes to common-sense administration?
7. What is your assessment of how George handled the vandalism problem? Would you have done it in a different manner? If so, how?
8. What is your assessment of how George handled the item relating to Chuck Christopher?

Controlling

9

Chuck Christopher, supervisor in a large community park and recreation department, has just been advised that he has exceeded his budget for playground equipment by $5000.

Lois McGill, recreation supervisor for the Waterloo Park and Recreation Department, has just noted that part-time summer staff under her direction have worked 100 hours of overtime, 50 hours beyond the amount allotted to her for this period of the program.

Angelo Plaza, park foreman for the Metropolitan Regional Park System has noticed that the department no longer has appropriate herbicides and pesticides on inventory that are used daily for maintenance of parks in his area.

These scenarios all have something in common—evidence of poor control and a need for corrective action. Angelo lacks the materials he needs to effectively maintain the park resources under his direction. A lack of proper supplies will delay his work and may cause deterioration of the turf within the parks. Lois must cut back to ensure that, at the end of her program, the budget will be balanced and that funds will be available for overtime during other parts of her program. Chuck justifies the overexpenditure on playground equipment as the effects of inflation. Each of these situations alerts the individuals concerned that some action will be necessary to correct, change, or justify the situation. Control systems are designed to alert the manager that deviations from expected standards are occurring, so that the adverse situation can be prevented or rectified.

Control is a management process concerned with the establishment of standards to measure performance and the determination of ways in which corrective action can be taken to maximize resources. In the example in the introductory paragraph, Chuck Christopher, supervisor of parks and recreation, knew that he had exceeded his budget for playground equipment by $5000. His authorization of expenses had exceeded the planned standard, and when comparing actual expenses with estimated expenses for playground equipment, he was able to detect a deviation from the standard.

The control process is concerned with three important areas:

● The establishment of standards
● The comparison of actual performance to the standards
● The initiation of corrective action

Figure 9.1 presents a schematic rendering of these three variables and their relationship to one another. The development of standards occurs at

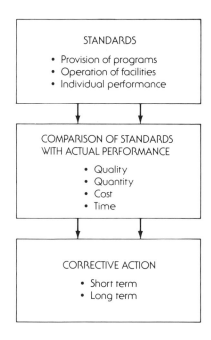

Figure 9.1   The control process.

the end of the planning process and the beginning of the control process. The recreation and leisure service organization initially develops a set of objectives to guide the organization. Once these have been established, the next step in the planning process is the development of standards. Standards are the link between the planning and control processes of management. Once standards have been determined, they can be compared with actual performance to detect deviations. The comparative analysis of actual performance to standards provides a basis for managerial action to ensure that the organization meets its intended goals and objectives.

Discussing control, Koontz and O'Donnell have suggested that its essence is measurement. They indicate that controls should reflect the following ten principles:

1. Control must reflect the nature and needs of the activity.
2. Controls should report deviations promptly.
3. Controls should be forward looking.
4. Controls should point up exceptions at critical points.
5. Controls should be objective.
6. Controls should be flexible.
7. Controls should reflect the organizational patterns.
8. Controls should be economical.
9. Controls should be understandable.
10. Controls should lead to corrective action.[1]

STANDARDS

In order to determine what constitutes successful performance in individual work activities, as well as in achieving broader organizational goals, standards must be established. Standards serve as a gauge for measuring behaviors, attitudes, services, facilities, and perhaps profit. Standards help the manager control use of organizational resources by defining success or failure, effective or ineffective performance. "The relative success or failure of everything we do is determined by accepted standards, whether they be in school grades, sports achievements, income level, height or weight."[2]

---

1.   Harold Koontz and Cyril O'Donnell, *Principles of Management: An Analysis of Management Function*, 5th ed., (New York: McGraw-Hill, 1972), pp. 586–90.
2.   George I. Morrisey, *Management by Objectives and Results* (Reading, Mass.: Addison-Wesley, 1970), p. 109.

Establishing Standards

Standards allow us to understand what it is that we must achieve in order to be successful, or to operate in an efficient manner. In order for standards to be employed, the manager must first determine precisely what is to be measured. Second, the manager must define a point of measurement for effective performance. In other words, the standard must be stated and then evaluative criteria must be developed in order to more precisely delineate what steps must be taken to determine whether the standard has been achieved. For example, there are evaluative criteria that govern the therapeutic recreation profession in the area of personnel practices. These standards might be written as follows:

Standard for personnel practices. The institution has personnel policies and practices that are periodically reviewed by its governing body and revised as necessary.

Evaluative criteria. There is a written statement of personnel policies and practices. A copy of the statement is given to each employee and kept on file in the department. The policies are periodically reviewed by the governing body and revised as necessary.

In this example, the standard is that "The institution has personnel policies and practices" and that these are "reviewed by its governing body and revised if necessary." The evaluative criteria to measure the extent to which the standard has been achieved are relatively explicit. The criteria suggest that: (1) there is an actual written document; (2) the document is presented to each employee, as well as being kept on file in the department; and (3) the policies are reviewed periodically. Two of these three evaluative criteria are specific and can be measured to indicate whether or not the standard has been achieved. For example, the existence of a written document can be verified. It can be verified that the document is on file and that each employee has been given a copy. The distribution of the document can be recorded by the manager and verified by asking each employee whether it has been received. The last of the evaluative criteria could be made more specific, and thus more useful in measuring the accomplishment of the standard. The term "periodically" could be revised to say "annually," "semiannually" or "quarterly."

There are numerous benefits associated with the establishment of standards and criteria. Morrisey has identified ten of these benefits:

1. Yardstick for determining the probability for reaching objectives.
2. Means of measuring individual performance:
   a) for compensation purposes;
   b) for employee development purposes;
   c) for work assignment purposes;
   d) for promotional purposes;
   e) for downgrade or disciplinary purposes.

3. Incentive for individual improvement.

4. Incentive for organizational improvement.

5. Incentive for innovative approaches to work performance.

6. Means of self-measurement and correction.

7. Means of interpretation of performance to others.

8. Means of making realistic forecasts:
   a) for man/loading purposes;
   b) for facility, equipment and material needs;
   c) for evaluating and making trade-offs on objectives;
   d) for pricing purposes (bidding on contracts).

9. Incentive and means for continuous and consistent reevaluation of methods and results.

10. Means of comparison with the performance of other organizational units, departments or companies.[3]

In which areas of organizational management should standards be established? Virtually all areas within an organization can develop meaningful standards and evaluative criteria that measure performance. Standards can govern such areas as organizational philosophy; objectives; organization or client confidentiality; discrimination; organizational structure; interdepartmental relations; relations with the community; budget; record keeping; public information; safety; personnel practices; job descriptions; hours of work; wages, salaries, and fringe benefits; recruitment; selection, and training of employees; evaluation of employees and programs; promotion of employees; employee assignments and work load; staff development; supervision; employee qualifications; needs and interests of clients; diversity of program offerings; development of program objectives; and areas, facilities, and equipment.

Several documents drawn up in Canada and the United States over the past several decades address the development of standards for the recreation and leisure profession. The majority of the standards within these documents focus on acquisition, development, and provision of areas and facilities. Documents such as *National Park, Recreation and Open Space Standards*, published by the National Recreation and Park Association and *Outdoor Recreation Space Standards*, published by the U.S. Department of the Interior, serve as examples of standards for recreation areas and facilities. The most comprehensive document relating to various components of the public park and recreation system is the document *Evaluation and Self-Study of Public Recreation and Park Agencies*, also published by the National Recreation and Park Association.

Within the past few years, the appropriateness of the development and use of national standards by local communities for parks, recreation, and open space has been hotly debated. It has been suggested that the use of

---

3. George I. Morrisey, *Management by Objectives and Results* (Reading, Mass.: Addison-Wesley, 1970), p. 110.

national standards by local communities is inappropriate. Most standards, especially those related to the acquisition and development of space, are quantitative and are based on the suggestion of a given number of acres, facilities, or types of parks per 1000 population. These standards that have been developed by "experts" often do not have an empirically supportable base and have been compiled by averaging various standards developed by communities throughout the nation. This process ignores the fact that each community is unique. Many leaders in the park and recreation field suggest that standards should be *community-specific*. Each community should go through the process of determining its own needs and resources, based on an understanding of the unique social, political, economic, and geographic conditions present. The authors endorse this view and, furthermore, suggest that the development of standards for other organizational functions should follow a similar *organization-specific* process. This is not to suggest that minimum standards suggested by national organizations or other bodies should not be considered, but that an organization should develop its own standards based on local conditions.

There are several approaches that managers can use to develop organizational standards. First, the manager can review *historical records*. By examining past performance, the manager can often determine what has constituted a successful level of production. In addition, the manager may be able to isolate the factors that influenced successful performance, as well as the achievement of organizational goals. Standards for future performance may be predicated on past performance in the areas of cost effectiveness, sales, number of participants, number of program offerings, and number of acres acquired and developed. Another method of developing standards is to compare the performance of different individuals, different administrative units, different organizations, or different communities. This is known as the *comparative-analysis* approach. This approach can be useful whenever conditions present in two situations are similar enough to offer a valid comparison. In the *subjective analysis* method of setting standards, a manager and others establish a set of ideals based on their subjective appraisal of the situation. The danger in using this approach is that the standards set are often unrealistic and may not consider past performance, current resources, and other relevant variables. The final approach that can be used in setting standards is known as *objective analysis*. The development of performance standards on an objective basis can be linked to the time and motion studies established at the turn of the century by such well-known management theorists as Frederick Taylor. This method is based on the application of quantitative methods to determine organizational standards.

Standards and Performance

In the opinion of the authors, there is a direct relationship between the establishment of high standards and employee productivity. When discussing work performance, one might think of standards as the expectations that the manager has for the individual employee's performance. The manager who is industrious, conscientious, positive, and focused on attaining the goals of the organization, will often have an influence on other employees. If the manager's work patterns reflect poor time management, sloppy work, unpredictability, a lack of focus on results and the processes used to achieve them, similar behavior may be exhibited by subordinates. Individuals in subordinate roles are unlikely to be motivated to operate in a manner that is different from the manager's demonstrated behavior. Thus, the manager's demonstrated behavior directly influences the behavior of employees.

The recreation and leisure service manager must not only lead by example, but must consciously encourage high performance by establishing high expectations for each individual within the organization. High expectations mean very simply that the manager expects nothing less than the employee's best effort. The manager should expect employees to work up to the highest level of their potential. When an individual is challenged to use his or her potential and views this effort in a positive light, the result will be individual growth. Individual growth, in turn, is directly tied to job satisfaction. When people feel challenged, they grow; when they grow they have the opportunity for satisfaction in the work environment. When the efforts of employees are channeled toward the fulfillment of organizational goals, the result is organizational growth. This is the purpose of management: to enable individuals to prosper, while enabling the organization to prosper and achieve its goals.

Often, the way that we view the potential of each employee will influence our expectation for that employee. A manager who views an employee as competent, well organized, articulate, and energetic will tend to have greater expectations for that individual. On the other hand, if a person is perceived in a poorer light, the expectations will be correspondingly lower. It is important for the manager to remember that perceptions of the capabilities and potential of an employee may be inaccurate. The manager's perceptions may be affected by a variety of factors that are not necessarily related to competence. It is the responsibility of the manager to attempt to avoid biases and preconceptions and view each employee in terms of actual assets and liabilities, and the way in which the assets can be used to benefit the organization.

The ability of the recreation and leisure service manager to view individuals objectively is a fair measure of professional maturity. When confronted with poor individual or organizational performance, the easiest avenue of action for the manager is to fire the employee. It takes a far better manager to recognize the potential of each employee, even an apparently nonproductive person, and to create the proper challenges or expectations that will result in productive human effort. Perhaps the best lesson we can learn with regard to expectations and performance is from the Japanese. A large portion of the Japanese work force is guaranteed lifetime employment. The Japanese manager does not have the option of terminating an individual for poor performance or because of personality differences. The manager, in order to be successful, must determine what the individual's needs are, what motivates that individual, and how the individual can be challenged to operate in a manner consistent with the goals of the organization. Because of this, Japanese workers are among the most productive in the world today. The Japanese manager is forced to understand human needs. If he has a problem, he cannot alleviate it simply by terminating an unproductive employee. He must create incentives that relate to the individual's needs. In most Japanese corporations, high expectations for quality, productivity, and loyalty are a part of the organizational strategy.

The expectations of the manager are often a self-fulfilling prophecy. As indicated, high expectations lead to high performance, low expectations lead to low performance. A good example of how perceptions can affect behavior and become a self-fulfilling prophecy can be found in a research project conducted in the educational field. A group of 18 elementary school teachers were told that 20 percent of the children in their classrooms were "late bloomers." Late bloomers were said to be children who had not yet demonstrated a great deal of proficiency in their subjects, but who were exceptionally bright and would soon excel in their studies. In reality, the students were chosen at random, and were not representative of any special selection process. The teachers, however, had high expectations for these students. As a result, the students identified as late bloomers did indeed excel over the year and were said by their teachers to be bright, industrious, and conscientious. In fact, children in the late bloomer group actually showed an increase in IQ scores over the course of the year's study.

The lesson to be learned by the recreation and leisure manager from the "late bloomer" study is the effect that expectations can have on the performances of employees, and even on the manager's own performance and perceptions. The above example could just as easily be reversed. The teachers could have been told that 20 percent of their children were delinquent and destined for jail. Most likely, by the end of the year, the teachers would have had negative feelings about these children and would have proved their expectations to be correct. In the same sense, the recreation and leisure service manager's expectations and perceptions, positive or negative, will affect employee performance. Discussing the influence that a manager's expectations have on employee productivity, Livingston has written the following:

- A manager's expectations of employees and the way he or she treats them largely determine their performance and career progress.

- A unique characteristic of superior managers is their ability to create high performance expectations that subordinates fulfill.

- Less effective managers fail to develop similar expectations and, as a consequence, the productivity of their subordinates suffers.

- Subordinates more often than not, appear to do what they believe they are expected to do.[4]

Thus, it is important for the recreation and leisure service manager to personally exhibit a work profile that sets an example for employees and to establish high expectations for each employee.

COMPARING STANDARDS TO ACTUAL PERFORMANCE

Following the establishment of standards, the next step in the control process is the comparison of performance with standards. This is the most important part of the controlling process. There are numerous ways of detecting differences between desired and actual levels of performance, including personal observation, work sampling reports, problem reports, delinquent status reports, time cards, quantity and quality trend charts, network analyses and reports, status reports, and inspection checklists.

In most recreation and leisure service organizations, there is little systematic analysis of the mechanisms used to gather information regarding performance. There is a need to systematically evaluate the methods by which reliable information can be gathered relative to performance. Factors to be considered when analyzing an information-gathering system are the cost of the information system; the reliability, validity, and value of the information obtained from the system; and the frequency with which the system will obtain information. An annual employee performance appraisal is obviously a necessary formality; however, if this is the manager's only attempt to evaluate the employee, the results will be ineffective. An effective manager should interact with the employee more frequently, even on a day-to-day basis if possible, so that accurate and comprehensive information can be gathered relative to performance. Some of the key questions that must be addressed when selecting control mechanisms to gather information are the following:

1. What specific variables will this control measure identify?
2. What significant variances may not be effectively identified?
3. How much time is required to take effective corrective action? Does this control measure allow sufficient lead time?
4. How much time and effort will be required to apply this control measure?
   a) Does the value justify the cost?
   b) Is there another less costly measurement method available?

---

4.   J. Sterling Livingston, "Pygmalion in Management," *Harvard Business Review* (July–August, 1969), as cited in R. Wayne Mondy, Robert E. Holmes, and Edwin B. Flippo, *Management: Concepts and Practices* (Boston: Allyn and Bacon, 1980), pp. 285–86.

5. What is the danger of over controlling (does the control mechanism create more barriers than useful information) by the manager?[5]

Control mechanisms can be compared to standards relating to quantity, quality, time, and budget.[6] *Quality control* mechanisms provide information concerning such factors as durability and workmanship. For example, a recreation leader teaching a judo class might be evaluated as to the methods of presentation, the content of the course, the depth of knowledge that he or she evidences, rapport with students, and the degree of proficiency demonstrated by the students upon completion of the program. *Quantity control* mechanisms deal with numbers. In recreation and leisure service organizations, quantity control might relate to the number of people attending an event, the number of acres mowed by a park maintenance man, or the volume of sales for a profit-making organization. The establishment of controls to review *dimensions of time* is generally concerned with the amount of time (in hours, days, months, and years) needed to complete a project. The time it takes to plan an activity, type a letter, line a baseball diamond, build a creative playground, prepare a report, or develop a brochure can be measured quantitatively and compared to a standard. Last, *budgetary* control mechanisms can be established that compare estimated expenditures with actual fiscal expenditures. A budget can be viewed as a control mechanism in that it is a major source of fiscal control for an agency.

CORRECTIVE ACTION

Once the recreation and leisure service manager has compared actual performance to the standards established by the organization, appropriate action must be determined. If performance is below the standard, the manager will engage in *corrective action*. The purpose of corrective action is to ensure that the organization is achieving its goals and that its resources are being used in an appropriate manner. For example, if the manager determines that the performance of an employee is not consistent with the organization's expectations, corrective action can be taken to ensure that the individual's efforts are directed toward the achievement of organizational goals.

When does corrective action occur? Two approaches can be taken in the timing of corrective action. *Formative evaluation* occurs when the manager systematically evaluates the steps followed in the development of a program, facility, or other activity. The focus of this type of corrective action is the immediate adjustment of the work of the organization in order to ensure that ultimately its goals will be achieved. For example, when

5. George I. Morrisey, *Management by Objectives and Results* (Reading, Mass.: Addison-Wesley, 1970), p. 132.
6. R. Wayne Mondy, Robert E. Holmes, and Edwin B. Flippo, *Management: Concepts and Practices* (Boston: Allyn and Bacon, 1980), p. 8.

planning a recreation activity, there is a need to promote it aggressively. If adequate promotional methods are not being used by a recreation supervisor, the manager might step in and ensure that appropriate methods are employed. The second process or approach is known as *summative evaluation*. At the conclusion of the activity, the manager and the supervisor will determine the extent to which the program and process used to produce the activity achieved its stated objectives. The manager might ask questions such as Just how and why did events stray from their planned course? What can be done to prevent a recurrence of this difficulty?[7] The goal of this type of corrective action is determination of changes that can be made to avoid repeating the same mistakes when organizing similar programs.

Corrective action is more likely to be needed when certain factors are present in the organizational environment. For example, future factors are often unpredictable and find the manager in a reactive rather than a proactive posture. Morrisey has suggested that there are four common *causes of variances requiring corrective action:*

Uncertainties. Some of the typical uncertainties that might cause a deviance in performance are possible change in leadership at a critical level, possible delay in receipt of materials, facilities or personnel, possibility of a contract cancellation, possible change in direction, and possibility that the original forecast was inaccurate.

Unexpected events. Events that were not anticipated include such things as loss of key personnel, new design development, and changes in the market picture. Such occurrences cause delay, acceleration, or change in the scope of work performance.

Failures. Failures are stoppages that are beyond the control of the manager and his or her subordinates. These include such things as machine failures, test failures, nonreceipt of critical material (parts, designs, outside instructions), and failure to get anticipated approvals.

Human error. Human error is largely within the control of the manager. Human error can be divided into two categories—honest error and incompetence. *Honest error* may occur as a result of miscalculation, lack of knowledge or skill, lack of proper instruction, an unusually heavy work load, or outside distractions or interferences. *Incompetence* refers to willful wrongdoing, gross negligence, or incapacity to perform the work satisfactorily.[8]

Morrisey has further indicated that there are three types of corrective action that can take place independently or in combination.[9] The first is *self-correcting action*. The employee engaged in self-correcting action independently assumes responsibility for changing work performance. Since a

---

7.   R. Wayne Mondy, Robert E. Holmes, and Edwin B. Flippo, *Management: Concepts and Practices* (Boston: Allyn and Bacon, 1980), p. 112.

8.   George I. Morrisey, *Management by Objectives and Results* (Reading, Mass.: Addison-Wesley, 1970), pp. 132–35.

9.   George I. Morrisey, *Management by Objectives and Results* (Reading, Mass.: Addison-Wesley, 1970), pp. 134–35.

major management goal is to have employees operate autonomously, self-correcting behavior on the part of employees is desirable. *Operating action* is corrective action that involves the use of a new or different management technique, process, or tool and the employment of a new strategy or type of technology. Last, *management action* is the process wherein the manager determines if his or her original goals, objectives, and expectations were appropriate. Management action often results in reorientation of managerial style and restructuring of management-employee relations.

WHAT TO CONTROL?

As previously discussed, the recreation and leisure service manager primarily works with four types of resources: human, fiscal, physical, and technological. A number of management tools and techniques are used to control these resources. The recreation and leisure service field needs management techniques that will be specific to the profession. Most management tools are borrowed from business and found in the management literature. These applied skills are adapted for use in recreation and leisure service organizations to meet the specific needs of an organization, rather than on a universal basis throughout the field.

Although we will discuss a number of management techniques and tools that can be used as control mechanisms for each of the four types of resources mentioned, the reader should keep in mind that it is often difficult to separate the control of one type of resource from another. For example, fiscal controls are tied to the control of human resources, as well as technological resources. The tools and techniques that will be presented in each of these categories represent those that are commonly used in recreation and leisure service organizations or those that could be applied to the profession. As mentioned, there is a close relationship between planning and control. Many of the management techniques and tools used in the planning process are also used in the control process.

CONTROLLING HUMAN RESOURCES

Human resources are the most important resources of an organization. It is through the organization of human effort that accomplishments are made and organizational objectives attained. Controlling human resources is a process of shaping behavior. The organizational climate, motivation, reward systems, and performance appraisal are elements that shape employee behavior. The recreation and leisure service manager, implementing control techniques, is concerned with the extent to which individual performance exceeds, is equal to, or is less than the performance expected by the organization. The manager must evaluate not only the amount of work that an individual accomplishes, but the quality of the work.

The management of human resources within an organization also includes many other variables, such as relationships with labor organizations and unions, employee turnover, absenteeism, wage and salary costs, and safety. All of these variables can be controlled by the establishment of appropriate management techniques and tools. For example, labor relations can be controlled by the manager who understands the bargaining process and the aims of unions. Absenteeism and turnover can be controlled by establishing management systems that challenge employees and encourage development.

There are a number of definable management techniques that can be used to control human resources. These management techniques vary from financial incentives to programs that are directed toward encouraging employee development. There are a number of specific performance appraisal techniques that are used by recreation and leisure service organizations. Following is a sampling of control mechanisms available to recreation and leisure service organizations.

Management by objectives.   Perhaps the most popular management tool used for control is management by objectives (MBO). As a control technique, MBO provides the manager with an opportunity to review performance, in a timely fashion, so that corrective action can be taken. The MBO process can be used to control the way in which individuals use their time and the organization's resources. In addition, it provides a mechanism for gauging the quality and quantity of performance. Because objectives are stated in advance and mutually agreed upon by the manager and the subordinate, deviation from these standards is obvious and hence can be controlled by the individual and by the manager. When the individual checks his or her own performance against objectives, the process is self-correcting. If this does not occur, correction requires management intervention.

Financial controls.   Many organizations in the private sector establish programs in which financial incentives are used as motivating and control mechanisms. Generally speaking, financial incentives are viewed as one of the major mechanisms for modifying behavior. In establishing financial control programs, it is important to ensure that the employee understands the relationship between the payment of wages or salary and the performance desired. Unless an employee understands this relationship, use of financial incentives as a control mechanism will be ineffective.

Personal observations and interviews.   The control mechanism most frequently used to assess performance is that of personal observations and interviews. In some cases, this process is extremely systematic and related to specific check lists. One has to exercise caution when using the personal observation and interview mechanism of control, because of individual bias and differences in perceptions. What may be viewed as a problem by one individual (for example, aggressiveness) may be viewed as an asset by another individual within the organization.

Complaint, accident, and incident reports.   Organizations also provide numerous forms to record complaints, accidents, and incident analyses. By using these control mechanisms, problems can be identified and performance can be evaluated. Another type of record that can be used as a control mechanism is a daily log. From a log, it is possible to analyze the way that work efforts are being organized, and the extent to which the employee is using time efficiently.

Status and recognition.   The value of status and recognition techniques as control mechanisms is dependent upon the value associated with such variables by the individual employee. If an employee feels that status and recognition are important, then they can be used in the control process. Many organizations have thoroughly developed status and reward mechanisms. Often these come in the form of recognition for length of service and quality of performance. For example, individuals who had not met standards for attendance and performance would not receive status and recognition accorded to those individuals who had met such standards.

Performance appraisal mechanisms.   Often viewed as control mechanisms, performance appraisal techniques are directed toward determining the extent to which the individual successfully fulfills the organization's role expectations. Some techniques focus on personality traits, whereas other techniques are more result oriented. Some of the more common performance appraisal techniques are rating scales, forced distribution, forced choice, and critical incident. Rating scales are perhaps the most commonly used of these techniques. Rating scales include descriptive statements of desired behaviors and a scale on which actual performance is plotted in order to determine the extent to which an individual has demonstrated the desired behavior.

Use of psychological principles.   Use of psychological principles in the control of employee performance is becoming more common. Two concepts, *operant* conditioning and *modeling,* or social imitation, are especially suited for use within recreation and leisure service organizations. Operant conditioning is a process in which the manager shapes the behavior of the individual in order to elicit a set of desired outcomes. Appropriate responses or behavior are rewarded, whereas inappropriate behavior is not, or receives negative reinforcement. Modeling and social imitation refers to the vicarious reinforcement that an employee receives when observing a model act appropriately and receive consequent reinforcement.[10] As previously indicated, the expectations that are created for individual performance can be a powerful tool in controlling behavior.

---

10.   Marvin D. Dunnett, *Work and Nonwork in the Year 2001* (Monterey, California: Brooks/Cole, 1973), p. 125.

When establishing control systems, it is important to have accurate information regarding individual performance. This is especially important for nonprofit recreation and leisure service organizations where expectations may be nebulous, results difficult to define, and work activities problematic. In profit-oriented organizations, where the net gain or loss associated with an activity is used as a yardstick to gauge individual performance, the control process is more quantifiable. In either case, it is important that the manager precisely define not only the objectives for each individual, but also the broader goals of the organization. Further, it is important that specific methods to measure performance be developed. These methods should focus on both the end results desired and the processes for achieving those ends. It is hard to measure performance without evaluative criteria that determine what constitutes success or failure. Last, the control system should be tied in some way to the reward system of the organization. Rewards, whether financial or psychological, tie performance and its measurement to work effort.

Corrective Action and Human Relations

It is critical for effective control that the manager be able to take corrective action in situations where human relations are involved. It is relatively easy to change the parts of a machine, reorganize work schedules, or introduce a new piece of equipment to the organization. The retraining of individuals to accommodate changes in the application of equipment or work processes is a management action that is usually received in a positive way by employees. However, when an individual is not operating at full potential, deviating from standard work procedures or organizational expectations, corrective action on the part of the manager is often viewed as being disciplinary and may be difficult to employ in a positive manner.

The perceptions of the employee and the manager are key concerns in the process of corrective action. If an employee views the recommendations for corrective action negatively, work performance may be adversely affected. The employee may feel dejected and embarrassed, and have a lowered sense of self-esteem. The manager's perception of disciplinary action will also influence whether or not the corrective action is transmitted in a way that is nonthreatening and results in cooperative behavior.

In Chapter 7, the authors introduce the concepts of Douglas McGregor, known as theory X and theory Y. These assumptions about the nature of human beings can directly influence a manager's leadership style and relationships with employees. Theory X assumptions are basically negative ones that suggest that individuals need to be controlled and coerced in order to operate competently. Theory Y assumptions suggest that individuals can be committed to an enterprise and can exercise self-discipline in conducting their work activities. When taking corrective action, a manager operating from a theory X posture is likely to generate hostility and resentment on the part of the employees. The theory Y manager will view corrective action as a growth-oriented process. Another key distinction between theory X and theory Y assumptions is in the way that managers view control and its sources. Theory X managers view themselves as responsible for control. They would see their jobs as overseeing individuals and detecting and correcting deviations in work performance. Theory Y managers view the employees as able to exercise self-discipline and to assume the responsibility for control. In this situation, the manager's role would be vastly different than that of the manager operating from a theory X posture. The theory Y manager would see his job as one of removing barriers and helping employees change their behavior in order to contribute to the goals of the organization. The manager would help employees identify and solve problems that hinder effective performance. In doing so, the manager might point out different strategies and approaches that could be used by the employee to overcome barriers.

Are organizations and individuals likely to use theory Y management assumptions when taking corrective action? Organizations within North American society today are not based on theory Y assumptions. Lacking in most organizations is a clear-cut organizational philosophy dedicated to not only effective and efficient service delivery, but also to the growth and dignity of each employee. Many organizations rely on the application of management principles that concentrate authority and power in a few individuals. Further, organizations tend to use power in a coercive sense to force individuals to be cooperative in the performance of their work. The overall organizational philosophy must be addressed, as well as individual managerial leadership behavior styles, in order to successfully build an environment in which corrective action is viewed in a positive light.

One way in which corrective action is taken is *coaching*. Coaching can be thought of as a process of verbal exchange that is designed to increase worker proficiency, while at the same time encouraging growth. Coaching helps to develop a positive, supportive organizational climate. Coaching can address several concerns within the organization. First, a manager can coach subordinates in order to close the gap between expectations and performance. The recreation and leisure service manager, by working with employees, can develop a set of mutual expectations regarding the employees' responsibilities, as well as the organization's level of expected performance. In the strictest sense, coaching is used in this situation as a process of corrective action. It may involve helping the individual identify reasons for poor performance and difficulties encountered in the work environment. The coaching process also attempts to encourage the employee to operate in a more independent fashion. Research studies have shown that effective managers spend more time in long-range planning and less time directing their subordinates. The consumption of the manager's time by subordinates can determine the manager's success or failure. Having individuals operate independently by means of corrective action through the coaching process will ensure that the organization's resources are maximized.

A management technique that can be used with coaching is known as *consensus evaluation.* This process is a simple one and can be readily employed in any recreation and leisure service organization. Basically, the manager determines two things: What are the tasks that need to be completed? How well do the tasks need to be done? The employee is then asked to answer the same questions. The manager and employee together determine the role expectations, what constitutes acceptable performance, and last, but most important, the extent to which the individual has understood the organizational expectations for performance.

It is interesting to note that the use of management by objectives in large organizations has increasingly been viewed as a way of coaching individuals. The MBO process basically follows the same format as consensus evaluation. In an MBO system, a set of organizational goals and assumptions is developed. In turn, employees develop their own objectives in relation to broader organizational assumptions and goals. As in the consensus evaluation process, the manager and his subordinates meet individually, and perhaps collectively, to negotiate work activities, processes, and measures of effectiveness. The Dallas Park and Recreation Department has utilized the MBO system in the recreation division for the last few years. According to the assistant director of recreation for this organization, the MBO process is best seen as a coaching technique: "A way of helping individuals more clearly understand their roles as well as providing bench marks to gauge their performances."

Again, the posture that is assumed by the manager or the leisure service organization when engaging in corrective action can be negative or positive. The organization should strive to develop a positive orientation when taking corrective action among its employees. The development of a positive organizational climate can be best accomplished through the establishment of a coaching process that emphasizes mutual trust and confidence between the manager and subordinates. Appropriate tools, such as consensus evaluation or management by objectives, can be employed by the manager to assist in this process.

Controlling Management Practices

The management practices employed in the control process can affect productivity and can influence the extent to which an organization is successful in achieving its goals. It is the responsibility of each manager to carefully analyze the work situation to determine whether or not his or her own behavior is contributing to low productivity or other organizational problems. There are a number of variables that can be controlled by the manager. Some of the more important ones are managerial leadership style, communication, task definition, autonomy, and staff cohesion.

Managerial leadership style. Research literature has demonstrated that different situations require different managerial leadership styles. In one situation, an autocratic style may be most appropriate, while in another situation a democratic style may be more effective. Leadership style also refers to the type of structure and support provided to employees. In some cases the extent to which the manager is consistant in management style will influence productivity. The effective manager knows which style is appropriate in a given situation.

Communications.   The source of poor communication can be the sender as well as the receiver. For effective communications to take place, the message transmitted must not only be understood, but accepted by the receiver. Another concern relative to communications practice is the selective distribution of information. It is important that the manager provide information that is timely and appropriate. Employees have a desire to be well informed about current organizational concerns.

Task definition.   The manager can control the way that jobs are designed and interpreted to employees. Moreover, the manager can control the efficiency with which activities are planned and operated. Good planning that is goal-oriented creates an atmosphere that encourages higher employee productivity. Lack of knowledge of procedures and regulations can create conflicting expectations that may result in hostility between the manager and subordinates.

Autonomy.   The manager can determine the extent to which individuals are allowed to exercise independent judgement and operate in an autonomous manner. Management should strive to create an environment in which individuals can operate in an independent and self-sufficient manner. However, many managers are reluctant to delegate responsibility and authority to individuals, preferring to maintain control over work schedules, decision making, and other variables. Often a manager will use the organization's policies as a way of maintaining control and discouraging employee independence. The greater the dependency of employees, the greater is the degree of control that the manager exercises over them. The use of some control mechanisms may inhibit worker autonomy and, hence, productivity.

Staff cohesion and support.   The manager can, of course, directly influence the extent to which he or she is supportive of subordinates. The manager can also influence the extent to which employees are supportive of one another. Generally speaking, employees are more productive in an environment where support for one another exists. Thus, by encouraging individuals to be friendly and mutually supportive, the manager helps to create a work climate that is conducive to high performance. In addition, the manager can actively promote social opportunities where employees are brought together and encouraged to get to know each other better. The Japanese have employed this socializing approach to management very successfully in building staff cohesion. North American managers often shy away from socializing with employees, viewing it as inappropriate. The Japanese view socializing as an opportunity to learn about employees' needs and to build loyalty and organizational cohesion.

These points represent most, though not all, of the management practices that can be directly controlled by the recreation and leisure service manager. When taking corrective action, the manager ought first to look inward. The manager ought to ask, Are my management practices the source of the problem? Can my behavior, actions, or processes be altered or controlled? This can be a very threatening exercise for the manager who lacks a strong ego and self-esteem. If the manager determines, however, that it is his or her behavior or practices that need to be altered, unnecessary adjustments that may be painful to employees can be avoided. One cause of managerial and organizational failure is the transference of blame. "Passing the buck" is an unwise and ineffective short-term solution to problems.

CONTROLLING FISCAL RESOURCES

The control of fiscal resources in times of inflation, recession, and government cutbacks, and reduced productivity is a major concern that all recreation and leisure service organizations, both public and private, must address. Profit-oriented recreation and leisure service organizations are attempting to improve their cash flow and reduce expenses to improve profitability. Public recreation and leisure service agencies are being challenged to do more with less and, in some cases, their very survival is at stake.

The primary source of fiscal control is the budget. A *budget* is a financial statement that is used in the planning and controlling processes. The budget is used to estimate expenditures for the development, organization, and implementation of services. When actual financial expenditures are compared with estimates, the budget can be viewed as a control mechanism. Budgeting is an ongoing, evaluative process wherein the manager constantly reviews an organization's expenditures in order to avoid overexpenditures. The budget can also be used as a mechanism to compare the various costs associated with producing individual programs, services, or products to gauge the cost-effectiveness of one service, as compared with another.

Many different control mechanisms can be employed when dealing with financial resources. Some deal directly with the current revenues and expenditures of the organization; others are involved more indirectly in the control function. Financial control mechanisms include budgeting procedures, accounting, and auditing procedures. Some of the specific financial control mechanisms are as follows.

Cost-benefit analysis.   Cost-benefit analysis determines the impact or effectiveness of a program in relationship to its cost. Cost-benefit analysis in the recreation and leisure service field is usually used to determine the cost of a program, based on the number of participants or user hours. This allows an agency to determine the costs associated with each program and compare these costs to determine which services are most cost-effective.

Financial ratios.   A ratio can be thought of as a way of comparing one unit with another. Similar to cost-benefit analysis, financial ratios employed as a control mechanism allow comparisons of programs, divisions, agencies, past and current performance, and so on. There are four types of ratios: liquidity, leverage, activity, and profitability. *Liquidity* ratios are concerned with the ability of an organization to meet its current obligations. *Leverage* ratios relate to the ability of an organization to use outside resources (i.e., their bond rating). *Activity* ratios are concerned with the actual use of the organization's resources. Overall operating efficiency and effectiveness is the concern of *profitability* ratios.

Breakeven analysis.   Breakeven analysis enables profit-making organizations to determine at what point profitability occurs. The breakeven point is the point at which the volume of sales exceeds the costs of producing a product or service. Beyond this point, the organization achieves a profit. In other words, an organization must sell *x* number of products or services in order to cover its fixed and variable costs. After these costs have been covered by sales revenue, profit occurs.

Organizational audit.   As discussed in Chapter 8, auditing is the process wherein accounting records are viewed in order to determine whether they have been appropriately kept. This involves checking ledgers, accounts, inventories, and other operations of the organization. There are two types of auditing: internal and external. Internal auditing is conducted by individuals operating within the organization. Their appraisal is continuous and ongoing. The purpose of internal auditing is to ensure that the accounting system is being properly maintained and that resources are being used appropriately. External auditing occurs when the organization arranges for an external source of review. This external source of reveiw ensures an independent and unbiased appraisal of the organization's financial management program.

Risk management.   Risk management is a control mechanism that is concerned with reducing financial loss resulting from organizational activities that involve risk. In order to control the risks to which an organization is exposed a manager identifies risks and attempts to determine which methods are best suited to control them. There are four basic methods for handling risks: avoidance, reduction, transfer, and retention.

Avoidance of involvement in an activity is an option that reduces exposure to the possibility of financial loss. Reduction involves changing the activity or facility in such a way as to minimize potential loss—for example, making repairs. Transfer of responsibility is an option in which other parties assume the liability for potential losses (an insurance company, for example). Retaining the cost for risks rather than transferring it to another party (as when buying insurance) might be appropriate for risks that are of low probability and low cost.

Program planning budgeting system (PPBS).   The main feature of the PPBS method of budgeting is that it allows systematic and rigorous appraisal of program alternatives. By specifying objectives for each program or unit within an organization, this method of budgeting facilitates the control process. Stating specific program goals enables the recreation and leisure service manager to ask the question, How effective have we been in achieving these goals? Program budgets also serve as control mechanisms by grouping with each program all costs associated with it. This allows the manager, as well as the public, to have a clear understanding of the actual costs associated with an activity, facility, or administrative unit (often indirect costs such as administrative overhead are not easily definable in other types of budgets).

Zero-based budgeting (ZBB).   The ZBB approach to budgeting is primarily a control mechanism preventing organizations from automatically expending fiscal resources on already existing projects, programs, services, products, and administrative support. Periodically (usually annually) programs are organized into decision-making packages and are justified according to cost-benefit analyses. This approach allows the manager to avoid automatically refunding programs that are no longer effective. In government as well as business, functions, administrative units, and program services tend to be perpetuated without consideration of their current usefulness. The ZBB process prevents this. ZBB also allows a monthly comparison of results with costs and thereby provides the opportunity for different levels of management to determine variations from the budget and develop a course of corrective action.

Typically, recreation and leisure service organizations will employ a number of different strategies to control fiscal resources. Sophisticated information systems allow continuous and systematic review of financial resources. It is unwise to undertake the controlling of financial resources on an annual basis (for example, when the budget is due). An organization that is precise and detailed in its budget preparations and engages in extensive planning, both long- and short-range, will provide a basis for more effective fiscal controls. One of the problems in the recreation and leisure service field is the lack of fiscal policies and standards upon which to base control.

CONTROLLING PHYSICAL RESOURCES

Controlling physical resources involves the management of areas, facilities, buildings, supplies, and equipment. The reasons for controlling physical resources are fourfold. First, the recreation and leisure service manager wishes to preserve and protect large capital investments. The cost of land that has been developed, as well as facilities such as swimming pools, recreation centers, amusement parks, tennis and racquetball courts, and ice rinks reflect a large investment on the part of the recreation and leisure service organization. This is the case whether the investment is made by the public at large or by individual entrepreneurs. The second reason for controlling of physical resources is to ensure that supplies and equipment are available when required. When a program is implemented, such as a basketball league, there is a need to make sure that the basketballs, scorebooks, timers, and other necessary supplies are on hand in order to conduct the activity in an orderly and efficient fashion. In park maintenance, the lack of an essential chemical or piece of equipment can cause unnecessary delays in park maintenance and may disrupt work schedules. Another reason for controlling physical resources is to prevent their misuse by theft, inappropriate use of equipment, or unauthorized personal use of organizational supplies and equipment. Last, the manager controls physical resources, especially supplies and equipment, in order to ensure that no more of the organization's fiscal resources are tied up than necessary. Rather than stockpile resources unnecessarily, the manager should control physical resources so that fiscal resources are maximized.

Strategies to control physical resources focus on three factors: preventive maintenance, corrective maintenance, and inventory assessments. When a facility is in disrepair or has been vandalized, the manager employs a corrective maintenance strategy, repairing the damage that has been done. Through preventive maintenance the manager controls the physical resources (repairs or replaces them) before they reach the end of their usefulness. Last, to determine the amount of investment in supplies and the number of items available at a given time, the manager establishes an inventory. Some of the control mechanisms that can be used to control physical resources are included in the following discussion.

ABC analysis.   ABC inventory analysis is built on the assumption that various items found in the inventory of an organization have different values. Those items of high cost are classified as A items, those of medium cost are identified as B items, and those with a low value are known as C items. This inventory approach suggests that a detailed control procedure should be established over the most important items and less attention should be paid to the items of less importance. ABC analysis also takes usage into account so that an item that may be of low cost but high in the priority of an organization will be controlled more closely.

Fixed-reorder cycle inventory system.   Using a fixed-reorder cycle inventory system, the manager determines the amount of items used over a fixed period of time. Periodically the list is reviewed and items reordered in accordance with predicted use. This system does not take into account unexpected variables that may interrupt the flow of supplies and equipment to an organization. It is also based primarily on subjective analysis of needs. Nonetheless, it provides a method of controlling the inventory of supplies and equipment, based on need and use.

Fixed-order quantity inventory system.   The fixed-order quantity inventory system, or economic ordering quality inventory system, is a control mechanism directed toward providing the most cost-effective inventory of supplies and equipment. It compares the cost of carrying supplies and equipment as inventory to the savings derived from large quantity purchases. The cost of carrying inventory can be predicated on several factors, such as depreciation, storage, obsolescence, and insurance costs. This particular system is a quantitative, objective approach to controlling inventory.

Check lists.   Practiced by many organizations in the form of work orders and supply lists, the check list approach to controlling inventory rests on the assumption that the use of supplies and equipment should be documented in a systematic fashion. This is done by checking off when materials are used and comparing that information with the quantities of materials on hand. This is similar to the fixed-reorder cycle of inventory, although a cruder approach. The purpose of this control mechanism is to determine how many supplies are being used and by whom. Check lists are also used to review maintenance needs for buildings and other recreation spaces. For example, a maintenance person might determine the current state of playground equipment, making notations about existing needs (or deviations from standards) and recommendations for corrective action. The check list approach to control is systematic in that it provides a prescribed list of supplies and equipment that must be checked.

Personal observation.   Personal observations offer a way of detecting deviations from standards. The more systematic, regular, and continuous personal observations become, the more useful they are in controlling physical resources.

As indicated, the cost of physical resources (facilities, supplies, and equipment) is often great. In some organizations, physical resources may represent a greater financial investment than any other resources. It is important that the organization protect its investment in these types of resources and initiate adequate control mechanisms to ensure that protection is effective. The alternative is deterioration of physical resources, perhaps to the point that they cannot be repaired and must be replaced.

This could involve the organization in unnecessary expense or loss. Thus, it is in the best interests of the organization to control physical resources and ensure that they are protected, preserved, and adequately maintained for future use.

CONTROLLING TECHNOLOGICAL RESOURCES

Technological resources are the processes, knowledge, routines, or methodologies used in the development, organization, and distribution of programs, services, and products. For example, a step-by-step methodology would be used in the organization and implementation of a recreation activity. Maintenance routines also represent a technological process. These processes can be made subject to control processes. Often the way in which services are produced and their resulting impact on individuals produces complaints, frustration, and consumer dissatisfaction. This consumer dissatisfaction must be controlled if the organization is to operate successfully. Analysis of technological processes can result in increased efficiency within an organization. For example, a decision to employ more sophisticated equipment (improved technology) in the pruning of hedges in a Midwestern municipal park and recreation department resulted in considerable savings of man hours and a shift in the way in which the park maintenance schedule was organized.

The expansion of knowledge, as well as the rate at which it is communicated, makes the review of technological processes an important area of consideration in recreation and leisure service organizations. The number of new products, chemicals, equipment, and electronic devices available present the recreation and leisure service manager with opportunities to assess the usefulness of such items in improving the effectiveness of an organization. An illustration of this factor is the range and diversity of swimming pool filtration systems available. An automatic filtration system may provide considerable savings in maintenance, chemicals, and labor costs.

Another area in which knowledge is expanding is the way in which the profession defines and identifies user needs. For example, tests have been developed to measure leisure attitudes, behavior, and interests. Thus, not only are new products being created by our expanding base of knowledge, but also new ways for programs to be organized and delivered.

Controlling technological resources involves the identification of the processes, knowledge, and methodologies that are used to create and distribute products and services. Once these processes have been identified, defined, and understood by the staff, standards can be developed, comparisons can be made between standards and actual performance, and corrective action can be taken. The technological process of an organization combines the resources of the organization—human, fiscal, and physical—to produce the desired product or service. There are several mechanisms that can be used by the recreation and leisure manager to help control technological resources.

Network analysis.   The two most identifiable forms of network analysis are program evaluation review technique (PERT) and critical path method (CPM). These two strategies are useful in planning, coordinating, and controlling the activities of a project. PERT and CPM are concerned primarily with the time associated with producing a product or service. A derivative of PERT/CPM, PERT/cost attempts to control the dimensions of time and cost. Basically, both of these forms of analysis enable the manager to determine the earliest and latest completion time for an activity and the most probable time for completion. In this way, the time predicted to complete a project can be identified and other variables more accurately predicted. When deviations from projected time paths occur, corrective action can be taken.

Information systems.   Use of computer-based simulation and information systems has broad implications for recreation and leisure service organizations. Simulation activities that determine interrelationships between environmental variables, logistics, and other factors can be used in controlling the use of resources. Simulation activities can determine use and capacities of areas and facilities and can result in the regulation and control of management and program strategies. For example, computer simulation of a wilderness river can predict the impact on the environment of use by different numbers of individuals. This can help in the establishment of regulatory policies, as well as the analysis of the physical variables in the environment.

Aggregate control.   Related to the product life cycle, the future aggregate demand for products or services can be calculated. An organization should plan the use of its resources to reflect the gradual build-up of work activity to produce the goods or services, the leveling-off period, and the period in which need for the product or service declines. Its use of its resources should correspond to the various stages in the product life cycle of take-off, growth, leveling-off, and decline. Obviously, an organization does not want to have resources allocated disproportionately to the stages in the product life cycle.

Maintenance schedules.   Schedules that detail annual, seasonal, weekly, and daily maintenance activities can be used for planning and controlling. A maintenance schedule details routine maintenance activities, repairs, and preventive maintenance needs. The maintenance schedule provides an estimate for the accomplishment of each task, as well as the standards for maintaining a facility or piece of equipment. Control procedures can be employed by determining not only the amount of work completed, but the quality of the work done.

Reports.   Reports that analyze the success or failure of activities and the mechanisms used to produce programs can be reviewed to assist in planning and controlling. These reports may detail such factors as the number of individuals attending a program and their reactions to the program. Further, the step-by-step process involved in organizing activities may be detailed, steps and routines may be reviewed, and deviations from acceptable levels of performance can be detected and corrected.

Personal observation and interview.   Often the best way to determine whether technological processes should be changed is by interviewing or observing those who perform a given activity. For example, a supervisor might observe the process used by a park maintenance man in pruning a tree and suggest a newer, more cost-effective method. Personal observation enables the manager to detect deviations from standards firsthand and take corrective action on the spot.

Acceptance sampling.   Acceptance sampling is a control mechanism used in business that has implications for recreation and leisure service organizations. Rather than examine activities on a daily basis, all activities and programs are reveiwed intermittantly and are sampled by the recreation and leisure service manager. The pitfall of this approach, however, is the possibility of a faulty generalization. The manager may, for example, observe a knitting class on a poor night and determine that the class is ineffective, when it is actually well received and effective the remainder of the time. Or the manager may view a poorly organized activity on a particularly good day and, again, make a generalization that is in error. Sampling is a necessity within leisure service organizations; however, the manager should keep in mind the possibility of error.

Management-organizational audit.   Recreation and leisure service organizations may use internal or external sources to audit their organizational structure, role expectations, and performance. An organizational audit usually occurs internally, on an ongoing basis, and occasionally involves the use of external consultants. A complete management analysis of the operations of an organization by an external appraiser can result in the employment of new processes for organizing and delivering services.

SUMMARY

Control is a process that involves the establishment of standards and the comparison of actual performance with these standards. It is through this comparative analysis that problems in the management of organizational resources can be detected and appropriate corrective action pursued by the manager. Standards determine what constitutes acceptable performance or behavior. Standards can be developed by reviewing historical records, analyzing other systems, and by conducting subjective and objective analyses. The level of the standard will directly influence the degree of work effort produced. Effective managers often create high performance expectations that subordinates fulfill. When comparing actual performance (the production of a product or service) to standards, the quality and quantity of the product or service produced and the time and finances involved in its production can be evaluated to determine deviations from the standards. Once standards have been established and compared with actual performance, corrective action can be undertaken. There are three types of corrective action: self-correcting, operating, and management.

The manager controls four types of resources: human, fiscal, physical, and technological. Controlling human resources is a process of shaping behavior. Some of the control mechanisms that can be used are management by objectives; financial controls; personal observations and interviews; complaint, accident, and incident reports; and performance appraisal systems. Both the behavior of the manager and the behavior of subordinates can be controlled; the control process is not a one-way street.

Control of fiscal resources is primarily accomplished through budgeting. Budgeting is a process of estimating expenditures and then controlling the distribution of financial resources in such a way that they conform with these estimates. Several control mechanisms can be employed, including cost-benefit analysis, financial ratios, breakeven analysis, organizational audit, risk management, and two budgeting systems: program planning budgeting system and zero-based budgeting.

In controlling physical resources, the manager is concerned with the protection of large capital investments and the use of supplies and equipment within the recreation and leisure service organization. Some of the control techniques that can be employed are ABC analysis, fixed-reorder cycle inventory system, fixed-order quality inventory system, check list and inventories, and personal observations. The control of technology within an organization refers to the measurement of the knowledge, methods, and routines used to produce recreation and leisure services and products. Some of the control mechanisms to be considered in this area are network analysis, information systems, aggregate control, maintenance schedules, reports, personal observations, acceptance sampling, and management-organizational audits.

STUDY QUESTIONS

1. What is the control process and why is it important in the management of recreation and leisure service organizations?
2. Define the terms "standards" and "evaluative criteria." What is the relationship between the two?
3. Identify the benefits of developing standards and evaluative criteria.
4. What is the relationship between standards and employee productivity?

5. What deviations from the standards within an organization might require corrective action? Identify and discuss three actions that can be taken to correct deviations from the standard within an organization.

6. What problems may occur when taking corrective action in situations where human relations are involved?

7. What can a manager do to "control" his or her own behavior?

8. Identify and discuss control mechanisms for fiscal resources.

9. Identify and discuss control mechanisms for physical resources.

10. Identify and discuss control mechanisms for technological resources.

CASE STUDY 12

The United Way Seminar

At the conclusion of the weekly staff meeting, Laurie George was relating to the senior staff some of his experiences at the recently held United Way Seminar on "Control in Nonprofit Organizations."

"Generally speaking," said George, "I found that the seminar was not worth either the time or the money that I invested by attending. I found that either the material presented by the instructor was just common sense, or the methods of control that he talked about just did not relate to the not-for-profit sector of society or for those of us in government service." When will people finally realize that we don't have a product that can be measured and that we can not be compared to industry? It is very easy to set standards and instigate control procedures when you are producing tractors, motor cars, or television sets, but you just cannot measure our products in the leisure service industry.

"Another point that really got me hopping was the insistence by this business administration type instructor that to have effective control all unit heads should develop their own budgets. Why, if I let that happen here everybody would spend so much money that we would soon be way over our fair share of the tax dollar! No sir! My method of control is the only one that will work in this organization. I'll decide how much money is to be spent for each department, and then I'll have control of how it is spent.

"And furthermore," Laurie continued, "now that we are discussing these United Way seminars, I notice that they now have seminars on public relations and communications, marketing for the nonprofit sector, leadership development, basic and advanced management and a host of other topics. I have been giving these seminars considerable thought and have come to the conclusion that, in general, we are not getting a good return on our investment by having staff in attendance. There is absolutely no way of determining if those in attendance have learned anything or not. Frankly, until it can be shown that we get a bigger bang for our buck than is now the case, I will not allow any more expenditures of this nature. And that is the kind of control we all understand."

QUESTIONS

1. Are control procedures basically the same for organizations that produce services and those that produce goods?

2. If, as George indicates, the organization is not getting a good "bang for its buck," could this be traced to any other causes?

3. Do you think that George's organization has adequately defined its objectives in terms of participation in the program; has it developed a plan of execution to see that these objectives have been reached, and, finally, has it developed some methods of corrective action to ensure that the program is meeting its original objectives?

4. Taking the process of control as outlined in this chapter, how would you apply it to George's comments and action in relation to the United Way seminars?

Managing Organizational Dysfunction

10

All organizations have problems. They may occur as a result of poorly defined organizational objectives, as a result of problems with individual motivation and interest, or for other less obvious reasons. It is not unusual for one to hear about problems such as lack of trust, low motivation, lack of productivity, poor organization, and low morale. These types of behaviors can seriously undermine the work of an organization.

It is important to recognize that organizational dysfunction can be managed. With proper consideration of causes, symptoms, and solutions, a manager can succeed in dealing with organizational problems. The manager should approach these problems as opportunities, that is, as situations in which management knowledge and skills can be applied to effectively meet the challenge presented and resolve organizational dysfunction.

ORGANIZATIONAL DYSFUNCTION

Any situation within a recreation and leisure service agency, involving an individual or group of individuals, that adversely affects the performance of the organization contributes to organizational dysfunction. Organizational dysfunction occurs when something is wrong within the organization that prevents it from achieving its stated objectives. One problem that occurs within recreation and leisure service agencies is that of conflict between individuals. Frequently, we hear If only John and Ted could resolve their personality differences, this would be a better place to work. However, it is important to recognize that organizational problems are not solely confined to conflicts between individuals. There can be conflicts between agencies, as well as conflicts between factions within the organization.

One of the most serious organizational problems is that of *goal displacement*. Goal displacement occurs when an individual's needs conflict with the goals of the organization. This is common in any organization. Each individual's perception of the roles of the organization may differ. This difference in perception can affect the method chosen to accomplish goals, as well as the ultimate achievements. The more closely the employees' personal needs are fused with the goals or purpose of the organization, the more likely it is that goal displacement will be avoided. Other sources of dysfunction within recreation and leisure service agencies are as follows:

Employee burnout.   Burnout, a growing phenomenon among recreation and leisure service professionals, results from occupational stress. Basically, burnout is emotional exhaustion. It often leads to poor relationships between the professional and clients. Some of the factors that cause burnout are case overload, overwhelming administrative duties, and lack of authority to carry out assigned responsibility.

Communications.   Often patterns and styles of communication create organizational problems. In hierarchically structured agencies, lateral communication can be confusing. In any type of organization verbal communication and written communication can be misunderstood. Communicative style can also contribute to problems within the organization. For example, a manager can be overly directive or possess poor listening skills. If communication is effective, directives should result in action.

Goals.   The way in which goals are established in a recreation and leisure service agency can create problems. The real issue in goal-setting is whether appropriate persons are involved in the process and whether long-range strategies are linked to day-to-day tasks. Often organizational objectives are not linked to individual needs, rendering the objectives ineffective.

Decision making.   The decision-making process can be cumbersome and contribute to organizational inefficiency. Problems can occur when decisions are made that are not linked to resources available to the organization or when decisions are made by individuals who do not have sufficient skills or knowledge. The problems associated with delegating authority for decision making can also be a problem.

Organizational conflict.   There are three types of conflict that organizations must manage. The first is interpersonal conflict, that is, conflict between two members within the organization. The second is intrapersonal, that is, conflict that takes place between factions within the organization. The third is conflict that exists between organizations as a whole. The questions should be asked, Does the agency have a way of dealing with this conflict? Does the organization's reward system promote or prevent conflict?

Interface relations.   Often within and between organizations there are overlapping responsibilities. These create an arena for organizational dysfunction. How are these overlapping areas of responsibility dealt with? Are the two units or individuals compatible? Do their interfaces result in conflict or unwarranted competition? Another interface relationship exists between the agency and its consumers.

Organizational roles and structure.   The roles that are created for individuals and the structure that blends these roles into a coherent unit often create dysfunction. Often roles do not allow an individual to maximize his or her potential. Jobs may be created that are not challenging and do not allow the opportunity for creativity.

Employee performance.   Inadequate employee performance is obviously a source of organizational dysfunction. Poor performance can be related to a lack of controls. Often, the appraisal system within an organization breaks down because the performance is not tied to a reward system in a meaningful way. Those conducting appraisals may not understand the full impact that a system has on the employee or the agency as a whole.

Managerial leadership styles.   Adjustment to various management styles can be a source of dysfunction within an organization. Whereas one individual may operate more effectively as a follower, another may require more independence. In addition, it may be difficult for some managers to alter their management styles to meet the needs of a given situation. Conversely, it may be hard for subordinates to mold their behavior to complement a given management style.

Individual expectations.   Often individuals within organizations are not rewarded in ways that satisfy them. The needs of each employee must be understood in order to produce the highest level of performance. In some cases, individual expectations cannot be met because the organization lacks the resources, or the philosophy of the organization is inconsistent with the individual's needs.

Failing to manage these types of dysfunctions can result in such common problems as employee turnover, absenteeism, slow down, low morale, sabotage, and lack of trust. These problems are symptomatic of a failure to plan effectively. Symptoms should not be confused with problems. It is important to treat the source of the problem, i.e., low morale, rather than the symptom, i.e., sabotage. Treatment of the symptoms, in an ad hoc, reactive way prevents the manager from devising long-term solutions. Further, it is important to recognize that problems may be inter-related. Communications, for example, may be related to decision making, objectives, and interface relationships.

DEVELOPING THE MANAGEMENT STRATEGY

Through effective management, organizational dysfunction can be prevented or contained. In fact, through proper management, problems can be corrected before they adversely affect the organization. There are a variety of strategies that can be employed to prevent organizational dysfunction. Perhaps most important is that of establishing a process of problem solving that enables the diagnosis of problems and consideration of alternate solutions. An ongoing problem-solving effort within a service agency will result in organizational improvement, increased competence, and increased organizational effectiveness. A planned management program is needed to prevent and solve organizational problems.

Management strategy to prevent and solve organizational problems should focus on ways in which problems can be identified, decisions made to alleviate the problems, and strategies for change implemented. For example, every recreation and leisure service organization should thoroughly review its objectives every five years. Questions should be asked concerning the future of the organization and the methods it uses to achieve its goals. Are the goals of the organization still relevant today? Are the methods, including the programs and services offered, appropriate? Are the talents and skills of all members of the organization used effectively in solving problems, or is problem resolution confined to a select group of individuals?

As suggested, organizational dysfunction should be dealt with in a comprehensive, organized manner. The manager should approach organizational dysfunction with a step-by-step diagnostic process. Problem-solving skills are central to this process. Problem solving can be thought of as the methods that an organization uses to diagnose problems within the environment and then to select the strategies or solutions that best solve problems associated with organizational dysfunction.

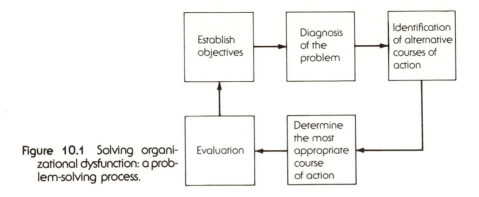

Figure 10.1 Solving organizational dysfunction: a problem-solving process.

Figure 10.1 presents a model that diagrams a five-step process of problem solving.[1] The first step is the establishment of objectives. This is followed by diagnosis of the problem and identification of alternate courses of action. The figure presents two major solutions to problems—structural and human. The last two steps in the process are determination of the most appropriate course of action and measurement of the extent to which the changes made are effective in preventing or resolving the organizational dysfunction. It is important to recognize that this process, organized as a systems design, requires continuous feedback so adjustments to the process may be made. A discussion of each of the five steps in this strategy follows.

Establishing Objectives

Organizational objectives give direction to an agency. They spell out what an agency is trying to accomplish and how it will accomplish it. Organizational objectives serve as the focal point for all decision making. With established objectives, the process of decision making has a foundation. Thus, decisions do not have to be made based on the arbitrary whims of an individual manager. Objectives lend support, justification, and credence to the decision-making process. It is important to point out that there are times when organizational objectives must be reevaluated. For example, personal communication with all employees might be an objective for a leisure service manager. However, as the organization grows in scope and diversity, the advantages of direct communication with each employee may be outweighed by the problems associated with it.

Objectives can be long- or short-term. Short-term objectives tend to focus on immediate needs. Long-term objectives focus on the needs of the organization over extended periods of time. Both types of objectives give direction to the organization and to the manager making the decisions.

1.   Adopted from Joseph J. Bannon, *Problem Solving in Recreation and Parks* (Englewood Cliffs, N.J.: Prentice-Hall, Inc., 1972), p. 47.

Diagnosing the Problem

Diagnosing the problem may be the most complicated and demanding task in the problem-solving process. It involves determining what the problem is and what causes it. Often, this part of the process is clouded because the manager deals with symptoms rather than causes. There are numerous ways that the manager may gather information relative to organizational problems. Some of the methods that a manager can use to gather information are listed as follows:

- *Interview.* Interviewing involves one-to-one interaction with employees to determine their preceptions of problems with the organization.
- *Survey.* Questionnaires can be designed to solicit employee and consumer opinions. Surveys can be designed to gather information regarding such diverse areas as motivating factors, job satisfaction, employer-employee relations, and adequacy of the job environment.
- *Task analysis.* The manager can determine the tasks that need to be done and order them sequentially.
- *Equipment and facility analysis.* Many problems in organizations occur as a result of misuse of equipment or a facility. Correction of problems related to equipment and facilities may involve the training of staff to more effectively use them.
- *Organizational analysis.* The manager can engage in activities such as analysis of communication patterns and organizational patterns in order to identify problems.
- *Appraisal of performance.* Appraisal of performance can lead to the discovery of problems within the organization.
- *Policy analysis.* The manager can review organizational policies to determine if they contribute to existing problems.

Basically, the role of the manager is to collect enough accurate information for the problems within the organization to be defined. Again, the point needs to be made that the inefficient manager may take a reactive approach, waiting for problems to emerge and then trying to diagnose them and find solutions. However, it is obvious that organizational dysfunction can be prevented by constant analysis and resolution of potential problems. A manager should constantly be engaged in analysis of work, equipment and facilities, and organizational structure, as well as the appraisal of individual and organizational performance.

Identification of Alternate Courses of Action

As indicated, there are two basic approaches to the solution of organizational dysfunction—structural and human. Structural solutions include changing the organizational structure, modifying the way that work is organized, modifying the job itself, and changing the physical environment. Structural solutions can be seen primarily as changes to the environment that affect the individual. These are indirect solutions, with behavioral changes occurring as a result of changes to a structure, a job, or the physical work environment. Human solutions to problems are those that directly focus on the skills, attitudes, and knowledge of the employee. They are direct in that the focus is on the individual, rather than components of the environment, such as the organizational structure.

The latter half of this chapter is devoted to a detailed discussion of specific structural and human solutions to organizational problems. It is important to recognize that the best solution to a problem may not be the obvious one. Therefore, a systematic appraisal of as many solutions as possible should be attempted. Short-term objectives may be best met using one solution, whereas long-term objectives may require a different solution. The identification of potential solutions should be a creative process based upon the involvement of all appropriate individuals. Often, the formulation of solutions is bound by individual perceptions, prejudices, and previous experience.

Determining the Most Appropriate Course of Action

In determining the most appropriate course of action, the manager must take a number of factors into consideration. First, the manager must choose a course of action that will solve the problem. However, there are other considerations that must be made, such as cost-effectiveness. A solution may be very effective but too costly. Another consideration is the extent to which the decision produces binding commitment from the individuals involved. If commitment is not an outcome of the problem-solving process, the decision, no matter how appropriate it is, will not be effective.

Although it would be desirable for an organization to achieve consensus on a given course of action, in North America the responsibility for decision making ultimately falls on the shoulders of management. It is therefore critical that the manager carefully weigh alternate courses to minimize the risk involved in selecting one solution. This means that the manager will employ the solution that is cost-effective, builds commitment, and solves the problem with the least risk to the organization. It is interesting to note that, in Japan, building commitment is an essential strategy in choosing the most appropriate course of action. The Japanese commit large amounts of organizational resources to decision making, involving their staffs in this process and allowing veto power to many employees. In North America, an individual manager usually has the responsibility and authority to choose the most appropriate course of action. This is the case with recreation and leisure service agencies.

Measurement and Evaluation

The last step in the diagnosis of organizational dysfunction is that of measurement and evaluation. We evaluate in order to determine the extent to which organizational dysfunction has been alleviated. Without knowing whether the method that we have chosen actually alleviates the problem, our efforts are incomplete. It is important to determine the exact effects of a solution on particular problems. Once this relationship is understood, a manager's efficiency can be increased because he knows that solution A will solve problem B.

There are two basic types of evaluation. One is known as formative evaluation and the other is summative evaluation. *Formative evaluation* takes place on a continuous basis, whereas *summative evaluation* takes place at the end of a process to be appraised. Both types of evaluation are essential in the diagnosis of organizational dysfunction.

SOLUTIONS TO ORGANIZATIONAL PROBLEMS

The next section of this chapter describes a number of different solutions—structural and human—which may be used by the manager to alleviate organizational dysfunction. Structural solutions include organizing work, job design, organizational structure, and physical environment. Human solutions include selection and placement of employees, training and development, motivation, and management-style training. Figure 10.2 represents these concepts.

STRUCTURAL SOLUTIONS

Organizing Work

Work can be organized in various ways to alleviate dysfunction. This is often an underutilized approach to solving organizational problems. There are a number of factors in the work environment that can be manipulated in order to deal with organizational dysfunction. Among these are work schedule options (e.g., flex time; a four-day, 40-hour work week; and accrual of time off), reward structures, and work structure (e.g., choosing an area of work).

Flexible time.   Flexible time formats have been used experimentally in large organizations recently. The concept of flex time has been practiced in professions for many years. The concept is predicated on the premise that the employee is in the best possible position to determine when and how many hours he or she will work. This means that an individual makes a

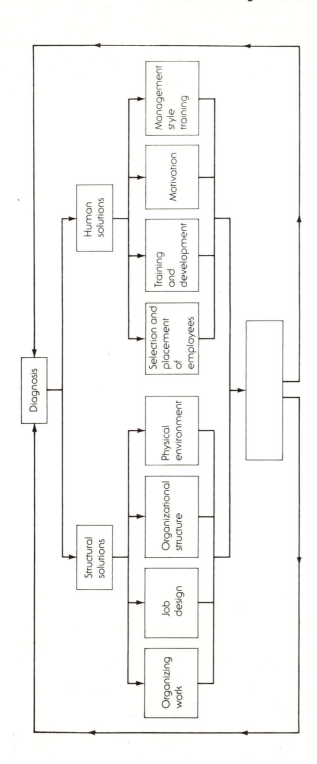

Figure 10.2 Solutions to organizational dysfunctions. (Adapted from Joint Financial Management Improvement Program, General Accounting Office, Washington, D.C. 20584)

decision when to start work in the morning and when to stop in the afternoon. Some people function more effectively in the morning; others would rather work later in the day. The eight-hour work day was established for the convenience of the corporation. Since the amount of time a person spends doing a job may not be related to output or to their lifestyle, flex time may be more appropriate to organized work.

Flexible time has significance for leisure lifestyle. Since the beginning of the industrial revolution, human life has been regulated mechanically. Work has governed when we eat, when we sleep, and when we play. Flexible time provides independence in making decisions regarding work and may result in the fusion of work and leisure values. One corporation that has employed this concept successfully is Hewlett-Packard, which has headquarters in Palo Alto, California. This electronics firm uses the flexible-time principle at all levels within the organization. The result is a more productive, satisfied work force.

The four-day work week.   The idea of a four-day, forty-hour work week has recently become popular. In this work design, an individual would work a ten-hour day, four days a week. The value of this approach is that it allows for a longer period of time away from the work environment. The incentive is this extended period of leisure time, which is earned.

Accrual of time off.   Most organizations employ this concept to reward employees for their longevity with the organization. That is, the longer that they remain with the organization, the greater the amount of time allowed for vacation. An individual might accrue three weeks of vacation after five years of service, six weeks of vacation after ten years of service, for example. Accrual of time off can be related to job performance. In this situation, an individual would be rewarded with time off for exceptional performance. Usually, if this concept is employed, the organizational guidelines are established to govern how this time is used. The two most common examples of this are leave for civic duties and leave for educational advancement. An individual with excellent work ratings might be given an opportunity to pursue an advanced degree with pay and be relieved of job duties until the degree is completed.

Reward structure.   New types of reward systems can be established in order to foster continuous commitment to an organization. In past years, rewards such as wages and fringe benefits were thought to be sufficient. New reward structures that emphasize interpersonal rewards such as social status, recognition, and friendship should be developed, as should reward systems that cater to intrinsic variables of work. Reward structures that emphasize the acquisition of skill and personal growth may be effective in fostering commitment and job satisfaction as well.

Choosing an area of work.   In some organizations, individuals have an opportunity to select or structure the work tasks that they are expected to perform. Allowing employees to choose what they are to do will directly affect their work performance and job satisfaction. For example, in the maintenance area, a list of tasks could be drawn up and individuals given a choice as to which tasks they want to perform. Each person might be given his or her first choice, and the other tasks might be delegated by the crew leader.

Working as teams or individuals. Work can be organized to be accomplished individually or within a group. An individual may be more comfortable operating within one or the other of these work structures. A group can be a positive or negative influence on a person's productivity and work satisfaction. A person might be placed in a positive group situation to reinforce values that are essential to effective job performance in the park and recreation field. Park maintenance tasks are often delegated to crews of workers. The reason for this is not only to increase efficiency, but to reinforce positive attitudes and behavior and ensure proper supervision.

Job Design

Jobs can be designed or redesigned to alleviate dysfunction. The way in which a job is designed can directly affect worker productivity and job satisfaction. Some jobs may be routine, tedious, and provide few challenges to the employee. Even a job that is initially designed to challenge the individual may at some point become boring and routine if it is not expanded. Consider the park maintenance worker. Pruning a bush the first ten times may be rewarding and challenging; however, after a period of time it may become routine because it does not provide personal satisfaction in itself. The employee may slow down, become sloppy, or avoid becoming involved in the task. The challenge to the manager is to design the job in such a way that it challenges the individual and provides opportunities for intrinsic motivation. In the case of the maintenance worker, the solution may be to teach him how to shape the trees in unusual formations and have a public display once a year.

Historically, the concept of job design can be traced back to Frederick Taylor and the scientific design of jobs. Taylor was interested in improving the productivity of individuals, and he suggested that jobs could be redesigned to become more efficient by using such techniques as time and motion analysis. Much of the early work in job design resulted in the specialization of work. For example, using assembly-line techniques, one person specialized in tasks related to one part of the total process of creating a product. This specialization ultimately led to the consideration of the effects of this factor on worker productivity. Although worker specialization was initially viewed as being more efficient and effective, it ultimately created dysfunction in many cases. As a result, a number of alternative concepts have been developed to modify jobs to make them more challenging and creative. Techniques such as job rotation, job enlargement, and job enrichment have been established.

Job rotation.   The basic premise of job rotation is that a person can be relieved of boredom and monotony if the job routine is varied. This involves moving an individual from one job to another. In professional positions, job rotation has been employed by a number of organizations. The city of Sunnyvale, California has rotated its top and middle-level managers successfully. For example, in this community the director of parks and recreation became the director of libraries for a period of three months. This process allowed for an exchange of ideas as well as opportunities for individuals to more fully understand the problems associated with other departmental operations. It also provided an opportunity to formulate and implement new solutions to problems.

Japanese corporations, recognized as leaders in the area of management, have used the job rotation concept among professionals very successfully. By rotating individuals through each department, individuals develop a comprehensive and thorough understanding of each unit within an organization. Decision making often occurs with this holistic perspective in mind. Further, a process of job rotation allows an organization to view its talent in different situations and determine what position might be best for that individual. Job rotation, however, has been criticized as being an incomplete answer to the problem of job motivation. Simply moving a person away from a routine job does not make that job any more desirable to the next person.

Job enlargement.   Job enlargement is an attempt to expand the work that an individual does. In management terminology it involves horizontal, rather than vertical, job load. Horizontal job loading involves a variety of different strategies that are formulated to challenge the employee to do more work. One way that job enlargement might be employed, although somewhat superficially, would be to ask a secretary who types 50 words per minute to type 65 words per minute, or to challenge a maintenance person to reduce the time it takes to mow a park. Another way that job enlargement is applied is by removing the difficult parts of a job. The theory here is that when difficult parts are removed and the task simplified, the person will accomplish more of the simplified tasks. Last, job enlargement can be implemented by assigning more tasks to the individual. For example, a maintenance person in the park and recreation field who is maintaining Sierra Park and Washington Park, might be asked to maintain Christmas Run Park as well.

This approach has limitations. First, job enlargement does not change the job. The person is simply being challenged to do more of what might already be distasteful. Also, removing the difficult part of a job might make the job more monotonous and boring.

Job enrichment.   Job enrichment is an extension and refinement of job rotation and job enlargement. It is based on Frederick Herzberg's motivation-hygiene theory. The reader will recall from earlier discussion that there are two sets of behavior, or factors, that motivate each individual—hygienes and motivators. Using this assumption, this concept of job design is aimed at enrichment of the motivators. Thus, job enrichment deals primarily with the design of work so that there are opportunities for achievement, recognition, responsibility, and growth. This is seen as vertical job loading. Vertical job loading might be done by removing controls and increasing individual accountability. It might be accomplished by allowing an individual to learn new tasks. It might also be accomplished by giving a person more authority, hence more job freedom. These three actions allow the individual increased responsibility, and in turn, increased opportunities for recognition, achievement, and growth.

Job enrichment might be used in a park and recreation system through the process of decentralization. For example, authority and responsibility that would usually be under the authority of the superintendent or director could be delegated to an area supervisor. Thus, opportunities for responsibility, growth, achievement, and recognition would be more available to the area supervisor. As individuals in our society become more educated and increasingly sophisticated, there will be a great need to enrich work to meet their expectations. This may very well be one of the key areas of successful management in the future. Increased responsibility and job freedom can be facilitated by using management tools such as management by objectives, with an emphasis on the coaching aspect of this tool.

Organizational Structure

The structure of an organization can be manipulated to alleviate dysfunction. As indicated in Chapter 5, organizing involves designing roles within personnel structures to accomplish organizational goals. Essentially, this entails designing tasks for individuals so that their work will be coordinated with that of other individuals within the organization. Roles are created so that the human resources of the organization are deployed in an efficient manner. It is important to recognize that organizational structures can become ends in themselves, rather than a means to the end of achieving organizational goals. If this occurs, restructuring of the organization is in order. Organizational structures are created by recreation and leisure service managers, and they can be dismantled, rearranged, eliminated or restructured by them.

What is the difference between reorganizing the organization and restructuring the organization? Restructuring the recreation and leisure service organization refers to the selection of a different organizational design to meet the goals of that agency. The reader will recall that there are a number of different types of organizational designs (e.g., bureaucracy, linking pin, project decentralization, federation, systems) and that these designs can be placed on a continuum ranging from rigid, mechanistic designs to flexible, organic designs. When making a decision to change the design, the manager is engaging in restructuring. Reorganizing refers to internal changes within a given type of design. For example, in a bureaucratic method of organization, this might involve clustering job functions in a different way.

Recreation and leisure service agencies often are involved in *reorganization*, but seldom are involved in restructuring. Reorganization efforts may be related to perceived dysfunctions, or may reflect the preferences of the manager. Reorganization should not take place without serious consideration of its impact. The reorganization must be calculated and done in such a way that the human resources of the organization become more effective. Successful reorganization is simply not a case of moving one person from one position to another, but rather a process that potentially could affect the entire structure. Given this fact, reorganization should be done with great care.

Restructuring a recreation and leisure service agency is more dramatic than internal reorganization. It usually involves a major philosophical change within the organization. Restructuring may occur for a variety of reasons, including the need to have the organizational structure provide more effective means of communication and opportunities for creativity, individual initiative, and responsibility. To improve communications, an agency may consider a decentralized form of organization directed toward improving the amount and quality of interaction that takes place between those providing and consuming services. As the reader will recall, the decentralized model of organization allows for more grass-roots communication at lower levels. Another factor that may affect the structure might be the role that the leisure-service professional plays. In some agencies, great emphasis is placed on having the professionals engage in direct service delivery. As a direct service provider, the professionals would be responsible for the organization, promotion, and implementation of programs. In other agencies, the professional is viewed as an enabler. In this role, the professional serves as a facilitator to individuals and groups, assisting them in the organization, promotion, and implementation of programs. Even after changing to the role of facilitator, few organizations restructure to better organize themselves to function effectively in the enabler role. Direct-service provision is best organized in a bureaucratic form, whereas the enabler role may be better structured in a federation form of organization.

Restructuring can allow creativity. The modular method of organization, which is a derivative of systems design, allows individuals to work together, coordinating organizational resources for a specific task, rather than through traditional positions. Through this system of organization, an agency can use the resources that will be most effective to solve a specific problem. This may facilitate creativity and individual initiative.

Physical Environment

How does the organization's physical environment affect worker performance? The environment can have both positive and negative effects on the individual. Worker performance can be adversely affected by a physical environment that is unpleasant, especially in terms of loud noise, clutter, and poor lighting. Human-factors engineering deals with the problems associated with the physical environment and their implications for personnel selection, morale, and other factors in management. The physical environment (defined here in a broad sense) may create psychological problems. Manipulation of the physical environment may be necessary in order to produce an atmosphere that is conducive to worker performance. Problems associated with the physical environment may seem simplistic; however, when they are ignored they can have deleterious effects. Some of the factors in the environment that may affect worker performance include the following:

Physical structures.   It is important to recognize that the physical environment can be structured in such a way that it produces desired behaviors. For example, an office might be arranged so that desks may be open to one another. This would allow for ease in communications, a feeling of openness and accessibility. The reverse would provide an atmosphere that is conducive to work requiring a great deal of concentration.

Lighting.   Proper lighting can help individuals work efficiently and can contribute to a safer environment. Good lighting also reduces fatigue caused by eyestrain. There are standards for lighting that are available for various types of work environments. The famous Hawthorne studies were done to determine the effects of lighting on worker productivity, and although the controls in this study were not rigorous, other studies have determined that improved lighting can result in more effective employee performance.

Color.   The colors in the work environment are also important. They are linked to depression, aggression, or pleasant feelings. Light, subtle colors within the yellow, pink, and green color groups are generally thought to be most conducive to positive emotional feelings. It is thought that a work environment that is so colored will benefit worker performance.

Decor.   It has been determined that clutter has an adverse affect upon individuals. Within the work environment, a cluttered look should be avoided. Clean lines and an uncluttered appearance should positively affect worker attitudes toward their work environment.

Acoustical design.   Acoustical design involves the effect of sound on people. Acoustical engineers are interested in the properties of sound as related to various environments. Certain tasks require quiet areas. Proper acoustical design can enhance worker productivity.

Human factors engineering is also concerned with interface between people and machines. At stake is the issue of compatibility. Careful consideration of research relating to human-factors engineering can be useful in avoiding problems associated with the person and machine interface. The physical environment should not be overlooked in solving and identifying organizational problems. It is easier to solve problems in the physical environment than to solve problems that arise from the interaction of individuals.

HUMAN SOLUTIONS

Selection and Placement of Employees

One area that contributes greatly to dysfunction within an organization is initial selection and placement of employees. Considering the amount invested in the organization's human resources, screening and selection procedures are not always adequate. For example, an individual may be hired as a director of parks and recreation at a base salary of $25,000 per year. Add to that salary an additional 25 percent, or $6,250, for fringe benefits, as well as the amount of the capital investments the director will be responsible for managing and the salaries of subordinates. This person would likely be invited to an interview with the city manager and others for only a day. The employer might receive letters of recommendation and, if industrious, might even call the candidate's current or former employers.

When an individual is selected to fill a position, the recruitment process is undertaken primarily to produce enough applicants to allow a differentia-tion between those who are qualified and those who are not. The agency hiring the individual should be thoroughly familiar with the requirements for the position in order to write a job description that will attract qualified applicants. The agency should not only be aware of the tasks that the potential employee will have to accomplish, but also understand the skills, abilities, interests, and personality traits that are important for the position.

Assuming that a job analysis has taken place, the process of selection and placement of employees can be broken down into five steps, as described in Chapter 6. They are recruitment, screening, interviewing, and testing. Each of these steps involves the location and placement of the most qualified individual for a position within an organization. Many problems can be alleviated if the hiring process is developed in a thorough and com-plete manner. There are a number of management tools that can be used to help in selection and placement.

Manpower inventory.   One of the management tools that can be used in the selection is the manpower inventory. Recreation and leisure service organizations often fail to plan their human resource needs effectively. Planning, if it occurs at all, is done haphazardly. Manpower planning implies that an organization, to be effective, should inventory its human resources. This involves understanding the strengths and weaknesses of employees and their potential for advancement. The recreation and leisure service organization must engage in planning in order to predict its future needs and to understand its current reservoir of talent, both actual and potential. The concept of establishing an inventory is not new to organizational management. However, the idea of cataloging existing and future human resource needs within organizations is often ignored. By establishing an inventory, organizations are better able to deploy their resources to ensure uninterrupted services.

Recruitment techniques.   Appropriate recruitment techniques can also be useful in the process of selecting and placing employees. Any organization, regardless of its size, should make an effort to locate and recruit the right person for each position. In the human-service professions, the potential of consulting firms, on-site recruitment, and other associated strategies is often overlooked. As indicated in Chapter 6, there are a number of available strategies. The key is to determine the most appropriate recruitment technique to produce an adequate supply of qualified applicants. Careful consideration should be given to the choice of recruiting techniques, according to the level of the position and the availability of qualified applicants. The organization that uses mass media to advertise its positions, producing a pool of unqualified and semi-qualified applicants, only serves to alienate employees and increase organizational inefficiency. Of course, every effort should be made to abide by appropriate legislative guidelines to ensure the recruitment of minorities.

Employee turnover.   One of the problems that is tied to poor selection and placement is the turnover of employees. Therefore, turnover reduction techniques should be considered. There are a number of analytical methods that can be employed to curtail high turnover. One of the best and most direct approaches is to determine why individuals stay on the job and why they leave. This information can be applied to selection and placement. For example, if analysis finds that an individual who has a low tolerance for others and lacks assertiveness is unable to function effectively in a position that involves the promotion of the recreation and leisure service organization, it would be appropriate to consider these personality characteristics in the screening process. The organization would look for an individual who interacted well with others and had a high degree of assertiveness. The amount of turnover within an organization can be influenced by such organizational problems as poor supervision, low motivation, and low wages. Turnover is often tied directly to the inappropriate selection and placement of an individual.

The employment of a variety of selection and placement techniques is desirable. Of the methods mentioned in Chapter 6, none could be considered perfect; however, they increase the probability that the organization will select the right person and place him or her in the right position. Most employee selection techniques are based on the assumption that one can study employees who perform successfully, those who perform adequately, and those who perform poorly, and isolate those variables that result in employee success. By employing individuals who have a high potential for success, according to selected criteria, and avoiding those individuals who are not likely to perform in an adequate manner, organizational effectiveness can be enhanced.

Personnel assessment centers.   A major trend in large organizations is the development of personnel assessment centers. Assessment centers have been established in order to determine the factors that are essential to success in management positions. A person being assessed should go through a comprehensive process of testing and interviewing. A variety of exercises can be used in personnel assessment, including management games, case studies involving decision making and fact finding, group discussion related to management functions, and the traditional interviewing and psychological testing. Because a candidate involved in this process is seen by many people and assessed in a variety of ways, an accurate appraisal of the individual by the organization is possible.

Training and Development

As indicated in Chapter 5, the half life of management knowledge is seven years. This means that within seven years half of the current management knowledge will be obsolete. New theories and practices are being developed at an exponential rate. The need to convey current, relevant information in training and development activities is critical.

Dysfunction often occurs because individuals within the organization do not have the skills, attitudes, or knowledge necessary to do their jobs accurately and efficiently. Sometimes an attempt is made to involve individuals in training and development before they begin their jobs, but, in general, we are engaged in ongoing training efforts that occur after a person has been placed in the organization. Training is the major method for renewing an organization, but it is surprising how few organizations have a structured plan for continued training.

Organizational development.   Organizational development as an activity is directed toward increasing the effectiveness of the organization on a long-term basis. It focuses on the use of the principles of applied behavioral science to improve individual, group, and organizational performance. Large organizations may hire an individual to implement a program of organizational development. Organizational development is seen as a systematic process implemented to upgrade and renew an organization. Organizational development, according to French and Bell, involves the following characteristics:

1. It is an ongoing process.
2. It is a form of applied behavioral science.
3. It constitutes a normative-reeducative strategy for change.
4. It utilizes a systems approach.
5. It is a data-based problem-solving model.
6. It reflects an experience-based learning model.
7. It emphasizes goal setting and the planning function.
8. It involves intact work teams.[2]

These authors also point out that organizational development involves the action-research process. Action reseach is a process of research that attempts to solve problems in an inductive, rather than deductive, manner.

It is important to note that we live in a society dominated by change. Organizational development as a process can be extremely useful in helping organizations plan for and adapt to changes. It allows an organization to systematically react to forces of change and manage these forces in such a way that the organization not only survives, but prospers. Historically, recreation and leisure service agencies have not adapted effectively to change and have been reactive rather than proactive. If recreation and leisure service organizations are to prosper, planning for change is essential.

Motivation

Many organizations admit that they have a motivation problem. The lack of employee motivation contributes to organization dysfunction and has a deleterious effect upon worker performance and employee satisfaction. It can result in such symptoms of organizational dysfunction as theft, slow down, sabotage, absenteeism, turnover, and low morale.

Chapter 7 presented ways in which motivation was tied to job performance. Without restating many of the basic concepts discussed already, it is important to recognize that motivation may be at the heart of many organizational problems. We have established that work meets a basic human need. We discussed two categories of factors that motivate individuals to work—hygienic factors and motivators. Hygienic factors focus on such things as type of supervision, interpersonal relationships, salary, status, and security. Motivators include recognition, achievement, responsibility, and opportunities for growth.

The crux of the motivation problem seems to lie in the failure to first

---

2. Wendell L. French and Cecil H. Bell, Jr., *Organizational Development* (Englewood Cliffs, N.J.: Prentice-Hall, Inc., 1973), pp. 45–64.

satisfy hygienic factors and then move to the more important motivators. To establish a management strategy to increase employee motivation, an environment must be created that provides continuous opportunities for self-motivation. A self-motivating environment will allow an individual to receive recognition, achievement, responsibility, and opportunities for growth as a result of his efforts. In discussing the creation of a motivating environment, Williams has suggested that there are a number of steps that can be used. These include the following:

1. Decide what outcomes each employee values. Remember this is an individual matter and each employee is different.
2. Determine what kind of behavior you desire. Sometimes managers talk in generalities about what they feel is good performance without really defining it. In establishing a good motivational environment, the manager must figure out specifically what his or her expectations are for good performance and make sure they are understood by the employees and rewarded when achieved.
3. Make sure desired levels of performance are realistic and obtainable. There is nothing more frustrating than working hard for something that is ever out of reach.
4. Link desired outcomes to desired performance. If an individual works hard for something and achieves it, his or her performance should be rewarded, and that reward should be meaningful in the eyes of the employee, not the eyes of the manager.
5. Analyze the situation for conflicting expectations. The manager needs to know if there are factors conflicting with the positive expectations set for the employee in the employee's mind. Motivation will be high only if people see a number of rewards associated with good performance. If a manager is unable to reward the hard-working individual because of pay scale limitations, this situation conflicts with the expectation of hard work.
6. Make sure that outcomes are large enough and adequately reflect performances. Minimal or trivial rewards result in trivial or minor effort whereas significant rewards encourage significant performance.
7. Check the system for equity. Obviously, inequity is very frustrating to employees. For example, the employee who works very hard side by side with an unreprimanded employee who dawdles will deduce that hard work is not worth the effort.[3]

Coaching.   An important step in the motivation process is that of coaching, or counseling. Dwight D. Eisenhower once said that motivation is the ability to "get him to do what you want him to do, when you want it done, in a way you want it, because he *wants* to do it." Coaching is the

---

3.   John G. Williams, "The Care and Nurture of Employees (or Greasing the Path to Productivity)," *Parks and Recreation*, 15:9 (September, 1980), pp. 69–76.

primary way this is achieved. Coaching involves a one-to-one relationship with an individual. The first step in the coaching process is a discussion with an employee about the behavior that constitutes good job performance. Following this, an attempt is made to arrive at a mutual agreement concerning the job itself. The next step in the process is recognition, on the part of the manager, of the factors that are motivating to the individual and ways in which poor performance can be avoided. Last, the coaching process involves an appraisal of employee performance.

Coaching allows the development of a self-motivating environment. It provides an opportunity for individuals to receive recognition, feel a sense of achievement and growth, and assume responsibility. The coaching process must be ongoing. Too often the coaching process is used sporadically to curtail problems as they emerge. If it is employed on a continuous basis, coaching can be a great aid in preventing organizational dysfunction.

Peer influences.   Another element affecting the motivation process is the influence of one's peer group. An individual's peer work group can be a significant motivator, having direct influence over productivity and satisfaction. Cohesive work groups that focus on organizational goals can be an important element in positive work behavior. Efforts aimed at creating a supportive, motivating environment should not only focus on the individual, but also groups within the organization. This can be achieved by promoting group participation in decision making within the recreation and leisure service organization. Unproductive work groups are one of the most pervasive factors causing organizational dysfunction.

Management-Style Training

Because of the importance of managerial leadership in recreation and leisure service organizations, the authors have included a discussion of this topic. A manager's style is central to success or failure. Today, more than ever, the responsibility for failure within the organization may be placed on the shoulders of the manager. In previous eras there was a tendency to place the blame for organizational failure on incompetent employees.

Even though there is a tendency to place responsibility on the manager to adapt his managerial leadership style to a given situation, the employee should recognize the need to adapt to different managerial styles. Managerial style is a result of a variety of factors. Some of these are personality, prior experience, and social and cultural factors. For example, an individual's need for controlling others might result in an authoritarian style. It is important to recognize that style changes can be learned and that individual employees may learn to accommodate a given manager's style.

The most well-known management-style training program was developed by Robert R. Blake and Jane S. Mouton. Their program, grid organizational development, helps organizations examine the managerial behavior and style of their executives.[4] The program is based upon the assumptions made in the Blake and Mouton management grid. This way of assessing managerial behavior suggests that there are two factors that comprise managerial leadership style. One dimension is concern for people, and the other is concern for production. Further, there are five different styles that one can assume. According to Blake and Mouton, the most effective managers are those who have high scores on both concern for people and concern for production. In the grid, this is known as a 9–9 managerial style.

The grid organizational development program is a six-step program that can last between three and five years. The purpose of the program is to enable individuals to explore their own management styles, strengths, and weaknesses. Further, the program helps individuals develop the necessary competence for effectiveness at all levels within an organization. This includes individual, group, intergroup and total organizational effectiveness. The first phase in the program, the prephase, involves the retraining of key managers who later will be instructors in another organization. They learn about their own management style, problem solving, and other skills necessary to implement the grid program. The next phase involves having these trained managers implement the program within their organizations. Again, the focus is on having organizational managers understand their management style and develop the knowledge necessary for the development of the grid program. The next two phases of the program focus on the development of teamwork and intergroup relations. The fourth phase in the process is devoted to development of an ideal organizational model. In this part of the process, long-range planning is undertaken, as well as an examination of various alternate strategies. Following development of an organizational model, implementation takes place. Last, continuous monitoring and critiquing is conducted.

Although the grid organizational development program is extensive and should be seen as a preventive measure for organizational problems, there are other short-term programs that can be used by a recreation and leisure service organization to serve similar ends. Many of these short-term individual assessment programs—personality inventories, psychological testing, and managerial-leadership-style testing—are available from management consulting firms. They can be useful as discussion vehicles to help individuals understand themselves and other individuals within their organization. When dealing with a problem diagnosed as poor management style, a manager should consider both sides of the issue—changing the manager's style and helping the employee to be more accommodating.

4.   R.R. Blake and J.S. Mouton, *Building a Dynamic Corporation Through Grid Organizational Development* (Reading, Mass.: Addison-Wesley Publishing Co.) 1969.

SUMMARY

Organizational dysfunction is any situation in which a problem, or problems, prevents an organization from achieving its stated objectives in an efficient manner. There are many sources of dysfunction within recreation and leisure service organizations. Some of the specific problem areas are communication, objectives, decision making, organizational conflict, interface relations, organizational roles and structure, employee performance, managerial leadership styles, and individual expectations.

In order to effectively deal with these types of problems, the leisure service manager should develop a problem-solving strategy to alleviate organizational dysfunction. Problem solving involves five steps, including establishing objectives, diagnosing the dysfunction, identifying alternate courses of action, determining the most appropriate course of action, and measuring and evaluating.

There are two types of solutions to organizational problems—structural solutions and human solutions. Structural solutions involve modifications or manipulations of the environment. Some of the structural solutions that can be employed are reorganization of work, job design, or organizational structure, and manipulation of the physical environment. Human solutions focus directly on the skills, attitudes, and knowledge of each employee. Human solutions involve such variables as selection and placement of employees, training and development, motivation, and management-style training.

STUDY QUESTIONS

1. What is organizational dysfunction?
2. What is goal displacement? Why is it a major organizational problem?
3. What are some specific areas that cause organizational dysfunction?
4. Discuss the need for a planned management program to deal with organizational dysfunction.
5. What is a process that can be used to alleviate organizational dysfunction?
6. What is the difference between structural solutions and human solutions to organizational dysfunction?
7. Identify and discuss different structural solutions to organizational dysfunction.
8. Identify and discuss different human solutions to organizational dysfuntion.
9. From your perspective, which type of solution, structural or human, is more difficult to implement?

10. Describe the ways in which various solutions to dysfunction can be employed by recreation and leisure service agencies. List some specific examples.

CASE STUDY 13

The Special Meeting

It is Tuesday afternoon in the council chambers of City Hall. Chuck Christopher, Lucy Brown, and Bud Smith have taken seats in the front row of the almost full council chambers. Since last Friday when the notice came to all members of the recreation and parks staff requesting them to be present at the special meeting of the Parks and Recreation Department, Chuck, along with other staff members, has been speculating on the reason for the special meeting. "Well, we'll soon know," he said to Lucy as Laurie George and the city administrator entered the room and closed the doors of the council chamber. Almost immediately a hush fell over the packed council chambers.

"Good afternoon, ladies and gentlemen," said Laurie George, who somehow seemed a bit less than his usual confident self. "Thank you for coming to this meeting, which has been called by our city administrator and myself to discuss a decision made at an in-camera meeting of the Recreation and Parks Board last Thursday night. Let me now introduce Mr. John Butler, our city administrator, who will fill you in on the details." "The plot thickens," Lucy whispered to Chuck as John Butler rose from his seat.

"Thank you Mr. George, and thank you all for making arrangements to be here on such short notice. As some of you are aware, a special in-camera meeting of the Parks and Recreation Board, the mayor, myself and Laurie George was held last Thursday night. This meeting was called at the request of six members of the Parks and Recreation Board and was held to discuss the overall efficiency and effectiveness of the department. After considerable discussion, the board has recommended to the city council that an outside management consultant firm be retained to study the current operations of the department and make recommendations for any needed change. The recommendation went to this morning's council meeting and has been approved. My job this morning is to tell you of this decision and to ask for your cooperation during the process. The firm will be responsible to council through me and will be commencing work as soon as possible. I should add that the decision to employ outside expertise is normal procedure and is an attempt to get professional, objective views on the operation of what has now become one of the largest and most expensive departments in the city. You will be informed of developments. Thank you."

QUESTIONS

1. If you were a member of the consultant firm employed by the city what kinds of information would you secure in relation to such topics as goals and objectives, organizational structure, employee performance and appraisal, decision-making processes, communication networks, employee relationships and turnover?
2. From your current knowledge of recreation and leisure organizations in general and the Canusa Parks and Recreation Department what kinds of organizational dysfunction might be anticipated?
3. Was this meeting conducted in a proper manner? Why?

Index